Why Muslim Women and Smartphones

Why Muslim Women and Smartphones

Mirror Images

Karen Waltorp

Routledge
Taylor & Francis Group

LONDON AND NEW YORK

First published 2020 by Bloomsbury Academic

2 Park Square, Milton Park, Abingdon, Oxon OX14 4RN
605 Third Avenue, New York, NY 10017

Routledge is an imprint of the Taylor & Francis Group, an informa business

First issued in paperback 2021

Cover design: Ben Anslow

Publisher's Note

The publisher has gone to great lengths to ensure the quality of this reprint
but points out that some imperfections in the original copies may be apparent.

A catalogue record for this book is available from the British Library.

A catalog record for this book is available from the Library of Congress.

ISBN13: 978-1-350-12735-7 (hbk)
ISBN13: 978-1-03-217433-4 (pbk)
DOI: 10.4324/9781003087380

Typeset by Integra Software Services Pvt. Ltd.

Contents

Foreword

Sarah Pink

In recent years I have, both individually and with others collectively, argued for and practiced a revised anthropology. Such an anthropology should account for futures not only as an object of study, but moreover as a site for exploring anew our ethics and our commitments to anthropological intervention. Instead of engaging only with what has already happened, a revised anthropology needs to focus on emergence, uncertainty, and possibility, and on the anticipatory feelings of hope, trust, and anxiety through which they are experienced. It is also an interdisciplinary anthropology, which engages visual and sensory modes of doing ethnography and that experiments beyond its boundaries to create new methods and techniques of knowing, critiquing, and intervening toward responsible and ethical futures. This might mean it sometimes cedes its conventional principles in the pursuit of encountering alternative ways of knowing to those the discipline conventionally adheres to. Finally, I believe in an anthropology that seeks to participate in processes of change, an interventional anthropology that understands how technologies and media are part of the way life is already lived out and imagines how they will be part of possible futures.

I am delighted to write the foreword to *Why Muslim Women and Smartphones: Mirror Images*, precisely because it is just the kind of book that a revised anthropology needs and that its scholars and students will be inspired by. Karen Waltorp gifts us a compelling example of what anthropology can be, when it takes a visual and sensory stance, once it is divested of its conventional structures and formats of writing and presentation, when it engages fully with the technological and mediated worlds that characterize everyday life, and when it moreover accounts for the different and maybe not immediately visible temporalities through which people experience events of their lives. We learn what it can mean to live in the midst of an everyday social, sensory, and affective world, entangled with the complexities of the continents, technologies, and intimacies that bind people together. And we are introduced to the anticipatory modes through which smartphones and social media are engaged as people carefully and skillfully navigate the complex environments they are implicated in.

Fieldwork

The inextricability of fieldwork and life is integral to the experience of the anthropologist, who must find a route through the ethics, friendships, and theoretical and methodological stances that guide her personal and professional commitments. More than two decades ago I found myself immersed in a life of fieldwork in Southern Spain (Pink 1997). I wove my time between the sometimes connected or contiguous world of bullfighting and a network of personal relationships and friendships, some of which have endured to the present thanks to social media. My life and research made a temporal trace, which I tracked with the help of an analogue camera, a pile of press cuttings and photocopies, and many written notes. I still cannot imagine how I could have done ethnography without photographing (and occasionally videoing), copying or saving printed images, and watching TV. That is, the materials of my fieldwork were necessarily composed of things that could not be written or always spoken. I was surrounded by, and participated in, a world that could not be separated from the media narratives of the time, as public events were made meaningful in terms of intimate possibilities and intimate relationships were understood through public narratives. My later projects have involved me researching in the intimate space of the home (Pink 2004, 2012), where I found that the recounting and reenacting of the most mundane everyday tasks of cleaning or laundry on video were capable of invoking stories of life's memories on the ongoingness of the sensory presence of others and of the intensities and loss of death and separation. Writing from the position of the intimate worlds of others, in which one has shared, is beautiful, difficult, and complex. This is to write from a position of privilege, but not in the sense of hierarchy or a privilege that one already assumes, but from the privilege of having been allowed and trusted to write about other people's lives. Being in such a position brings with it perhaps an obligation to acknowledge how our own lives are likewise part of the story. And to do so assumes both responsibility and vulnerability. It requires that the anthropologist becomes and allows her research to be vulnerable to her informants. As Waltorp shows, this means both inviting them to set the boundaries and simultaneously taking up her own responsibility. For the visual anthropologist this position is emphasized still further, since the personal and professional, the intimate and public, and the ethnographic and the theoretical, become connected through the processes of making, showing, sharing, and concealing videos and photographs. My own fieldwork in the 1990s, in a bullfighting world with a vibrant local and national visual culture, was often shaped around photographing, having printed, sharing, and tracing the connections made through analogue photographs. As we seek to collaboratively document the lives of others, they bring us into their images and they incorporate us through own visual practices, and as such into their visual cultures and worlds, on their terms (Pink 2013). As Waltorp shows, when such relationships are articulated in contemporary sites of which the smartphone and Internet are inextricable parts then digital images and their attendant uses and sharing across social media apps and platforms become both modes of understanding how people live, feel, experience, and imagine, and bonds between researcher and informants. These are the visual and mediated sites and fields in which in-depth ethnography now often happens; Waltorp's discussion offers new researchers a pertinent insight into how the visual anthropologist might engage with and learn through such relations ethically and responsibly.

Narrative

The particular fieldwork site, informants, and questions that Waltorp engaged with invited her to navigate a complex narrative. To cope with this, she makes a typically anthropological move. Anthropologists have long since argued for the importance of engaging with the epistemologies of our participants and giving these equal weight to that conferred on those which are privileged by science. There are different views among anthropologists regarding how this might be best achieved and where and when universal theories might be best applied in the discipline, as shown in a debate between Tim Ingold and David Howes regarding the question of sensory anthropology (Ingold 2011, Howes 2011). Paul Stoller eloquently offers us the possibility of what he refers to as tacking between the intelligible and the sensible (1997), as he interweaves different modes of ethnographic and theoretical writing into his work in such a way that enables us to engage with different modes of knowing and understanding. Waltorp's work likewise follows this commitment to bringing together theoretical ethnographic writing and, as a visual anthropologist, also images, as she draws explicitly on the intermediate realm between the intelligible and the sensible: the imaginal realm. She also offers a new twist of the anthropological attention to other people's ways of knowing and being, in her adoption of the Arabic notion of *harakat*, which was so integral to the lives of the women she worked with. *Harakat*, which Waltorp tells us is "used to denote smart, skilled navigation of situations," is not simply an object of study in *Why Muslim Women and Smartphones*. Rather Waltorp doubly engages it as a principle through which to narrate and visualize lives, feelings, and places that readers would otherwise never encounter. The "tactical moves" of *harakat* endure throughout the book, and they enable her to tell stories that cannot be told, places that cannot be identified, and photographs and videos that cannot be seen. Waltorp does this by bringing forth the fragments, moments, and feelings through which we learn to appreciate a sense of the essence of the lightness, intensity, joy and pain, and hopes and anxieties of the women whose lives she invites us to empathetically contemplate. On the one hand we can see how the tactics of *harakat* play out in the intimate lives of the women whom Waltorp videos, photographs, and writes about, while on the other they lend themselves to shape the very tactics and structure of the book itself.

Futures

The temporalities of anthropology, as I have alluded to above, need to shift, both in how we research and how we engage with societal questions. Waltorp's work responds to a particular movement in anthropology, led by the Future Anthropologies network, which has been decisive in pushing such an agenda forward (Salazar et al 2017). Her attention to the anticipatory and imaginative dimensions of life for her informants, in Denmark and in relation to their transnational families and social media worlds, enables us to comprehend how life as documented in anthropological description, video, and photography refers not simply to what has already happened, but to what might happen in an uncertain world, within the realm of possibility, hopes, and dreams. While, as I have discussed elsewhere, conventionally anthropological writing has focused on what has already happened, and what we and others might already know, a growing focus on how what we and our research participants cannot know and have not (yet) and perhaps never will experience is emerging as a central concern for some contemporary scholars (Pink and Salazar 2017). Such a futures anthropology has implications for how we write, film, and photograph ethnographically—because it shifts the tenses and temporalities that such anthropological media refer to. In the work of the visual anthropologist, possible futures are not only imagined and experienced through what people tell us and what we see them do but are detectable in the ways they use images, both as part of their own visual cultures and in their relationships with us.

A focus on futures also requires us to think carefully about the ethics of anthropology since it relocates our practice outside the comfort zone of the ethnographic past and situates it in the discomfort of an uncertain future (Pink 2017). That is, when we participate, as anthropologists, in what might happen, rather than documenting what has happened, we accrue new responsibilities and commitments, which have been little considered in existing discussions of ethics or reflexivity in anthropology. By comparing her own with participants' feelings about current and possible future events and feelings, Waltorp shows us the importance of learning with others, in this case about how the specificity of Muslim religious interpretations of temporality and agencies bring forth particular modes of imagining and engaging with uncertainty and futures. Waltorp's work shows how she was not only responsible for documenting and studying how her informants experienced uncertainty and lived out hopes for their futures, but rather she was sometimes ongoingly implicated in informants' investigations about what might happen next or what might be possible. That is she participated, along with the smartphone, in how scenarios for the future were discussed, particularly in moments and events when her own and her participants' worlds more intensively intersected. It is through her skillful *harakat* moves that Waltorp takes responsibility for these engagements with uncertain futures in her text and images; that is she uses the same tactics to enable her readers to know what they need to see, and to cover what they should not, as do her informants, while at the same time offering us the illusion that we have encountered something akin to that which she experienced while immersed in the site where they played out.

A new generation of anthropology

In *Why Muslim Women and Smartphones* some of the central principles of conventional anthropological practice endure. Waltorp keeps the ethnographic-theoretical dialogue that is at the core of the discipline. The habit of referring to participants in ethnographic research as informants is something that she chose to maintain through her work. Yet while holding up these conventions, Waltorp simultaneously disrupts the modes through which anthropological practices and terminologies are traditionally played out. *Why Muslim Women and Smartphones* introduces us to what I see as a new generation of anthropology, which also departs from the traditions that have guarded the mainstream of the discipline for so many years.

This book is an inspiring example of what anthropology can be when it is divested of its conventional structures of writing, when it takes a visual and sensory stance, and when it engages fully with the technological and mediated worlds that characterize everyday life. In the wake of the postmodern turn in the 1980s and 1990s there was a surge of what were at the time experimental writing and formats, seeking to decenter the anthropological mainstream, some more successful than others. In the present experimental anthropology is emerging anew, as represented in Adolfo Estalella and Tomás Sánchez Criado's recent edited collection (2018). Waltorp's work is an example of what this can be when developed in the form of a monograph.

Why Muslim Women and Smartphones speaks to anthropologies of gender, mobile technologies, social media, religion, migration, futures, and much more. It interweaves the traces that these different themes—which are often separated out into fields of study of their own—make through lives and worlds and show how they configure in the contingent circumstances of individual experiences in different ways. This book also provides valuable insights for scholars of anthropology's cognate disciplines and interdisciplinary fields of study. For instance for the mobile media studies scholar, who might be drawn to the title of this book, there is also much to be learned. Waltorp performs a non-digital-centric digital ethnography (Pink et al 2016). This provides an example of what we can learn when research about and with smartphones is undertaken as part of anthropological fieldwork that sets these technologies, and the social media apps and platforms that they connect us to, within the specificity of social relations that span the intimate and the public and that take us right to the core of what is most important in the lives of the women who use them. As such *Why Muslim Women and Smartphones* is a book that has the potential to demonstrate the value of anthropology, not only by presenting a particular mode of anthropological practice to the discipline itself, but also by demonstrating why anthropology matters to the disciplines and interdisciplinary fields that it rubs shoulders with.

If we need a new anthropology, and it is my argument that we do, then *Why Muslim Women and Smartphones* is an ideal starting point.

Acknowledgments

My first and most profound thank you is to the women I met in Blaagaarden, Noerrebro—as well as many family members and friends of theirs. For all the time given, the availability, and the attention given across Copenhagen, Tehran, Esfahan, Dubai—as well as the availability and attention given online. Since 2010 we have been working together on chronicling your neighborhood and your lives, with images being our common ground. There would have been no book without these collaborations.

In those early days in Blaagaarden, Chilie Thode believed in me and connected me in ways I will always be grateful for. Before and beyond, there are webs of connectedness, inspiration, and feedback that inform my work. I trace these webs to the Department of Anthropology, University of Copenhagen, where I graduated in 2007 and held a teaching position between 2011 and 2013, an affiliation to the African Gender Institute at University of Cape Town in spring 2006, and to the Department of Anthropology at Aarhus University, where I was part of starting the MA track in experimental visual anthropology and which has been my academic home since 2013. Research stays at Department of Anthropology, University of California, Berkeley, in spring 2016, and the Digital Ethnography Research Centre at RMIT University, Melbourne, in spring 2018 gave me the opportunity to present the research that this book is built on.

During the research for this book, I benefitted from support from the Faculty of Arts, Aarhus University, and a grant from the Danish Research Council as part of the Camera as Cultural Critique Research Group, headed by Ton Otto, who has also been kind enough to read parts of this book. In this research group I was fortunate to inquire about the role and potential of images and image-making as cultural critique alongside him, and Arine Høgel, Peter Crawford, Christian Suhr, and Christian Vium. The latter is not only my closest colleague, but also my life partner. He read the manuscript several times along the way, and where my ideas end and his begin is sometimes impossible to untangle. I am lucky to share an environment at Moesgaard with so many amazing colleagues at the Department of Anthropology. Line Dalsgaard, my former PhD supervisor, provided initial support and her boldness in writing experimentally is a continued inspiration. At the time I wrote the book, Mikkel

Rytter was Head of Research. He has been most supportive and believed in my work, and read an early iteration of the full manuscript. Morten Nielsen was the one pushing me to focus on writing the monograph, and also commented several chapters, as did Pierre du Plessis. I also wish to thank the students at the department, who have challenged and developed my thinking over the courses that I have taught.

At Department of Anthropology, Berkeley, I wish to thank Stefania Pandolfo, Cori Hayden, and Trinh T. Minh-ha for their comments. Lisa Sang Mi Min, Annie Malcolm, Annie Danis, and others in the Experimental Ethnographies Townsend Working group also made my stay in 2016 joyful, and contributed valuable feedback when inviting me to lead a Roundtable on Experimental Ethnographic Forms. I further extend my thanks to George Marcus, who kindly invited me to present my research to colleagues at University of California, Irvine. I had the pleasure of sharing time in California with Brit Ross Winthereik who pushed my thinking on STS and infrastructures in my material and my method.

I thank Sarah Pink at Emerging Technologies Lab at Monash University, Melbourne. She has been a mentor to me in thinking about digital and visual anthropology, questioning our ethnographic practice and our commitments and entanglements—both during my research stay at the Digital Ethnography Research Centre, RMIT University, Melbourne, in spring 2018 and her visiting professorship at Department of Anthropology, Aarhus University, in the fall that same year. Sarah started the EASA Future Anthropologies Network with Juan Salazar in 2014, assembling a very diverse group of scholars who have challenged me greatly in thinking about our commitment to a future-orientation and world-making in our ethnographic practice. Débora Lanzeni has been my co-convener of the EASA Future Anthropologies Network since 2016, and she pushes for new ways of thinking data and the digital-material. Tomás Sánchez Criado and Adolfo Estalella, conveners of the EASA #Colleex network, I thank for challenging discussions about experimentation and new modes of collaboration, latest in the Experimental Collaborations PhD course co-taught with Adolfo at Aarhus University in 2019.

To Laura Marks at Simon Frazer University, I owe a special thank you for an engagement with my work at an early stage that helped shape my thinking around the virtual, Islamic philosophy, and the flow of images. Andrew Irving at University of Manchester, my former co-supervisor, has informed my thinking about sensory anthropology and the visual. Emma Tarlo, Goldschmidt, was part of my assessment committee with Sarah Pink and with Kasper Tang Vangkilde at Aarhus University as chair. Their engagement with my thoughts around materiality, surfaces, clothing, and (modest) fashion has had effects in my writing of this book. I am grateful and hope for continued future collaborations with all of these scholars.

Miriam Cantwell approached me in London at the Royal Anthropological Institute's Conference on Art, Materiality and Representation in 2018 and soon made me realize that the right home for my book is with Bloomsbury, and I thank her for that—as I thank Lucy Carroll for continued excellent work in preparing the book for publication. Jannie Møller Hartley at Roskilde University has offered feedback on chapters and is a valued discussion partner on media, (Big) Data, and on Bourdieu—about which we coedited a special issue together with Ida Willig in 2015. With Sine Plambech, DIIS, and film director Janus Metz, I enjoy ongoing discussions about migration and the power of visual anthropology in portraying this global phenomenon in grounded and intimate ways. Film director Andreas Dalsgaard, who also has a background in anthropology, afforded me a space and facilities to edit my film material in Copenhagen. All the women in the network group Netwerket—counting film directors, fiction writers, artists, journalists, etc.—have been an inspiration since 2008.

My closest friend Jane Pedersen, I would like to thank for both support and patience. My brother Jens Waltorp, fellow anthropologist, has read parts of the manuscript and I appreciate his feedback tremendously. My sister Mette Waltorp both supports me and offers a different perspective on things, from her discipline of law. My Dad, Peter Sørensen, is a rock and a constant support. He has informed my outlook and approach more than anyone. I thank my mother-in-law Kätte Bønløkke for taking an interest in my work, and not least for helping out with the children in intense writing periods. Christian Vium—my partner, collaborator, teacher, and fellow traveler—the most deeply felt thank you is to you and our two sons Carl and Vitus, who have shared fieldwork experiences and life entwined, who have been patient with me, and whom I owe attention and availability and continued love. My mother always gave me love unconditionally. From her I learned to listen closely and pay attention. She is not here anymore, yet with me every day. To her, I dedicate this book with love.

Introduction: Al-Harakat

We're sitting all together, a small group of women in a dimly lit living room. The curtains are drawn tight. The TV is turned on, showing a reality show that no one is paying much attention to. All of us have found space on the large corner sofa and we are chatting. Smartphones lie around, beeping, lighting up when a notification or message ticks in. Voices change from Danish to Arabic, to Farsi, and back to Danish again, depending on who receives a call. I film Mariam as she returns from the kitchen and sits down at the other end of the sofa. She reaches for her smartphone. The message she receives is from someone special. All her attention is focused on the small screen. Through the viewfinder of my video camera I see how her chest moves up and down faster, her breathing becoming heavy. I zoom in on her chest and lower face, knowing that I cannot show images of Mariam without the hijab, which she is not wearing now. Time stands still, while everything continues as before for everyone else in the room. I feel my own breathing change, and my own heart beats faster. Mariam bites her lip and quickly replies to the message. She exhales and puts the smartphone down on the table, reorienting herself to the present, physical world.

Muslim women and smartphones in Blaagaarden, Noerrebro

The online, digital realm is very real for the women I worked with in the social housing area Blaagaarden in the Copenhagen neighborhood of Noerrebro. The women's relations to people and places, possible futures, even questions of life and death are all aggregated in their smartphones. The smartphone and, most importantly, its image-making technology constitute an infrastructure for seeing, thinking and knowing—not just for the women—but also for me as an anthropologist engaging in fieldwork. The use of images has long been important to me in my research, and I had already worked on a participatory photo project in the Blaagaarden area in 2010–2011, several years before I began the research that forms the basis of this book. In this earlier project, the importance of cell phones and smartphones for the young women in the area became clear to me. They used it prolifically to consume, produce, and share images, and they used it as a relational device in specific ways. In this book I start from the smartphone, and throughout, I return to the smartphone. The book, however, is not *about* the smartphone in itself, but rather about what it enables and invites for, for my informants and for me, the anthropologist. I explore its affordances (Gibson 2015 (1979)) as a relational device, as a knowledge-making device, and as "virtuality"—through the power and the flow of images. Throughout the book, I intentionally avoid the term "virtual reality" to denote the online and the digital realm, instead drawing on the notion of the virtual as real, but not actualized (yet)—real without being actual, ideal without being abstract (Bergson 1920; Deleuze 1989, 1994; Marks 2000, 2010, 2015). As with Mariam whom we meet in the opening vignette, the present physical world of sociality in the living room is very real, so too are the interactions and exchanges taking place—and possibilities opened up to—through the Internet-enabled smartphone.

Blaagaarden is a social housing area in Noerrebro, Copenhagen, where 65.5 percent of the inhabitants have a migratory history.[1] From February 2014 to December 2015, I conducted ethnographic fieldwork among young Muslim women with Middle Eastern, Central Asian, and North African backgrounds, as well as what they themselves described as "a mix" (et mix) when having parents with different national or ethnic background. All the women grew up in Denmark. We spoke in Danish together, and I learned a few phrases in Arabic, Farsi, and Urdu. I embarked on this work because I was curious and intrigued by the affordances of the smartphone in relation to young Muslim women in Blaagaarden, whom I had seen use smartphones ubiquitously in their everyday life—and especially in making and sharing images. I followed the young Muslim women across on- and offline realms, as they navigated often conflicting sets of expectations and ideals while "keeping cool and staying virtuous" (Waltorp 2015). I went with one informant, Neda, to visit her suitor in Dubai, with whom she had been in a strictly online relationship for 2 years at the time. I traveled to the Islamic Republic of Iran with two informants, Zara and Bita, to stay with their relatives in Tehran and visit friends of the family in Esfahan. I received generous invitations by other women I worked with to join them on travels to Pakistan and Jordan as well but did not have the opportunity to go with them. I regret this as I recognize that there is no immigration without emigration and acknowledge the importance of understanding the two as always in relation (cf. Sayad 1979, 2004). Time and budget did not allow for fieldwork in all these locations, and the main focus has been on Blaagaarden and how the women who were born and raised here engage—through the smartphone—with each other and family in the countries that their parents fled or emigrated from and with family members settled in other countries and regions of the world (cf. Hage 2005). To provide a sensorial context to this ethnography, following this introduction is a Playlist that readers can listen to, with a compilation of music that was played by informants in Blaagaarden in 2014 and 2015; most of the individual tracks will be referred to in the book. A few tracks are from the following year, as the fieldwork did not stop abruptly when 2015 ended, but contact continued through social media and occasional visits.

The main question that guided my research was: what does a smartphone *do* in the hands of a young Muslim woman from Blaagaarden: a young woman in the Scandinavian welfare state of Denmark, who is the daughter of immigrants or refugees from countries in the Middle East,[2] Central Asia, or North Africa? What does a smartphone afford a young woman who moves street-smart and skilled in this specific urban environment and who has strong transnational links to family and friends across countries? What does it afford her in terms of managing relations—local links and networks that she might have to be discrete about, as family members, neighbors, or others in the local community might question the nature of these relations? The research carried out was situated at the junction of the smartphone and social media, the young Muslim women, and the urban social housing milieu of Blaagaarden, explored together as an assemblage.[3] Face-to-face fieldwork in a shared physical environment with my informants, focusing on their use of the smartphone, in combination with systematic, intensive online fieldwork, helped me tune in on distinct and concrete configurations of (digital-material) social relationality. What do you write to someone on Facebook, who do you pose with in the pictures you post on Instagram (see p. 32–33 for an introduction to various social media platforms and their use). Who do you "like?" Does your "snap score" show you sending and receiving more snaps to this person than that person so they appear in your "streak" and as your "top friends?" Who do you call, or Facetime, and who do you text most frequently? How much time passes before you get back to someone? Looking at how these kinds of questions are made manifest through smartphones and social media brings the social relation and the reciprocity entailed into view: how large a part of me you are—and how large a part you want me to be of you? That is, the smartphone entwines the online digital realm in everyday, emplaced, embodied living and webs of reciprocity[4] such that "being online" is a fundamentally social practice to my informants, but one in which it is carefully chosen whom one is visible to, how, and when.

Why Muslim women—the mirror image and the book's double focus

The title "Why Muslim Women and Smartphones: Mirror Images" alludes to a double gaze and a double focus. The twofold aim of this monograph is to provide an ethnographic description of the lives of young Muslim women in the Copenhagen social housing area Blaagaarden and how smartphones figure in—and configure—their lives, *and* to attend epistemologically to how this description entails its own mirror-image. Chapters A, B, C, and D introduce the ethnography; a number of "images" from fieldwork: images of the smartphone as used by my informants; of the neighborhood; of hijab (Islamic headscarf), desire, and social control; and dream images and digitally circulated images relating to the imaginal realm (the *alam al-Mithal*). Interspersed are chapters a, b, c, and d, which revolve around epistemology, methodology, and new questions and perspectives emerging from the ethnography. The form of this book is thus twinned chapters. This effect is called *refraction* and the light is said to be refracted[5]—the mirror images in the commentary, in the small-letter chapters can be approached as refracted mirror images. The mirror image that you see when you look into a plane (flat) mirror is an image, a reflection. An important effect with transmitted light is that its direction of travel can change as it crosses the boundary between materials.

In the four chapters of this book—marked with capital letters A, B, C, and D—I seek to show how the Internet-enabled smartphone is both a concrete *relational device*. It aggregates significant others, relatives, friends, and new acquaintances spread out geographically across different parts of the world— and, at the same time, *real virtuality*, in that it affords reciprocity, networking, and liaisons as well as invites for imaginings and experimentation that extend the "range of possibilities" (Zigon 2009). In short, online spaces do *not* figure as parallel worlds for the women; they are an integral part of the worlds they live in, a part of the environment they move in, across the on- and offline. In these chapters with capital letters, I focus on what the women *do* with the smartphone. What does it afford, for good or ill, in terms of connection, simultaneity, and secrecy? How does it show how much one is part of the people one (visibly) invests in across the on- and offline realms? I further discuss the urban habitat: Who is the typical Blaagaarden girl? What goes on in "the Ghetto," in the central square and behind the curtains in the apartments in Blaagaarden? Smartphones and social media are very much a part of this habitat and the not their goings-on. I recount how Facebook flirts led to a deathly stabbing of a participant in the photo project I carried out in the area. The ways in which the women strive for—and inhabit—modesty and piousness while being fun and attractive simultaneously are described. Hijab and desire are at the center of debates about, and conversations among, young Muslim women about the proper way to comport oneself. These ethnographic descriptions also engage with the dynamic denoted "social control" in the Danish context and the differing sensibilities relating to the notion of "freedom" at play in my field.

In asking "*Why* young *Muslim* women and smartphones," I introduce a questioning of anthropological knowledge-making, its imperative and interventions. Why produce knowledge about specific groups of people? For whom is this knowledge produced? What is its motivation and purpose? In attempting an experimental intervention in the politics of representation in the specific case of Muslim women in Denmark, I do not assume a "realist" approach to studying culture in which one simply describes social reality but acknowledge that "the exercise is not more context-free than its subject matter" (Strathern 1988:8). Experimental problems must first be embodied in an intensive assemblage prior to their being solved (DeLanda 2002:177), and the experimentalist (anthropologist) is always part of the assemblage interrogated. In these mirror chapters, I seek to make evident the knowledge claims on which this book is based. The small-letter chapters are concerned with methodology, epistemology, and take a closer look at where the questions pursued in the capital-letter chapters stem from. They are concerned with what those questions tell us about the anthropologist's culture(s), the observer observed (Bateson 2000). What emerges at the interface of what Laura Marks terms the "new cultural formations of Western metropolitan centres," which have resulted from global flows of immigration, exile, and diaspora, where people of different cultural backgrounds now live together in the power-inflected spaces of diaspora, post- or neocolonialism (Marks 2000: 1–2).

In between the chapters, through the montage of descriptions and reiterations of questions posed, a *composite* image is conjured up—one of the young Muslim women in Blaagaarden as embodying a composite habitus: parts of different wholes. This image implicates the anthropologist, her "culture," and the "we" of the anthropological knowledge-making practice. The smartphone has been key as a particular kind of knowledge-making device for me as an anthropologist in the field. Through my fieldwork, these multiple qualities of the smartphone have entailed the formation of new kinds of sensibilities— including relations between the physical, digital, and imaginal realm. In Eastern Islamic philosophy, the imaginal realm is a realm of images, in Arabic denoted also as *alam al-mithal* (world of images, or world of analogies) or *alam al-khayal* (imaginative world). It is conceived of as more real than matter (Marks 2016) and the analogy of images in this realm is the reflection in a mirror, thus describing the relation of images to the empirical world (Chittick 1994; Corbin 1976). From this view, all ideas and all potentials for manifestation are held suspended "as if in a mirror." The twinned chapters and the continuous mirroring throughout the book, might evoke a sense of déjà-vu. According to Henri Bergson the illusion of déjà-vu is due to a recollection of the present, contemporaneous with the present itself: "Our actual existence, then, whilst it is unrolled in time, duplicates itself along with a virtual existence, a mirror-image. Every moment of our life presents the two aspects, it is actual and virtual, perception on one side and recollection on the other" (Bergson 1920:165).

A mirror image is—strictly speaking—the description of a reflection of an object, which appears almost identical but is reversed front to back (reflection). The smartphone has a "front-facing camera," first developed for the iPhone 4 in the expectation that it would be used for the FaceTime app. The young Muslim women use the smartphone's front-facing camera to see the person they are speaking to, but also as a mirror and to take "selfies." Figuratively, the smartphone also functions as a mirror in that you make out who you are in the reflection sent back to you by others. The self emerges through interaction with significant others through socialization, as described in classic social theory (Cooley 1922; Mead 1962). The mirrored analogy thus extends to ethnography. Anthropological knowledge-making has been said to have a mirror function: looking at ourselves through the contrast with the other (Novaes 1997; Strathern 1988; Wagner 1981 [1976]). Margaret Mead, for example, famously gave Americans reason to reflect on gender norms and sexual mores in adolescence through the mirror she held up in her description of coming of age in Samoa (Mead 2001 [1928]), itself a mirror image and reflection as the subtitle alludes to "A Psychological Study of Primitive Youth for Western Civilisation."

The representations of the self—this reflection of oneself prompted by contact with an *other*—imply confrontation between different value systems as a result of which one speculates about oneself and others (Novaes 1997:47–48). This was a key subject of debate in the 1980s explored in "Anthropology as Cultural Critique" (Marcus and Fischer 1999 [1986]) differently in "Writing against Culture" (Abu-Lughod 1991), and with experimentation at the forefront and in newer iterations troubling the self/other in reconfigured fieldwork in increasingly mediatized and globalized environments (cf. Otto et al. 2018; Estalella and Criado 2018). Images, media, and new technologies were central in the research project

"Camera as Cultural Critique" that I was part of (2013–2016), paying attention to how "televisualist anthropology" has its own implicated Western epistemologies (Weiner 1997) and that "our own metaphors reflect a deeply rooted metaphysics with manifestations that surface in all kinds of analyses. The question is how to displace these most effectively" (Strathern 1988:12). This work has been deeply informative and integral to the conceptual development of this book and its refracted, material (chapter) form.

According to Roy Wagner, historical anthropology mirrored the ideology of the late colonial and supraethnic empires of Britain, France, Central Europe, and others (1981:107–108), and Orientalism has been described as, in essence, a (distorted) mirror image of the Occident (Said 1978). This book aims to challenge this anthropological tendency pointed out by these scholars while acknowledging the mirrored representational work of ethnographic writing (see Strathern 1999). I do so by scrutinizing how the smartphone and video camera allowed for what I call a "Cyborg optics," drawing from Strathernian "partial connection" as co-elaborated by Donna Haraway in the Cyborg Manifesto (1985). I entered into affinities, not possible without the digital tools and technologies for seeing and sharing images, generating knowledge with the women involved. I suggest that this allows for a parallax, moving between, and entering into, different configurations for seeing—with or without prosthetic (optical) devices (Waltorp 2018a, b). In this discussion of optics, perceptions, mirrors, and mirror images, I draw on Ibn al-Haytham (Sabra 1989) and his *Kitab al-Manazir*, the Book of Optics, or "Perceptiva" as the Latin title reads. I enter into a dialogue— or circulation—of knowledge, philosophy, and science in the Arab world and Europe, going back to the Greeks, over the Islamic "Golden Age" in 800–1200 with translations of old Greek texts into Arabic, and from Arabic to Latin and back into the circulation of European philosophy (cf. Sedgwick 2016). I discuss in this book how new (technological) possibilities for affinity also raise questions and (im)possible challenges that call for a "Cyborg ethics" in the globalized and digitalized world we live in.

Drawing on Gregory Bateson, I question "what circumstances promote that specific habitual phrasing which we call 'free will'?" (Bateson 2000:163). This is entangled in debates in Denmark and elsewhere around whether or not "Muslim women need saving" (Abu-Lughod 2013), implicating (neo-) Orientalism in new figurations and increased state control to counter what is called "social control" in the political discourse. I could only start to answer and, more importantly, reconfigure questions I posed in my research after I had imploded them (Dumit 2014). An implosion is "a violent collapse inward," a force bringing multiple dimensions together, connecting them. By using this term, I am making a claim for heterogeneous and continual construction through historically located practice, where the actors are not all human. The multiple dimensions that make up objects also make up ourselves, as well as our categories (Dumit 2014; Haraway 1988). The mirror image that is enacted in the small-letter chapters is both reflection and refraction; it is concerned with methodology, epistemology, knowledge-making, *and* future-making. The small-letter chapters sometimes displace the questions raised by the ethnographic material but always speak back to the capital-letter chapters, returning to them with reconfigured questions, which acknowledge the situated habit of seeing and take the specific apparatus of vision that is implicated into account. Ibn al-Haytham (Sabra 1989) wrote about optics, perspective, and how we are able to see. Drawing on him and the ecological psychology of James J. Gibson (2015), concerned with the same issues, I ask, what's in a field? How was *this* particular field delineated, accessed, and what configured the questions posed? I trace my affections for the neighborhood (Hanan al-Noerrebro) and how—through fieldwork—I began to *perceive* the affordances of the area, which was also my own neighborhood where I lived with my family, differently. This leads me to suggest that this urban habitat, this field—and the subject position of being a young Muslim second-generation immigrant—is conducive of what I term a "composite habitus" (Waltorp 2015).

To sum up, the form of this book is twinned chapters or refracted mirror images of each other. In capital-letter chapters A, B, C, and D, I follow the young women, smartphone in hand, in their everyday life in this specific environment at this specific historic time. In Chapters a, b, c, and d, in turn, I attempt a figure-ground reversal (Wagner 1981[1976]) and the figure that emerges is the knowledge-making practice itself, which now becomes object. The ethnographic, descriptive chapters are denoted with capital letters and the refractive mirror images in small-letter chapters. The small-letter chapters do not explain or analyze the content in the ethnographic chapters, for the analysis is in the montage of the ethnographic text, and in the friction in-between repeated concerns and questions in capital-letter chapters and small-letter chapters. They are on the same level, so to speak. In an attempt to tear down the wall that "stands between narrative (associated with subjective knowledge) and analysis (associated with objective truths)" (Narayan 1993:682), the book's form mixes lively narrative and rigorous analysis that "involves enacting hybridity, regardless of our origins" (Narayan 1993). The analytical object of this book is the everyday of young Muslim women in Blaagaarden, what their smartphones afford them—and with equal weight—the analytical object is anthropological knowledge-making.

Informants and anthropologist: Women, collaborators, interlocutors, friends

The women I worked with were born in Copenhagen or had moved there (migrated or fled) at an early age. I moved to Copenhagen from the countryside, the North West coast of Denmark, when I was 18 years old. I am a woman, mother, wife, daughter, sister—and a friend to those of the women with whom I shared most time and life lived. They are also women, some are wives and mothers, and they are daughters, sisters, and friends. I am also a majority ethnic Dane in the Danish nation of 5.6 million people, and the women are part of a Muslim minority estimated at 300,000. I acknowledge that we are in differing positions and have both overlapping and different experiences and struggles. I do not intend to "imply, however, that all women suffer the same oppression simply because we are women ... to distort our commonality as well as our difference. For then beyond sisterhood, is still racism" (Lorde 1983 [1981]:95, 97). I am an anthropologist and the women I worked with have informed me in all respects and across registers in the research that I have carried out together *with* them. They are collaborators, but doing research, analysis, and dissemination is predominantly my work. They have a stake in my work but have their own jobs, education, and aspirations to attend to. I have chosen the term "informants." The women are my interlocutors, a more recent term in anthropology, but so are my colleagues, students, many acquaintances, and those who inspire me through their own writing. "Informant" might be perceived as a dated term that implies the problematic history and even violence of the anthropological endeavor of *knowing-as-ruling* minorities, indigenous people, and colonized people. The term carries a lot of baggage, and by insisting on using it, I attempt to be conscious of this history and acknowledge it and strive for an accountable knowledge-making practice, not brushing over the responsibility of knowledge-making and -sharing and never thinking there is a position from where to lead "non-innocent conversations" (Haraway 1988). I attempt to start from the productivity of "staying with the trouble" (Butler 1990).

In learning by doing, or by interacting and adjusting to materials, machines, and models, experimentalists progressively discern what is relevant and what is not in a given experiment. In other words, the distribution of the important and the unimportant is slowly brought to light in the process of defining an experimental problem and as the assemblage stabilizes itself through the mutual accommodation of its heterogeneous components. In this assemblage the singularities and affects of the experimentalist's body are meshed with those of machines, models, and material processes in order for learning to occur and for embodied expertise to accumulate (DeLanda 2002). There is a general self-referential paradox underlying all observing systems. Every record has been somehow subjected to editing and transformation either by woman or her instruments. No data are truly "raw," as Gregory Bateson has it, as it is always formed by the instruments used and the person using the instruments. Still "the data are the most reliable source of information, and from there the scientist must start" (Bateson 2000:xxvi).

All of the women I have worked with self-identify as Muslim; yet, I am not a scholar of Islam. In this study, the women showed me when and how religion was important in their lives. Within the study of Islam in Europe, there has been a debate between the so-called "everyday Islam" scholars (cf. Schielke 2010, 2015; Schielke and Debevec 2012) and those who focus on piety, ethical self-transformation, salafi- and ultra-orthodox Muslims (Fadil and Fernando 2015a, b). Like Saba Mahmood and Talal Asad before them, Nadia Fadil and Mayanthi Fernando seek to denaturalize the conventions of secular thought and praxis and point to how liberalism and secularism (and not just Islam) operate as moral fields enacted through everyday practices (Asad 2002, 2009; Fadil and Fernando 2015a; Fernando 2013, 2014; Mahmood 2004, 2009). The same movement of seeking to denaturalize secular thought and praxis is relevant in displacing my own cultural metaphors and challenging the conditions and grounding of the questions to which I pursue answers: "examining the entanglements between ethical selfhood, concrete praxis, and (religious or secular) norms" (Fadil and Fernando 2015b:99). At the same time, the sentiments of "everyday Islam" studies resonate with my empirical material in that the women I worked with did not foreground their religious practice with me, or with each other, but Islam was a part of an everyday taken-for-granted aspect of life, sociality, and cosmology through a temporal ordering of the day (in five prayers), the week (Friday as the most important), the year (with *Ramadan*, the month of fasting, and *Eid al-Fitr*, the celebration of its ending) as well as life-cycle events with religious rituals and traditions around marriage, birth, death, and burial, and the desired pilgrimage to Mecca—the place also ordering the spatial orientation wherever one is in the world (placing one's prayer mat in the direction of Mecca when praying). The constant negotiating between pious attitudes, norms and morals, is part of an "everyday Islam," that is also influenced by digital media and new opportunities and spaces opened up by these (cf. Menin 2018).

In addition to being a Muslim woman (in the age group between 20 and 30), residence in the local area of Blaagaarden, Noerrebro, was a criterion guiding whom to include in my study. The assemblage I was interrogating entailed physical, geographical place as well as imagined, remembered and online, digital space. A few (ethnic) Danish women, some converted to Islam, were part of the peer groups that I did fieldwork with. Living in the area and being part of the everyday sociality there, they also made up part of my study, however not as key informants. My main informants had origins in different countries in the Middle East, Central Asia, and North Africa (Jordan, Palestine,[6] Lebanon, Syria, Iran, Iraq, Pakistan, Morocco, Tunisia). Most of the women referred to themselves as immigrants ("indvandrere"), even though they were born in Denmark and their *parents* had emigrated (or fled) their home countries (or in the case of Palestinians arrived from Lebanon or Jordan). A few of the women would use the term "second-generation" or "of other ethnic background," and in the official national census, they would be categorized as "descendants from non-Western countries" ("efterkommere") (Danmarks Statistik 2014). I have occasionally identified them as "Muslim, second-generation immigrant women," and while I regret how it collapses the complexity of the lives and trajectories of these women, it does speak to a joint experience of a "subject position," which is shared. At the same time, the women I worked with defy clear-cut categories: they constitute a "new urban culture" of peer groups, across Danes and immigrants of various backgrounds. The women, no matter their ethnicity or where their parents came from, agreed that, as young Muslim women, they share the same experience growing up in Denmark with roots both here and elsewhere, different sets of expectation to live up to and reconcile, and the same set of stereotypes to navigate. I draw on the wide range of research done within the field of migration studies in the Danish context,[7] where this group of young people born and brought up in Denmark— children of immigrants, *not* immigrants *themselves*—are less often portrayed.

I anonymize my informants and change various facts in all publications, including this book. Yet some of the informants are very "revealed." Some have asked that I use their real name, and, not least, many of the informants feature in an experimental ethnographic film I produced as part of my research. However, despite their willingness to reveal themselves in this way, I remain concerned that those of the women who have agreed to show their face will not just be associated with their own particular story but also carry the weight of the stories of the other non-identified women, whose stories are shared as "ethnographic cases" in this book, but who have chosen not to be in pictures. As a result, when presenting my informants in this book, I have had to conceal parts of their story. I have changed names and small details, following a tactics (Waltorp 2018b) of "not showing" as a cultivation of particular moral sensibilities as "ambiguity is a favourite strategy for simultaneously revealing and concealing"

(Ewing 2006:100), since "ambiguity allows deniability" (Ewing 2006:102). As long as there is ambiguity, there is the possibility of deniability—maintaining this ambiguity mirrors the type of tactics the women apply in their lives in order to maintain ambiguity while they navigate various sets of expectations simultaneously, and where the individual young woman's reputation reflects on the whole family. The need to be ambivalent, and let some things be evoked, without being too literal in the way they are conveyed, is mirrored in this book to some extent—in the form of *hijab latif,* putting up a thin veil allowing for different interpretations according to who is reading and the depth of their understanding. Ambiguity is central to the notion of *harakat,* which I introduce below. Aligning different areas of one's life is made possible by ambiguity—something that the smartphone allows for.

Harakat movement

From looking closely at the ways my main informants move physically across neighborhoods and countries, and the way they move in online spaces, it's clear that notions of personhood and space are being reconfigured with new digital technologies. These reconfigurations of personhood and space also bring into view the ethnographic theory of *harakat* movement. I was in a shop on a Saturday afternoon, with two informants looking at cosmetics. They noticed that there was a sale on support compression stockings. The mother of one of them had a bad knee and needed such supportive stockings. For some reason, only the small size was on sale; yet in a swift move, a price tag had changed place from an on-sale item to the right size for my informants' mother. We paid and left, the two informants high-fiving each other as we walked down the street. "What just happened there?" I asked, and they laughingly said that they did not let me in on it because I don't do *harakat.* I follow rules and do not move in a very *harakat* way. I always buy a ticket when taking the bus, and so on. The term *harakat* would be used to denote smart, skilled navigation of situations to the advantage of the person, but on different scales. In the Danish online slang dictionary, it is the newest entry, with the explanation "Harakat betyder ballade—Eow vi laver harakat!" ("Harakat means trouble—Eow we're making trouble!," slangster.dk), or the urbandictionary.com site, which has a similar explanation: Arabic meaning of going out to make trouble "Abdul—Wanna go make some harakat?" (added March 5, 2018). In the latter example an Arab male name is added, indicating who is expected to be making this kind of trouble.

The explanation catches the double aspect of making fun/making trouble but is lacking the dense meanings of the world depending on who uses it. For the women I worked with, it was more charm and cunning that was valued as *harakat*, what they would explain as "to play a trick on someone or in some situation," shifting between positions and playing on people's different expectations, rather than the more criminal *harakat* of young gang members, who focus on outsmarting opponents and/or the police. The specific subject position of being "second generation" creates a range of possibilities for a type of movement that are *harakat*—more tactic (informal acts) than strategy (formal structures and planning); An ad hoc, subversive, cunning way to move around and about structures not of one's own making. I was introduced to the term *harakat* by my informants and had heard them use it in different contexts without comprehending the meaning. I noticed it being used in a hip-hop tune by local artist Amro (see Playlist). The chorus "*We do a harakat on your sorry ass, we do a harakat on your harakat*" and "*we do a harakat on the police*" on YouTube is accompanied by the following homemade explanation:

Ha·ra·kat [ħarə'kæt]
Noun
1. Movements (arab.)
2. To do harakat; to play "tricks", avoid something, make a move:
Ex.: "We do a harakat on them!"

In the case of *harakat*, playing on people's prejudices sometimes is part of a subversive, rebellious everyday "making do" while having a laugh. You need to have attitude to "pull it off." Finally, it is the word for Arabic diacritics: marking short vowels in Arabic script. The *harakāt* literally means "motions" and denotes the short vowel marks that move around the vowel, small diacritics but with an impact on how the pronunciation and meaning are actualized, determining the way a letter is pronounced.[8] In art and calligraphy *harakāt* might be used simply because it is considered aesthetically pleasing.

To sum up, *harakat* is an Arabic term signifying motion or movement. In the local slang of young Muslim people in Noerrebro, however, *harakat* means to "make a move" and to "play a trick" on someone in a cunning, smart, or charming way. The young women you meet in this book, and second-generation immigrant youth in Copenhagen at large, commonly employ the notion *harakat* to denote and appreciate such moves. This move can be concrete, or it can be understood in the sense of "general tactics" applied in the everyday navigation across often conflicting sets of expectations and values. Applied in this way, *harakat* changes and overflows the meaning of movement and becomes a movement trick. It is symptomatic of being street-smart in the area of Noerrebro and of being formed by the place where one grows up. The smartphone is crucial to this navigation; it offers a specific set of opportunities as a *relational device* to my informants. They are trying to balance various sets of sociocultural, moral, and religious norms and expectations and maintain networks and relations across these. This includes negotiating differing notions and practices of public, private, and intimate spheres and the complex interfaces between them. The notion of *harakat*, as used in Noerrebro slang and performed in "vernacular movement," is reflected in the Islamic philosophic notion of *al-Harakat*: and *harakat al-wujud*—the flow of being (Marks 2016). The know-how of moving skillfully became even more apparent through travels with informants to Iran and United Arab Emirates. Hanging out with family members, especially cousins the same age as themselves, made it obvious how they are not "at home" in their parents' country of origin yet manage to move across countries and different sets of norms, codes, and hone the "trans-contextual" (Bateson 2000) skill set necessary for an everyday lived across contexts and expectations, keeping futures open.

The specific emic-cum-analytical notion of *harakat* that I am developing here has its own empirical flavor yet grows out of a subject position in which one is not in a place where one can plan and strategize; it is subversive. *Harakat* is a necessary skilled way of moving in an insecure environment in which one is not in a power position to make the rules; it finds parallels in Michel de Certeau's conceptual pairing of the "strategy" used by those in power, to the "tactics" used by the weak (1984, see also Scott 1985). The analytical notion of tactics and "se debrouiller" or "making-do" has been developed ethnographically by many anthropologists: examples of this are Henrik Vigh's concept "social navigation" (*dubriagem* is the emic Portuguese term that inspired it) to describe the young men in Guinea Bissau's conflict-ridden landscape with few options and many risks (2006, 2009), and Christian Vium's rendition of the emic notion of "Tcheb-Tchib" denoting former nomads making-do-tactics in the Mauritanian capital of Nouakchott (Ould Ahmed Salem 2001; Vium 2016). I use the term *harakat* in this book to denote a specific skilled mode of moving in one's environment (counting here both the online, physical, and imaginal realms). It resembles the dynamics in the studies above: using tactics to make the best of things, the most of what you have, and in the case of *harakat* not least have fun while doing it. Below you will find the Playlist and images: collages from fieldwork, film stills from the experimental ethnographic film and images shared in social media. Choose a track and watch the images in the collage of this place you are invited into.

I have a thousand brilliant lies
For the question:
How are you?
I have a thousand brilliant lies
For the question
What is God?
If you think that the Truth can be known
From words,
If you think that the Sun and the Ocean
Can pass through that tiny opening Called the mouth
O someone should start laughing!
Someone should start wildly Laughing—Now!
(Hafez, Persian poet 1315–1390—meme shared on Instagram)

I

II

III

V

VI

VII

VIII

IX

X

XI

XII

XIII

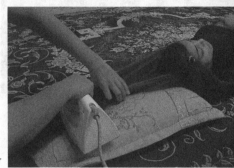

XIV

Joyous are the eyes that see you

XV

XVI

XV

XVIII

XIX

XX

 XXI

XXII

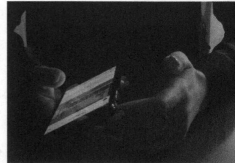

XXIII

XXIV

XXV

XXVI

XXVII

XXVII

XXIX

XXX

XXXI

14

XXXII

Image list

I	The eyes tell a story. Driving along the lakes in Copenhagen. Still from Joyous Are the Eyes That See You, Waltorp 2017b.
II	Touching the images of family members far away—on the Smartphone screen. Still from Joyous Are the Eyes That See You, Waltorp 2017b.
III	Driving, Tehran. Still from Joyous Are the Eyes That See You, Waltorp 2017b.
IV	Contemplation. Inside an apartment in Blaagaarden. Still from Joyous Are the Eyes That See You, Waltorp 2017b.
V	The Student Lake (Peblinge Soe) seen from Noerrebrogade, Queen Louise's Bridge. Wassim and Felix' photo diary, Ghetto NO Ghetto project.
VI	With friends of the family. Growing up together. Apartment in Blaagaarden. Fatima's photo diary, Ghetto NO Ghetto project.
VII	Veiling in preparation of leaving the apartment, Blaagaarden. Still from Joyous Are the Eyes That See You, Waltorp 2017b.
VIII	Staircase in apartment building in Blaagaarden. Still from film accompanying Ghetto NO Ghetto project.
IX	Old family photo, children's birthday in Blaagaarden. Fatima's photo diary, Ghetto NO Ghetto project.
X	Blaagaarden. Still from film accompanying Ghetto NO Ghetto project.
XI	Taher's photo diary, friends cruising in Blaagaarden.
XII	Blaagaardsgade. Still from film accompanying Ghetto NO Ghetto project.
XIII	Present while absent through images. An image of the father on display, Blaagaarden apartment. Still from Joyous Are the Eyes That See You, Waltorp 2017b.
XIV	Straightening hair, Tehran. Still from Joyous Are the Eyes That See You, Waltorp 2017b.
XV	Title Screen. Still from Joyous Are the Eyes That See You, Waltorp 2017b.
XVI	Grandmother, welcoming/waving goodbye, Tehran. Still from Joyous Are the Eyes That See You, Waltorp 2017b.
XVII	A daughter's love for her mother. "Paradise is at the feet of the mother." Still from Joyous Are the Eyes That See You, Waltorp 2017b.
XVIII	Jordan, footage from film accompanying Ghetto NO Ghetto project.

Playlist

Call to prayer:
https://www.youtube.com/watch?v=fe8qRj12OhY
Call to prayer in London:
https://www.youtube.com/watch?v=3paZoyU-1aE
Amro: Noerrebro (2013)
https://www.youtube.com/watch?v=9PZjp4Ro-Iw
Xander feat. Nadia Gattas: Mit Hjerte Brænder (2013)
https://www.youtube.com/watch?v=CkFaC9DstDg
Amro feat. Gilli: Korrupt (2014)
https://www.youtube.com/watch?v=Ztgr7quKZjA
Mazen: Lige nu (2016)
https://www.youtube.com/watch?v=HSnKy-dLjaM
Mohammed Assaf: Ya Halali Ya Mali (2014)
https://www.youtube.com/watch?v=jCOfMdXNSzs
Amro: Harakat (2012)
https://www.youtube.com/watch?v=NT6-s2kZE3g
Beyoncé feat. Jay Z: drunk in Love (2013)
https://www.youtube.com/watch?v=p1JPKLa-Ofc
Mohsen Yeganeh: Bekhand (2014)
https://www.youtube.com/watch?v=2CqWmHCfjSg
HDM: AFRO TRAP Part. 4 (fait la Mouv) (2015)
https://www.youtube.com/watch?v=4OaEf9zeyI8
SIVAS: Kbhavana (2013)
https://www.youtube.com/watch?v=dktOk2LoOIE
Ammar al Koofe: Arab Idol (2015)
https://www.youtube.com/watch?v=J1SI3hMNYII
Gilli: Orale (2015)
https://www.youtube.com/watch?v=BXJEs7C6aLQ
Gilli: Knokler Hårdt (2014)
https://www.youtube.com/watch?v=RRLLPavaSwo
Maître Gims: Habibi (2015)
https://www.youtube.com/watch?v=Yi8toWtoqtw
Mohsen Yeganeh: Behet Gol Midam (2016)
https://www.youtube.com/watch?v=cDNDVtoJhik

A

Smartphone

Affordances of the smartphone

"What does the smartphone mean to you?" I posed this question directly to Bita, Ilham, and Dunya, just before reaching the top of the mountain Bame Teheran with the Teheran skyline as backdrop. A long "selfie-session" was about to take place. We were sitting in the shadow of a few trees along the dusty road to catch our breath in the burning heat of the July day in 2015. I had taken out my video camera and pointed it at the women. "What was the question?" Bita asked. Ilham explained on my behalf: "The smartphone—what does it mean to you?" Bita responded without hesitation:

> Bita: "Oh—it means everything ..." (holding the smartphone in her hand).
> Ilham: "No not everything—depends on who you're with, if you're having a
> good time (*hygger sig*) ..."
> Bita: "Yes, of course—but when you're not with the people you care about—
> that makes it very important, for example."

I turned to Dunya: "What do you think?" She was sitting a bit afar, looking at her nails, showing them to the video camera, and asking what I thought of her nails, instead of replying. She then proceeded to take out her smartphone, in a move that crystallized how varied the affordances of the smartphone are to her. She pointed it toward *me* sitting with my video camera and started recording: "Now we'll do a short interview with you." I responded to her questions about whether I enjoyed my stay in Iran, meeting her family and so forth, smiling at the lens on her smartphone directed at me, aware of the potential audience. Roles shifted. Was it a video she would send? To whom? I knew it could not be sent as a so-called "snap," as the app Snapchat, which was much used in their lives in Denmark, was prohibited and did not work in Iran. Dunya put the smartphone down and the others got up from the ground where they had been resting in the midday heat: "Interview's over, come let's go," she concluded. This moment shared in real time was reiterated and made present again on many occasions since, courtesy of the smartphone. I received pictures of it while back in Denmark and saw the images on Instagram and Facebook where it received comments and drew in other people. We were continually made present in each other's lives through these and countless other replays like them.

As alluded to in the opening vignette, the smartphone is ubiquitous among young Muslim women in Blaagaarden as in many other places in today's technologically mediated world. Smartphones figure as central networking devices to people inside and outside of the social housing area and in broader transnational networks. The smartphones shape, register, and impact what is communicated through them. In addition to their uses for accessing information and for communication, smartphones are applied in a multitude of ways in Blaagaarden: As a tool for protection, gossiping, alliance-making, flirting, bullying, or trafficking drugs. They are used for reading the Qur'an, keeping track of prayer time, geo-tagging (subversively giving other coordinates online than one's actual physical location), paying bills, raising money for humanitarian causes[1] for communicating with municipal offices and social services, and for entertainment and "flashing" one's economic and technological capital. It is a relational device, as Bita points to in the quote above from the interview on Bame Tehran "when you're not with people you care about." It makes people part of you and partly present, even though they are absent.

The most-used apps and social media platforms that I refer to in this book are the Snapchat photo messaging application that allows users to take "Snaps"—photos or videos with added text, filters and drawings—and sends them to a controlled list of recipients, the content automatically deleted after a set time limit of maximum 10 seconds; Instagram, an image-sharing platform with filters and editing tools that enhance the appearance of the images; Facebook, the world's largest social networking site that affords both public displays on "the wall" and private communication through an inbox system; the Messenger app, which also has video, or VoIP ("Voice over Internet Protocol"), and file-exchange capacity; also widely used in communication among my informants is the WhatsApp application (with 1 billion unique users worldwide, as of 2016), which integrates photos, text, short sound recordings, and small video clips with messaging and video VoIP, and allows group communication; FaceTime, a video application that makes it possible for the parties to see each other while on the phone; Skype and Viber, which are instant messaging and VoIP applications, where users can speak and text as well as exchange images and other data files.

Texting (iMessage, WhatsApp, SMS, etc.), calling, snapping, and checking "Insta" (Instagram) and Facebook were done frequently and at all hours by most of my informants. Images sent and shared could be an image of a pack of cigarettes; a cup of coffee and manicured nails, saying "have a nice day my peeps" from *fajr* (morning prayer); images from the day at the workplace, educational institution, social gatherings, often of food set up nicely on the table or a plate in a café; images from the living room showing what's on TV and a sentence added with one's opinion; yourself in your room; in the car with friends; on outings with family etc. My informants would use the term "apps" or the specific brand name of the app rather than discerning between channel, platform, and media when talking about their practice, saying "I just snapped it to her," "I'm going to put this on Insta right away," "Don't post this on Facebook," "Facetime me later, ok?" These apps were used for contacting people across their social and familial networks; indeed, a day would seldom be spent without the women being in contact with close family and friends through these apps. Viber, having taken over the platform that Skype previously occupied as the primary face-to-face video phone service, was often used to communicate with siblings who had married and settled elsewhere—usually in their parents' countries of origin, in Dubai, or in other cities in European countries. In semi-public and intimate spaces both on- and offline, my informants experimented with both virtuous versions of themselves and, on the other hand, tried out behavior and relations that would be gossiped about if they occurred in public. The intersections of gossip and the off- and online social networking in Blaagaarden are intricate, and they touch on nearly every element of the lives of the women whom I did fieldwork with.

On a late summer afternoon in 2014 in Khadija's living room on the outskirts of Copenhagen, we had a conversation that highlighted the way smartphones enable the probing of values at various levels, including those associated with bodily and aesthetic norms. At the same time as those norms were expressed, they were transformed through a continuous, effortless discerning between what to share via which media channels or platforms, and to what audiences, thus showing the affordances of the smartphone in navigating public and private interfaces and gray zones. Together with Amal and Nour, I had taken the bus to visit Khadija, who moved here from Noerrebro with her husband and son when she was pregnant with their second child. Later Mona and Jamila joined us. We brought along cakes, bread, humus, olives, and other snacks from the halal places in Noerrebro. After greetings and kissing cheeks, we sat down in the living room around a sofa table with a large glass plate as surface. Smoke from a water pipe inhaled and exhaled. With my camera I panned across the table full of plates of cake, the colorful mix of fresh and dried fruits, candy, and soft drinks. I zoomed in on a Coca-Cola can. Light summer rain on the windows. Nour grabbed her phone and said: "Come, we do a selfie." We moved closer together, eyes to the tiny lens on her smartphone. The pictures she took were quickly decorated with a few emoticons and sent as a Snap to girlfriends who were not there with us in the moment, and who only saw the picture in the moment they received it, since a snap will cease to exist after 10 seconds. Other pictures were arranged in montages of pictures of the cakes, the fruit on the table, and us smiling to the camera. A filter was added in a photo app and the photo posted on Facebook, receiving comments from friends and acquaintances. In these pictures, the women wore hijab, as a varied audience is able to look at what is uploaded to Facebook. It is a semi-public online space, as opposed to the physical private space of the living room, and the private online space of the Snapchat platform.

I panned over the four women sitting on two black leather sofas. Although they go veiled in public spaces, here in the private space of the home they removed the veil, long cardigans, and the "outer layer" of clothes they are wearing. This is safe and allowed as long as no men except those from the immediate family (*marhram*)[2] are present. Nour was in her black leggings and a tight black blouse. She had removed just part of the hijab from her head and kept on the inner part, which functions like a hairband. Khadija was wearing a short, comfortable dress in a stretchy jacquard material, and her hair in a ponytail. She was 5 months pregnant and the bump showed clearly now. Jamila did not remove her headscarf—"bad hair day," she said. She sat with her legs curled up under herself on the sofa, in elegant trousers and a small jacket. Mona arrived late, with a water pipe wrapped in two H&M plastic bags, and arranged it on the table. She was wearing jeans and a tunic top. I was in tight jeans and a black T-shirt, seated next to Nour. My thoughts drifted, until they were called back by the women's voices getting louder:

> Amal: "If you're psychologically tired of your breasts, then it's allowed, I'd say it's allowed."
> Mona: "Depends on your husband."
> Jamila and Amal protest: "No, no, no, no, no not the men."
> Amal: "I'd do it for my own sake. My husband says, no, that he doesn't want me to do it. But I want to do it—why: because I feel uncomfortable when I'm naked and my breasts are small."
> Jamila: "Listen, if your husband tells you to do something that is really wrong and lousy, would you still do it just because, yani (you know), he would be happy?"

Mona: "No, I'm just saying …"

Nour: "If it's for him, and he's happy about it, he won't look after other women!"

Jamila: "Even if it's haram, you'd do it?"

Voices overlap and interrupt each other as the discussion heats up. My camera follows the discussion and zooms in on facial expression and the simultaneous handling of messages on the smartphones.

Jamila: "Ok, so it's not haram to have your breasts operated, it's not haram. If God created you, God gave you some nice breasts, a really nice size, then you do not need it," she changes into Arabic, and then back into Danish, turns to me and the camera, letting me in on the main points in Danish as my Arab-language skills are poor. Then she turns to face the others: "We humans are greedy, we just want, want, want—maybe if I have nice breasts, I'll say I don't need it [the operation] but if I have a nose that's crooked, then I'd off course want to fix it."

Mona: "If you have a sickness or a crooked nose, if it's something like that, then you're allowed."

Jamila: "Narook she had her breasts done, she asked an Imam, and they'll tell you: 'Yes, if it's something you feel that makes you look like a man, masculine, then you have a right to have it done'—but not to show them off to others. It has to be done in a way so that they fit you—feminine!"

Jamila: "I've talked to an Imam, I called …."

I film Amal who gets excited and yells in Arabic. But Nour interrupts her:

"No, no, no, you don't have the right to say that. If you think, think, think, and"—she leans back in the leather sofa to illustrate—"When she has to have sex with him, she only thinks about her breasts—wrong." She sits back up and inhales on the water pipe. She turns to me and says directly into the camera: "She [Amal] needs to have hers done 100%—she's got only nipples."

Amal and Jamila talk about how disgusting (*ulækre*) they feel, with only nipples and not fuller breasts. We talk about another friend who has large breasts but would like even bigger, something that is condemned by everyone in our company.

Jamila: "She wants extra-large. I have a butt, that doesn't mean I need a whole other arse. You see what I mean? There are people who have, and just want more!"

I film Amal who turns to her older sister, Mona, laughing: "What about you? Do you have a big arse? Let me feel," and she pinches Mona's butt in the sofa. I film Nour who measures the size of her own breasts with her hands. Everyone agrees that a 75B is a good size. We talk about what happens after breastfeeding, and my camera tilts a bit, as my gestures aid my explanations. We discuss a device that Jamila brought home from Jordan in the hope that it would fulfill its promise of enlarging the breasts naturally.

Mona: "You can have too big breasts too. I have a friend who had fat removed, because she had back pain."

She's interrupted by Nour, who jokingly remarks: "I know what we'll do—then you, Amal and Jamila, you could all contact that woman, who got the fat off from her breasts, and you get that for yourselves."

Amal turns toward me and the video camera: "Karen—Why don't you use push-up bras? You actually have a nice pair of tits, you should wear bras that show it. Your husband would appreciate it, I'm sure."

Nour: Yeah, we talked about that—why don't you?

My camera grows increasingly unsteady as I'm drawn into the discussion, defending my choices, and being asked about my friends'. A few days later, Nour brings me a selection of push-up bras in a variety of colors. She won't be using them herself as they don't fit her. She guessed they would be my size.

The above example unfolds an everyday social situation among the women, slightly altered and made into an event by my being present (with video camera). In the situation, the smartphone is used in various ways: to take selfies and share them on the Snapchat platform with friends, to take other pictures for a different audience on the Facebook platform (wearing the hijab in the pictures for Facebook), and for texting and talking with friends and family. The posts and texts shared during this social gathering were not explicitly related with the subject of breast surgery and beauty ideals in the conversations taking place. Such private or intimate subjects are necessarily avoided while being "openly" joked about in the closed social group of women. The values and norms revealed in any conversation and every post in a social media platform mediated through the technology are related to what is appropriate to share with whom, when, and in what form. A sensibility in terms of appropriate concealing and revealing is part of the habituated social media use of the women.

Like most young people in the Western world, the young Muslim women engage in various media platforms on a daily basis when using their smartphones. As mentioned above, the most important of these are Snapchat, WhatsApp, Facebook, Instagram, text messaging, VoIP, and telephone conversations. They carve out distinct private spaces for themselves within public and semi-public contexts, where they meet and exchange text, images, videos, and links. They then modify, censor, or reveal according to different purposes and audiences (Waltorp 2013b, 2015, 2016). Their creative experimentation with parallel worlds and possible futures emerges within and articulates dominant social, political, and moral conceptions, including that of female Muslim virtuousness as well as other dominant perceptions perpetuated by media and public discourse, such as that of "the ethnic other" vis-à-vis majority Danes. If the online (semi-)public Facebook wall is the only part of the myriad of online "places" that exists, it might seem that it is rather conforming and "conservative" how one presents oneself. Yet with select audiences and confidantes it might play out otherwise.

Touch and crucial connectivity

Smartphones became widespread following the release of the Apple iPhone in 2007, and most smartphones produced from 2012 onward enable wireless access to high-speed mobile broadband, fiber optic cables running under water and across landscapes. A smartphone is a mobile phone, or cellular telephone, with a mobile operating system (IOS or android) combining a computer operating system with the features of a mobile phone: calling and text messaging, calendar, media player, video games, GPS navigation, and the like. It can access the Internet and can run (third-party) software components called applications (apps). A significant difference from the telephone and earlier models of cell phones is the surface of the smartphone—dominated by a touchscreen, where the user via a virtual keyboard (the technical term for the keyboard that appears on screen and disappears when not in use) can type words, numbers, and emoticons and press the icons on the screen to activate the different apps. The touchscreen further enables "swiping" with the fingertips and provides a particular tactility to the use of the smartphone. The smartphone has a digital camera that enables photography and video recording, which was one of the pivotal functions of the smartphone for informants, as noted. The touch of fingers on the surface of images, enlarging by placing index and middle fingers at the point one wants to enlarge or zoom in on, and moving the two fingers simultaneously in opposite directions on the screen could also be done by thumb and middle fingers, depending on habit.

All of my informants owned a smartphone. The preferred brands and models at the time of my fieldwork in 2014 and 2015 were Apple iPhone 5 and 6, and the Samsung Galaxy Models Note 3, 4, 5 and Note Edge. These were the models and brands in fashion and with the best cameras, according to informants. The camera in particular was very important for all of my informants and largely determined which specific smartphone they had chosen. Engagement with photographs involves embodied movement and perception, as does touching a screen with fingers, which is how many people today engage with digital photographs. All of my informants had a photo stream, which they valued looking at—and touching—returning to it in times of boredom or to show something. Due to the Internet access of smartphones, it is possible to share the instant capturing of a moment immediately. This access shifted when in other geographic locations, and with other countries' policies and different available subscriptions, which for example saw my informants chasing *kiosques* across Tehran to buy airtime for their smartphone. Even for those images that were received and saved, and for those not meant for sharing but for oneself to keep as an archive, the revisiting and tactile engagement was fundamental; my informants would touch their phones with their fingertips and scroll with thumb, or middle finger and ring finger: the sound of long, manicured nails scrolling a broken screen (several of them had broken the glass by dropping the phones) is a very particular sound, nothing like the barely audible sound of fingers with bitten-down nails scrolling and touching. The young women would hold their phones to their ear, place them in their lap when driving, and at times hold them close to their chests, kiss the (picture on the) screen, or even throw the phone when particularly upset by a message received or a message that did not manifest or elicit the hoped-for-reply.

The mothers of several of my informants had re-photographed old black-and-white family photos with the camera in their smartphone. They could look at these images in their photo stream whenever they wanted. Wherever they were, the smartphone was in their pockets or very close by, and so were the family members and important moments in their personal archive in iPhoto and other software. Such pictures would be examples of images on the smartphone screen that would be kissed and caressed—images of relatives far away in other countries or deceased. In some instances, it could be images of someone of the opposite sex, whom one had not met but hoped to develop a deeper relationship with (platonically) never knowing where this might lead, perhaps toward romance and even marriage. The force of the smartphone as relational device also opens it up for relations beyond—or not yet—actual. The smartphone opens up to remembering, to futures, and to virtuality.

I was introduced to the family members of one close informant through the photo stream on the smartphone of her mother Mona. Faces of siblings, parents, and of times past looked back at me from black-and-white images on the small screen, accompanied by the soft "bloop" sound that the phone gave off every time Mona clicked to enlarge a photo. I struggled to understand the Danish of

Mona, while she struggled with the kinship terms in Danish, her daughters and niece commenting and correcting her from the other side of the living room, where they were watching TV, when she used a wrong term. I saw three young girls sitting next to each other looking seriously to the camera. Mona pointed and enlarged the image by touching the screen with her thumb and middle finger and moving them away from each other: "This is my sisters. This one she lives here, and this sister ... she is dead. In Tehran." She showed me other photos of relatives living across Iran, Sweden, and Denmark. She showed me pictures of herself as a young woman, laughing, and photos of herself with her husband, now deceased. More than a year after, I was at the grave of her husband and the sister who had died, with family members living in Tehran. We bought red roses from the flower sellers close to the graveyard and placed them carefully around the portrait on the tombstone. I knew the images on the graves from Copenhagen—from the photo stream on a small smartphone screen—*and* I now encountered the images here physically on a grave in Tehran and at the same time they existed in the smartphone of Mona. When revisiting my own footage of a session of looking at photos together on the smartphones, I realized that I now recognized all of the young children in black-and-white photographs. I had met them as middle-aged men and women in Tehran, and one sister I had met at the Imam Ali Mosque in Copenhagen. Other mothers of informants likewise had "photo streams as archives" as well as the pleasure of sharing voice messages on WhatsApp with family members far away, also becoming "familiar" with new family members born, which they could see and hear through the smartphone.

The smartphone as a relational device seemed to be more oriented toward the close social circles of the young women I worked with. The people they were most in contact with would be the ones whom they saw often, sometimes daily (for girlfriends and sisters, not for a potential suitor possibly living far away). The necessity of having the smartphone, and thus one's social circle and social life, close by was evident in the care practice around charging. When arriving to an apartment together, someone would identify a power outlet and a charger (or have brought one themselves) and, when putting their own phone to charge, ask others if they needed to charge or had remembered to charge their phone. It was a standing joke that I often ended up with a flat battery on my smartphone as I did not pay attention or had the same careful routine of making sure to habitually charge when the possibility was there prior to—or as a natural part of—settling down and socializing.

The smartphone would sometimes be keep an informant company through sleepless nights, and when sleep arrived, it would be tugged under the pillow. I knew from sleepovers at informants' houses that the smartphone would either be in the charger or in bed with the woman. It has a status of an intimate part of the person, as archive, connecting and relational device, and as a device for virtuality. This is not to indicate that these aspects are in a unilateral way adding positively to people's everyday living: new possibilities of relating to others and to oneself—past, present, and future—pose as many challenges as they open opportunities. The pressure of showing the care that has now been made possible is deeply felt also as pressure, surveillance, and source of many conflicts. The technology paradoxically affords a monitoring and surveillance in new ways, while simultaneously offering new spaces to be carved out.

Secrets and smartphones

I have sent a text message to Sana to let her know I am almost at her apartment block in the "red bricks," the apartment buildings that make up the social housing area Blaagaarden in the inner-city neighborhood of Noerrebro, Copenhagen. I buzz the door entry phone. Sana comes down the stairs. We exchange greetings: a kiss on the right cheek and then the left. Then we move. Quickly. We are late for an appointment with the tailor, where she is having a dress made for her older sister's wedding. Sana is upset, and we walk hurriedly away from Blaagaarden so that we can talk discreetly. In Noerrebrogade, Noerrebro's busy main street (and my home at the time), we hide in the usual gate of a courtyard in a side street for Sana to be able to smoke discreetly. "Good (Muslim) girls do not smoke in public." Frantically inhaling on the cigarette, Sana tells me of the recent breakup with her secret boyfriend. She explains how the breakup came about:

> You know, we always say good morning to each other; the first person to wake up sends a text to the other. He didn't answer, and yet he was active on Facebook. How can you have time for Facebook, but not be able to reply? I wrote him again, and I called him several times until he finally picked up his phone. Then he was just in a bad mood, telling me that he's only getting out of bed now, and wants to eat his breakfast in peace. I swear, Wallah [by God], I got furious. I'm concerned, waiting, and he's not able to reply? Shouldn't I be his first priority? I waited for hours again, now he should be finished eating breakfast, and he's still online on Facebook. So I call him up again, and he starts yelling at me, telling me to stop monitoring him, "være hovedpine" (be headache), and rather leave him alone. I excuse the fact that I worry by saying that since he was beat up badly by that other guy, I become nervous if I don't hear from him. But he just keeps repeating that I should leave him the fuck alone, go hang myself and stop making problems

for him. I told him "fine, if this is what you want, I will really leave you alone,
even though I love you, I will leave you alone. Goodbye, Hassan."

Sana shows me her iPhone with the text messages they sent each other as part
of the conversation. As we enter the tailor's shop, a text message ticks in from
Hassan: a picture of a cartoon figure holding a heart with the words: "I know it's
not much, but this is what I can offer." We agree that this is an excuse, but vague
and ambivalent, claiming the right to behave this way. The following day, Sana
shows me another picture and quote he has sent. I look long and hard at the
rather abstract picture but cannot make out what is depicted. Sana explains that
it is a young man and woman holding each other in an embrace, and a tree, the
branches, and the contours of the couple forming a fetus inside a womb. Finally,
I am able to make that out too. The text reads: "If you're in love, you'll see the
picture." We look at each other. He is insinuating love, wanting to have babies.
Sana saw the picture in his message right away: she must be in love.

Sana met Hassan on Facebook. Over time their relationship grew deeper.
They communicated solely online for the first 8 months. Later they began
seeing each other very briefly, never including more physical interaction than
a kiss. Sana has to be careful constantly, plan for the right time and place in her
everyday life, where she could get away to secretly text or talk to Hassan online
using Facetime or Viber. Being with Hassan is in itself a form of experiment
into the limits of the morally acceptable. She acknowledges that what she is
doing—being in a love relationship with someone when they are not engaged
or married—is *haram* (forbidden according to the Qur'an). Yet Sana negotiates
the relationship within a religious framework, pointing to how it is a good
thing that Hassan is "moving closer to God, and started praying" because of
her: "He didn't fear God before—now he fears him, really!" In this connection,
the stance of fear toward God is a very positive one; the fear reminds you to
honor God by being a good Muslim, a good person, and do what pleases him.
When Hassan then does not appreciate her time and effort, and the risk she is
taking in being with him, but is online and active on other media platforms and
paying more attention to that, Sana becomes jealous and, at times, furious. It is
an insult. Not being available, making her wait instead of answering a telephone
call is hurtful. Attention and availability are paramount across on- and offline
realms, a currency that is continuously negotiated, and a constant source of
either conflict or gratification in interpersonal relations. This is the case in love
relations not just between couples, but also between close girlfriends. Attention
and availability—and the time it implies—is a precious gift, something you

give of yourself and receive from others—it makes you the person you are. Had the relation between Sana and Hassan been shared publicly, it would have been highly problematic. Gossip-invoking behavior in cases such as this could be detrimental to the woman's reputation, her ability to marry well, and, consequently, to the reputation of her family.

Once you befriend someone on Facebook, add them as a WhatsApp or Snapchat contact, or are followed by someone on Instagram, your activity shows (unless you are really careful). Not being available and not paying attention to a friend or partner is a clear signal that warrants a reaction. The reciprocity of whom you invest in online and who invests in you can be "read" by others, and it shapes the picture of you, your relations, and your social standing and status. Depending on how you use them, smartphones and social media thus afford a carving out of spaces to be yourself, or rather be your different selves, while at the same time enabling a constant monitoring and tracking, as the above vignette alludes to.

In her monograph *Veiled Sentiments* (1986), anthropologist Lila Abu-Lughod writes extensively on the subject of honor as intricately related to the wearing of the veil and relations between the sexes in Islam. I see parallels in the way the Bedouin women she worked with use the expressive modality of poetry (*ghinnawa*) as a vehicle to express (non-virtuous) sentiments that are not necessarily talked about in the open[3] and how my informants communicate (secret) messages layered with multiple meanings and sentiments in social media. My informants are experiencing intersecting and conflicting structures and move across on- and offline realms in a *harakat* way, never being sure that someone will not "do a harakat on their harakat."

On social media platforms, the usage patterns of my informants without exception were much more exclusive than mine; they knew how to utilize privacy settings, use aliases, and many have double accounts. They would show different versions of themselves to different audiences[4] and with varying degrees of formality. The audience would mostly be their closest girlfriends, where a very informal tone, joking and selfies without the *hijab*, would be shared. The most censored image of oneself is typically on the Facebook page where one can encounter family and people of the older generation, something that calls for a different "tone" and type of images. On their "official" Facebook pages, where people use their real names and pictures, the content shared on the Facebook wall ranges from food, fashion and beauty, children and family gatherings, certain political crises and causes (Palestine and Syria mostly) to also include (opposition to) Danish right-wing politicians, work- and study-related postings and humorous memes. Most of my informants have profiles on semi-public social media sites such as Facebook. On these sites, some share their devotion to the Prophet Muhammad and his teachings. These displays have their own recognizable aesthetic with pictures and drawings, often quoting *ayat* (verses in the Qur'an), shared on the person's Facebook wall.[5]

All of the above belongs to a public online sphere. Simultaneously, however, the young women carve out spaces for themselves in which they modify, censor, and reveal—depending on audience and context—within otherwise seemingly very "public" platforms. Some posts can even communicate different opinions and sentiments to discrete others. Depending on how intimately the audience knows the person posting these images and quotations, different layers of readings are possible. Working with the technique of *"hijab latif"* (thin veil) allows for memes with text and images to be read in differing ways depending on people's prior knowledge. But as the below example shows, being skilled in moving in a *harakat* manner on- and offline does not make one safe or certain that it will work every time. In some instances, family members are keeping a close watch on subtle messages being sent and posted on Facebook. A seemingly innocent status update on Facebook by Hadia, a 22-year-old woman of Jordanian origin, read: "Oh, I feel so happy today (emoticon with a winking smiley)." This update stirred controversy among several of her uncles, however. The uncles contacted her mother and asked her to control her daughter and be aware of "what people might think." They implied that people could start talking about Hadia being happy for "non-virtuous" reasons, since the update could be read as implying a relationship to a man who was making her happy. The mother was in tears, and the incident made an impact on the whole family. Discussions ensued regarding what takes place in social media. Hadia, then, did what many young women do: she deactivated her account, only to reemerge under a new profile with a different name and with no pictures of herself that might lead a larger audience to identify it with her. She became very restrictive regarding whom she allowed to be her "friend" under her alias profile. In her fieldwork in Turkey focusing on Facebook strategies among young people, Elisabetta Costa (2016) recounts the story of Aynur who "unfriended" all of her male friends in Facebook (2016:200). Her boyfriend Besim had asked her to do it, and she said that she agreed with the actions taken, pointing to the importance of not losing morality. Costa and Laura Menin in their introduction to a special issue on the pervasive presence of digital media in the Middle East and North Africa point to how smartphones have reconfigured people's everyday lives, especially focusing on love, romance, and premarital relations (Costa and Menin 2016:137–138). Menin notes from her study in Morocco that practices of using digital media have created new contested and uncertain moral normative orders around love and premarital romances—due to the accommodation of desires that could not be satisfied previously pre-social media (Menin 2018).

Returning to the case of Hadia, the strategy of changing her social media identity involved hyper-vigilance, and new types of behavior, activating and deactivating profiles in pursuit of a place of one's own—many of these women do not have a room of their own, pace Virginia Wolf—living in social housing with few square meters shared between large families. As we see here in Hadia's story, the smartphone and the virtual arenas it opened up became highly contested, and what some senior family members perceived as looking out for the young woman's reputation and, thus, that of the whole family, was more of a gray zone for many of the young women I spent time with. Often informants and their network of family and friends would monitor each other in terms of inappropriate or indiscreet online behavior. Discretion to my informants meant discerning between what sort of content would find its way onto the public Facebook wall and what should be kept within private messages in WhatsApp or Snaps.

The relational work going on in the physical world was extended and augmented by the online platforms, reconfiguring the way that "being attentive" is understood. Returning to Abu-Lughod and the modality of poetry, romantic relations and sentiments have obviously existed and found ways to be lived out before the advent of the smartphone and social media. Physical places that allow for entering them without being seen as non-virtuous, yet holding the capacity for being seen by the opposite sex (and see yourself with a double gaze) emerged through spending time with informants. When I say emerged, I mean to indicate that these places did not occur to me to hold that potential, as I have not had reason to seek it out, and the potential and thus contested nature of such places and events were lost on me until explained and experienced *with* others, for whom these affordances were "virtual and real" and at times actualized. One such place would be the Copenhagen Central Square during a rally or demonstration for causes that were in line with politics of the ethnic or national group one belonged to: pro-Palestine demonstration, demonstrations in support of Syria, for defending the rights of immigrants and asylum seekers in Denmark, or at festive occasions such as Turkish Festival.

"My brother did not appreciate at all, that we were going here, he was giving me a hard time," one informant lamented as we entered the Copenhagen Central Square. "Why," I asked, "does he not support the case?". "It's not that, don't you see how much flirting is going on? People *come* here to flirt." I challenged her on that, and she coolly stated, "Just pay attention to how much care people took (hvor meget folk har gjort ud af sig selv)." As we left the demonstration via one of the narrow streets of inner-city Copenhagen, a fancy car pulled up and the guy behind the driver's wheel made contact with my friend, signaling to her out of the car window and asking for something mundane in Arabic. She politely said she couldn't help him and moved on, giving me a telling look and adding "You see?." Other spaces that have been referred to as having that potential, and for some even a reason to avoid such places because it is "too much," are the main street of the neighborhood Noerrebro, Noerrebrogade in Copenhagen, and the large shopping area Bazar West in Gellerup in Aarhus. Time of day is of the essence too in changing the capacity of such a place—the affordances of the place to different people. The road going along the beach Amager Strand in the neighborhood of Copenhagen called Amager is not a "flirty place" during daytime per se, but if someone is cruising in a car after 9 or 10 o'clock at night, it might be perceived as entering a problematic gray zone—you might have to find a really good reason for being in that stretch of road at that time of night. Places for clandestine meetings between young people that are couples would be more "generic"— deserted parking lots or in general a car parked in a discrete place (Waltorp 2013b). In relation to this, I find it important to stress that my informants believe that God is all-seeing, so they are constantly negotiating with themselves what is permissible and not. It is not sexual encounters ending in intercourse taking place in a car parked somewhere; it is intimate talking, being private, perhaps kissing, holding hands. It might be "petting," but that would indicate a very trusting and long-term relation. It is a risky investment on the part of the young woman. The woman is acutely aware that she would be seen differently by her romantic interest if she went further than that: it might foreclose the possibility of the relation going further and him becoming a suitor, fiancé, and husband eventually. She would also "lose" her own idea of entering into marriage as a virgin, which is very important to the young women I worked with.

During my fieldwork, a friend of an informant married her (secret) boyfriend of 7 years. The electricity in the air and in the car with her close friends as we were following them from the wedding party to the apartment was palpable. They would now move in together and spend their wedding night, this their first night together under the same roof, here. Many a stolen moment had been spent in parks, cars, etc., and now the wedding night had come and years of expectations and build up would hopefully culminate as the marriage would be consummated. All of the honking horns and *kell* (a lililili-sound made by the mouth, also called driii-drii'ing) and loud music when driving in the cortege to the apartment was like a communal outburst of all of that excitement. I am not here advocating or romanticizing the idea of virginity. I am drawing attention to how places in my home town held different capacities for the young women I worked with. An array of values and expectations were shared by them in parallell with them negotiating and slightly transgressing those same values, "stretching" how they could pursue happiness and "augment their social being" (Hage 2014). An important point is that this practice did not begin with the smartphone, but the smartphone reconfigured the spaces and possibilities in ways relevant to my informants. Some informants would be set up on dates, through the use of smartphones and social media, by discrete friends who understood the delicate nature of meeting and "dating" before introducing the idea of the person as a suitor to the parents. The smartphone and social media were integral to this process, potentially leading to platonic dates in such places as the airport or nearby Malmö, where one could go for a stroll and get to know each other without being exposed.

Returning to the affordances of the smartphone, the intense use of it and the focus on attention and availability are radically relational: "you are part of me, as I am of you." In technologically mediated images, messages, and likes, one is "given time" by someone. That someone shows that he or she is part of you by making the relationship visible—there for others to see and witness via social media platforms. Discussions and conflicts ensued if people felt over time that the attention they deserved could be "tracked" as going in another's direction in online platforms. Examples of this include one informant who complained that one of the women in their circle of friends did not respond to her texts sent individually yet was active in a WhatsApp group where several of them were part of the same "thread" (conversation). This was similar to the way Sana, whom I described above, became upset when her boyfriend did not prioritize communicating with her yet was online and interacting on various platforms with others. If a person does not react to your text messages, calls, snaps, pictures posted, or even to being "tagged" in a post, this person slowly becomes "invisible," moving out of your inner circle and your starred friends on your snap (those you communicate with the most often) and they will stop being a "visible" part of you (in the digital dimension). A severe action or sanction toward people who have disappointed one is to unfriend, unfollow, or, the extreme action, "block" someone. This will not just end all correspondence and contact but will make it impossible for the person to initiate contact or follow what you are sharing in the digital realm.

Let it matter what we call a thing …
Let me LOOK at you.
Let me look at you in a light that takes years to get there.
(Sharif 2016)

a

Cyborg

Cyborg ethics and multimodal anthropology

I continuously discussed with the women I worked with how I understood their everyday life, hopes, dreams, and the role of the smartphone in their life. I had conversations with my informants about how they might be presented in my work in different modalities: articles or papers presented, I would read aloud (translated into Danish), not with everyone, but those who were most "visible" and central in the written material. The two women most involved in the experimental ethnographic film (Joyous Are the Eyes That See You 2017b) were also part of the editing process. Some of the most interesting discussions during my research followed from this, even though it is excruciatingly awkward to shift from being with people on their turf, "doing sociality" on their terms, and into being scholarly and presenting "knowledge" and "insights." Someone you have come to regard as a friend is cast as "object of research." At times it prompted them to speak about my representation of them—the figure of themselves—in the third person. At these moments, the feedback process felt crucial, opening up to new questions and reflections for all involved. At other times it was to an extent a matter of my informants putting up with my "boring mode," as they defined it. Something they did out of care for me, rather than due to any need they felt.

As I transitioned into the mode of talking project and feedback, I apparently became the most boring person to be around. What happens when the encounter turns into the mode of official "feedback?" Am I to determine the form of the feedback encounter? Whom am I having this conversation with, after all? The principle I believe in first and foremost in fieldwork is that we should not forget to follow our interlocutors' leads. So where does this/they lead me? In what shifting registers does mutuality emerge and come to "count," and for whom? I have described elsewhere (Waltorp 2016) how two interlocutors broke out in laughter (flækkede af grin) at one of them parodying me when I wanted to "talk about my project," as she said, making quotations marks with her fingers in the air. She imitated my voice, but in a particularly slow and monotonous way, "Then you start talking really 'Dane-like,'" she says, directed at me, and turns to her friend, who is also participating in the project: "And after half an hour you'll hear Karen ask: 'But did I get it right? Do you see it this way?' And you'll just affirm, 'Eh yeah yeah, and you didn't understand a word, ha ha ha ha.'"

We were out having a coffee in a café in downtown Copenhagen and talking about what had happened in our lives since we saw each other last and filling in the details, which we were not already updated on through social media. I had moved to another city, and we did not see each other so often. From that day, I have a picture of an interlocutor taking a picture of me in a train carriage that is about to leave Copenhagen, her friend standing next to her laughing. I was taking a picture of my interlocutor taking a picture of me, and my reflection in the window is caught in the picture I was taking. I received the picture she took of me as a snap immediately after (you cannot save an image in the app and only send later; it must be "in the moment"). I went against the ephemerality of the snap and quickly pressed with my left thumb on the lower round button and the right thumb on the button on the upper right side of the smartphone—a screenshot. Saved. An actual image that I can go back to and look at.

Sometimes the feedback process was straightforward when I discussed themes and emerging insights with the young women I worked with, and sometimes I was laughed at, as described above. Being made fun of in my serious or boring mode serves to underline that we are not "collaborators" or co-creators in my project as such. The scholarly goals are intricately connected to my stake in the research, but not necessarily to theirs. The responsibility for the scholarly product rests with me, however many collaborative methods and feedback-moves I attempt. In the café that afternoon, they were doing a *harakat* on me, albeit a loving, mild one. They were letting me understand that they were cool to hang out with me, but not in the mood to be cast in the role of "informant" and object of research, no matter—or perhaps especially—if that meant giving feedback. The knowledge I gained sprang from mutual reflections and discussions with informants, certainly, but mostly from "being with," body and mind, feeling embarrassed and challenged at times, especially when trying to navigate interfaces and perform in an appropriate manner. Noor, one of the women in the café, used the word *moralhed* (moralness), which is not in the Danish vocabulary, when we discussed "morals" as a concept—and I was asking whether she felt she was influenced by particular Islamic moral sentiments as a Muslim:

Nour "Moralness is, let me explain it like this: How do I treat you?"
Me "Ehhmm—Good, good, I think" (not prepared to be quizzed).
Nour "What do you think of me!"
Me "Well, I think well of you, I like you!"
Nour "Yes, I know, I feel that as I get the same thing back from you. Sometimes
you don't, I mean … even though you treat people well. But then you know
yourself, deep down inside, I know I'm a good person—and Allah knows,
he sees everything and keeps score …."

Zara, the other friend with us, added: "God has created us so that you can
'shame yourself'" (*flove sig*). The phrase does not exist as such in Danish. To be
embarrassed is the meaning of the word "flov," and the phrase is made active in
the way she is using it here.

God has created us so that you can "shame you" (flove dig). How you behave
towards other people, the good deeds towards people, the respect. God is
"calculating" for you, what you do towards people, it's *akhlaq* (the practice of
virtue, morality, manners, character or ethics). It's a lot about the upbringing,
tarbia/tarbiyya (upbringing or training); it's difficult to have a good moral if you
do not have a good upbringing, even though it is possible, depending on your
personality. I have it (good morals) towards my (girl)friends: deep down inside,
I know that. At the same time, you can have double standards (dobbelt moral)—
also unconsciously, it's the *nafs* (ego/soul).

As I became closer with my informants less time was spent with more formal
questions and answers, and more time was spent with participation. I found that
semi-structured interviews and language were less helpful in understanding the
situation of my informants and that the smartphone gathered places and people
together for them in ways that made visible both who made up parts of them and
how they made up part of those people—images being of paramount importance
in this exchange. In the first couple of months of fieldwork, I drew up kinship
diagrams, time lines, and Venn diagrams (Chambers 1997). These helped me
get acquainted with, and not least remember, each individual woman's family
relations, the story of how her family arrived in Denmark, how she usually spent
her time, and what she prioritized in her everyday life. In addition, it was very
helpful in instigating conversation around which family members lived where,
who had married and settled where, and why. This naturally led onto discussing
how the individual woman kept in contact with those family members, as well
as how she herself felt about staying or moving elsewhere when marrying. After
years of knowing some of the women I worked with (several had been involved
in the photo project with me in the area in 2010–2011), it seemed somehow

awkward to initiate a formal interview. On many occasions I would check something specific with them, such as the meaning of a word or concept, but trying to resume the role of interviewer and interview subject beyond this made both parties uneasy.

The close relation I have with some of the young women grew over years, and this offered me the opportunity to see many of the women's different selves and performances, including the more intimate and vulnerable ones. At the same time, this made other, more straightforward data-gathering methods more difficult to engage. In several academic settings I have been asked questions along the line of: Is the work less scientific when you become too close "personally" with informants? How close is too close? What is the optimal distance? Close enough for people to want to disclose and share, but without developing the relation with them that typically follows from this involvement? Or, on the other hand, letting the relation develop with the friction that this also entails when politeness is shed? Reading through old field notes and revisiting photo and video material bring back the intense feeling of "early days" of fieldwork, taking part in social gatherings while still being "tested," treated as part of the group of friends sometimes and at other times met with arrogance or indifference. That insecure, humiliating part of the social game had me close to tears on a few occasions. That attitude is linked to what I came to think of as "the bubble." There is a certain mood when moving with some of the women I worked with (not all); that is hard to capture in words, but the dynamic is one of being out and about, free from worries for a while and having fun, taking up space when in the urban environment and being clearly minority "headscarf-girls" (tørklædepiger), fashionably dressed, young and pretty. The *harakat* aspect is about being just a little too loud, laughing too much, playing music loud, and using the surrounding people in the street/café/venue as spectators and "extras," whereas the important audience for one's "goofing" is the girlfriends accompanying one. I was let into that bubble but was also always highly aware of whether other people found this group behavior slightly irritating or offending—habitually acting differently and composing myself differently in public space, never having been in the same position of using subversively my presence and reactions to it. It is an in-group dynamic, and what is happening inside the bubble is what "augments your social being" (Bourdieu in Hage 2014). The bubble is both very seducing and holds importance in that the fun is part of being a young (minority) woman with a lot on one's shoulder; worries and struggles in one's everyday life, bearing the responsibility for sick parents, brothers, contributing to the household economy.

I asked my informants to critique my tentative analyses, as mentioned above. I would translate my articles and read them aloud to them in Danish via Viber if I was away. When in Copenhagen, I would conduct these feedback sessions in the homes of informants or in cafés. When giving feedback on the experimental ethnographic film, there were very different reactions. Some felt it was very true to experience but hard to watch. One woman felt that it was like being transported back to those times again, while another felt that she was made to appear less cool and collected than she was, and that the film showed her to "too unmade"; too fresh-faced and without her hair and make up done properly in many scenes. She was always with meticulous makeup when outside the house and in images shared in social media, where she had quite a large following. I had deprived her of that image by showing her in the vulnerable state of waking up, washing her face, brushing her teeth—with no makeup and "at ease." I liked those images and found them beautiful; she disliked them and felt exposed. We changed, edited and cut out, but that feeling lingered. The aspect several of the women were missing the most in the video piece was more scenes depicting "when we're having a fun and cosy time" ("når vi er ude og hygge os, og har det sjovt"). This refers back to the "bubble" described above.

A "politics of inviting" (Lindström and Ståhl 2016) shaped my project, and the initial framework was renegotiated continuously during the long-term fieldwork. Collaboration can simply be about inviting feedback, but more profoundly, collaboration is a kind of affinity or interface and a "seeing with" those whose lives I try to understand. Do the women I work with have a "correct impression" of the consequences of being portrayed in article-, book- and filmic form? Most probably not, and neither do I, to be perfectly honest. How could I? I have shared with them the scenario I could imagine: most likely, the scientific written work will be read by colleagues interested in some of the themes treated in them. But as it is digital content, those articles could be linked to on Facebook in a split second and someone who knows my informants might try to trace *who* could be the women in the examples. I have little means of controlling this process, so I have made sure to change names and small factual things, as mentioned above, so that no one person's story is identical to someone that could be readily identified—at least always only in part.

All informants without exception note the widespread gossiping in the area of Blaagaarden: neighbors keeping an eye on who is wearing too much makeup or clothes that are too tight or is in the company of someone of the opposite sex who is neither family nor friends of family. The *hijab*, and the hyper-vigilance concerning clothes and makeup striking a balance between beauty, cool looks, and modesty, was reflected in an increasing interest in surfaces on my part. With informants I discussed ideas of adding layers to the film—for example in the form of curtain or cloth—in scenes that would allow the audience to see the women as silhouettes only. They could then dance as they did when we were having a fun night or sit at the hairdresser preparing to attend a wedding—and the footage could be shown to an audience.

We seldom carried these ideas out; yet, our discussions informed me, especially about what could be shown directly and what must be concealed. For example, the women would dress casual and maybe sexy for female-only social events and get-togethers, while in public this would not be permissible. I was allowed to bring my video camera, though, as we had an agreement that they would be allowed to see the footage before the editing was finished and let me know if someone or something was not concealed properly, which was the case in the majority of scenes. Footage could not be shared or made public when informants or family members were not wearing veils or were not properly covered in general. There were several scenes I was sad to have to remove, such as a woman smoking secretly in the street, in a back alley or someone's yard. Even smoking in their own room could not be shown on film. Smoking is a practice done only privately, and discreetly, if you're a young Muslim woman in Noerrebro, not (disrespectfully) in the street in front of older Muslim people to see. But to me, the intimate moment was what I wanted to share—as that showed other sides of the women than the stereotype they were so tired of being perceived as embodying—the subdued veiled woman. Yet these could not be shown—the very intimate feel (and practices) caught on film could not be shared *on* film, exactly because they were that intimate, exclusive "not to be consumed in public." I was also sometimes unable to share footage with an audience if the women were talking about certain things that could not be shared widely.

The filmed material still informed me and transported me back to events and atmospheres. In this way, the filmed material worked as a frame, within which we could talk concretely about the taken-for-granted, tacit, embodied knowledge of what could be exposed to whom, when, and why. Some things must remain unsaid, or at least only partly revealed, in the contexts in which the young Muslim women move. This is reflected in both the filmed and textual material. An accountable "cyborg ethics" in anthropology must be shaped in dialogue with the field and with a sensibility toward what being "online" in different modalities might mean to different people in a digital world. An accountable cyborg ethics insists on devoting time to account for the eyes that see, how they see, why they see, and what apparatus of vision that is entailed in seeing.

Kitab al-manazir and cyborg optics

What was I allowed to see and hear? What was I *able* to see, hear, and sense? What I was able to perceive changed with time spent in place, and time invested in relations (across on- and offline), and it was bound up with the devices I perceived *with*. Raw data do not exist independently of the researcher and her instruments (cf. Bateson 2000: xxv–xxvi). My body, with the prosthetic devices, visualization techniques, and other technology I make use of, configures a distinct infrastructure for seeing, thinking, and knowing. Haraway was not speaking of smartphones in the 1980s when she offered her vision of the Cyborg figure and possible affinities in/through technology as alternatives to, yet entangled, the military visions and capitalist power. Yet I take a cue from her line of thinking that "vision requires instruments of vision; an optics is a politics of positioning" (Haraway 1988:586) and propose that the smartphone and its image-making and sharing technology afford knowing and sensing together in new ways and that a new way of seeing and sensing changes the affordances perceived in the environment (Gibson 2015 [1979]:128–135). What we as anthropologists are able to see and know depends on how we interact with the field and with the people we work with. We often look without seeing, and the camera and images can help us here as "evidently a different nature opens itself to the camera than opens to the naked eye" (Benjamin 1986:236).

With the images made and shared with the smartphone, I am allowed to stay with the details and to revisit them. Working in different "modalities," beyond the verbal, stringing material together in montages (with the temporal aspect) or collages, allows for new forms of analysis. It is a way of challenging and opening up to "unconscious optics" in Walther Benjamin's terminology (see Waltorp 2018b) and paying attention to what we do not "perceive" initially. In analysis, it acts as a safety against thinking that "general knowledge" of something makes us able to analyze it, without paying attention to ethnographic details of each new situation, context, assemblage of elements, and entities. Filming as part of fieldwork has helped me stay with movements between elements of the self and between different states and spaces. My audiovisual notes have allowed me to return to what people said, *and* how they said it, their tone of voice, the context, and mood: shifts and negotiations between us. And I have perceived dynamics, significant details when reviewing footage: things I was not able to perceive when filming and being in the situation the first time around. Our interaction is also in the audiovisual material—my own way of seeing, being in the situation, and interacting. Filming situations where informants prepared to go from the private space of the home and out into the public sphere, as well as changing behavior and dress when someone entered the home, helped me trace and tune into the obvious as well as more subtle shifts. During my fieldwork, I used myself as an important tool—the technological prosthetic devices of smartphone and video camera included.[1] I focused on the smartphone as a fieldworkers' device in today's world. The smartphone became a device for experimenting with collaboration in research, and it is part of specific ways of seeing and perceiving.

> The topography of subjectivity is multidimensional; so, therefore, is vision. The knowing self is partial in all its guises, never finished, whole, simply there and original; it is always constructed and stitched together imperfectly, and therefore able to join with another, to see together without claiming to be another. Here is the promise of objectivity; that is, partial connection. (Haraway 1988:586)

Donna Haraway presents the alternative idea of "apparatuses of visual production, including the *prosthetic technologies* interfaced with our biological eyes and brain" (1988:589, emphasis added). As she writes, "Vision requires instruments of vision; an optics is a politics of positioning" (1988:586). Ethnography, whether in fieldwork practice, dissemination, or representation, is a "particular type of performative and collaborative activity" (Cox et al. 2016:3).

In my case, this performative and collaborative activity entailed a specific attention to images and image-making. Engaging in a flow of images is part of a striving to implode Orientalism and stereotypic orientalist imagery. As images are so variously received by audiences, there is no guarantee how this plays out between filmmaker, protagonists, and audiences. Even the filmmaking process itself, as pointed out by James Weiner (1997) in his "Televisualist Anthropology," draws on technology developed in the West and from a very specific optics as politics of positioning. Laura Marks considers how films and videos that she denotes "intercultural" actually offer a variety of ways of knowing and representing the world. To do this they must suspend the representational conventions that have held in narrative cinema for decades, especially the ideological presumption that cinema can represent reality: "Formal experimentation is thus not incidental but integral to these works. Intercultural cinema draws from many cultural traditions, many ways of representing memory and experience, and synthesizes them with contemporary Western cinematic practices" (Marks 2000:1–2). With this in mind, I propose that (moving) images afford "de-familiarizing" in analysis (Marcus and Fischer 1999). Defamiliarizing is an artistic technique originating in Russian Formalism's *ostranenie* and the *verfremdung* of Brecht's theater (Brecht 1964). By presenting mundane or taken-for-granted things or phenomena to audiences in an unfamiliar or strange way, the habitual perception is unsettled and thus perception of the familiar enhanced (antithesis). This registers in ways other than scholarly discourse with audiences.

The analytical frames and theories that we work from inevitably shape our way of seeing *and* slowly morph with the field, as we are changed by the field (Waltorp In press). The very moment a camera is brought into the field or existing visual images are engaged, the entire human sensorium and imaginative faculty are part of the dialogue and knowledge emerging (Dattatreyan and Marrero-Guillamón 2019; McDougall 1998, 2019; Otto et al. 2018). Scholarly representation (such as an article, book, or film) is not the endpoint of research in a multimodal approach, but a catalyst for accelerating the reflection and dialogue between researchers and their collaborators: dialogical sites for knowledge in the making, requiring the conventional distinction between knowledge producers and knowledge recipients to be reconfigured. Audiences, correspondingly, are not simply recipients of scholarly work, but active participants in the creation of anthropological knowledge (Strathern 1999:7). Audiovisual representations and statements have effects upon the world (aesthetics and politics are fundamentally entwined) (Waltorp et al. 2017). These modalities offer less clear and closed analytical arguments but invite the viewer/reader/audience in (see Marks 2000, 2015; McDougall 2019). My previous research grounded in participant-observation and participatory audiovisual methods (Irving 2006; Pink 2006, 2007, 2012, 2015; Rouch and Feld 2003; Thomas 2005; Vium 2014, 2017; Waltorp 2013b, 2015; Waltorp and Vium 2010) motivated a consideration of technological tools simultaneously as an object of study and an integral part of my methodology. I engaged with the smartphone and with digital media and technologies in a broader sense, both as part of the world I wanted to explore and as part of the toolkit I used to explore that world with. I understand and employ digital technologies "in a way that goes beyond their status as technologies to disseminate representations or be used for communications, but as sensory technologies with other forms of presence, affordances and qualities" (Pink 2015:67).

Theories of perception have been divided into empiricist and idealist since Descartes's dualism, and people have grappled with how interior worlds and exterior worlds relate: empiricists assert that perceptual processes are guided by representations, which have been incorporated into experience. Idealists counter this assertion by arguing that perception is organized by a priori categories in the mind that does not refer to experience. As early as the eleventh century, Muslim mathematician and astronomer Ibn al-Haytham (Alhazen) engaged with these fundamental questions of how we perceive the surrounding world. He was the first to argue that the center of optical activity in the perception of the object was the object itself that, when illuminated, produces rays of light in every direction. This was contrary to the widely held theory at the time that the eye itself is the source of emissions. He wrote *Kitab al-Manazir* (Book of Optics), with the Latin translation "Perspectiva." In the books—there were seven of them—al-Haytham argues via the phenomenon of "afterimage"[2] against the "extramission" theory (which postulates the existence of visual rays emanating from one's eye). Al-Haytham believed in "intromission," but the theory he developed was radically different from those of his time, including the Aristotelian theory that in the presence of light the eye perceives an object by taking on its form (Pelillo 2014).[3] Alhazen showed through experiment that light travels in straight lines and carried out various experiments with lenses, mirrors, refraction, and reflection. And he did experiments with camera obscura and "pinhole camera" (Pelillo 2014).

Johannes Kepler, key figure in the seventeenth-century scientific revolution, built directly on the conceptual framework of al-Haytham in his theory of the retinal image. But the theory on the retinal images—assuming that an image is formed on the retina copying what is in the phenomenal world—is an idea of vision as "snap shot" vision. This builds on experiments of how the eye functions if exposed to one "image" at the time, the head resting in a fixed position. In contemporary science this understanding of images and vision was assumed for a long time, whereas the ecological psychology of Gibson[4] differs from this and is more in line with the theory of al-Haytham, who was the first to explain that vision occurs when light reflects from an object and then passes to one's eyes and to point out that *vision occurs in the brain, rather than in the eyes*. In the same vein, rather than focusing on the retinal image, Gibson introduces ecological optics where the eyes form part of larger perceptual system that encompasses the eye-head-body and the supporting earth; the perceptual system is always part of the person in the world (Gibson 2015, see also Ingold 2000). This demands a subject—a body—that moves around in the environment and thus implicates ambient vision (the head moving around) and ambulatory vision (the body moving around in an environment). "Vision is a whole perceptual system, not a channel of sense … one sees the environment not with the eyes but with the eyes-in-the-head-on-the-body-resting-on-the-ground" (Gibson 2015:195). He underscores that what we perceive is always bound up with and implicates the viewer herself

(2015:132–133), as "to perceive the world is to co-perceive oneself. The awareness of the world and one's complementary relations to the world are not separable" (2015:133).

In Gibson's terminology, "exteroception" and "proprioception" presuppose each other. This is wholly inconsistent with dualism in any form, either mind-matter dualism or mind-body dualism. Al-Haytham's work on "binocular disparity" is also interesting in this present discussion on perception and is something Gibson has also devoted attention to. It refers to the difference in image location of an object seen by the left and right eyes resulting from the eyes' horizontal separation—that is parallax. Parallax is also motion parallax and moving—on different levels—to be able to change perspective. Below I discuss how moving to change perspective was a *harakat* move on my part in my fieldwork in Blaagaarden. I make a detour to Mozambique and Julie Archambault's fieldwork with young people and the way they navigate uncertainty, mobile phone in hand (2011, 2017). In similar ways to mine, Archambault explores the ways in which young people navigate competing demands and expectations as they attempt to craft everyday lives and futures. Although in a very different environment, the way her informants must carefully manipulate information, and hone their social maneuvering skills, she alludes to with the notion of *visão* ("vision" in Portuguese). One with *visão* knows how to read the social landscape, while playing on the visions of others, but one with *visão* also knows when to look away and feign ignorance, and the phone is a particularly useful tool in an array of practices that includes an assortment of tricks and technologies aimed at "invisibility" or "embellishing reality often through concealment" (2017:43). Vision, always a question of the power to see, is discussed further below. What I learned from my research was, paraphrasing Solmaz Sharif quoted at the end of the last chapter, to appreciate "looking at someone in a light that takes years to get here." By this I mean that unlearning ways of seeing, having one's usual perspective displaced, and perceiving differently take time.

Parallax as a harakat move and a speaking nearby

The notions of reflection, refraction, and diffraction are central to the anthropological investigation in this book—and so is the related notion of *parallax*. The term "parallax" is derived from Ancient Greek (*parallaxis*), meaning "alternation or the apparent displacement or the difference in apparent direction of an object as seen from two different points" (Merriam-Webster

Dictionary). "Vision is *always* a question of the power to see—and perhaps of the violence implicit in our visualizing practices. With whose blood were my eyes crafted?" (Haraway 1988:192). As Joe Dumit underscores, drawing on Haraway's interrogation of both "seeing" and the "apparatus of seeing," this interrogation is not a reflexive practice of the seen and the seer, because *reflection* implies a self-presence, a comfortable sense of one's identities and stakes. Rather, it is *diffracted*. One only sees at all through eyes that are themselves devices with histories of their own. Non-innocence and complicity are necessary if one is to confront world histories that one is part of and accountable to (Dumit 2014). Diffraction is, technically speaking, the bending of waves around obstacles, openings, or edges of an object. There are diffracted mirror images in this book in relation to stereotypes and clichés. As a sort of *harakat*-movement trick these diffracted mirror images are always also dependent on the structures and strategies, which they seek to circumvent: Non-innocent and complicit, but seeking to bend around the obstacles that are the stereotypes and clichés and histories, sedimented.

The various *harakat* moves on my part in the field—and in the analysis "at the desk" (see Strathern 1999)—were attempts or opportunities to see from different angles, to achieve a parallax effect, as when one ventures into a hall of mirrors, where the slightest change in perspective refracts the image, bringing about new visions, new partial understandings. I forward the argument that motion parallax *is* ethnographic fieldwork; we move closer for an extended period of time to perceive better and from a different point of view—speaking *nearby* other people, instead of *for* them (Trinh 1989, 1991). As anthropologists, we pay attention to how *others* perceive; we share the environment with other people, and by being attentive to this environment (or habitat), we may begin to perceive differently through guidance from the people we spend time with. Following Gibson: "Affordances are properties taken with reference to the observer. They are neither physical nor phenomenal" (Gibson 2015:135). "Only when each child perceives the values of things for others as well as for herself does she begin to be socialized" (Gibson 2015:133). The image of the fieldworker as child, learning anew how to act, resonates here, because this is how humans learn. Taking it back to the tradition—and the modality—of visual anthropology, Faye Ginsburg draws on ethnographic filmmaker Jean Rouch's concept of *regards comparés* (compared views), which resembles the idea of the parallax effect (Ginsburg 1995). Beginning in 1978, Rouch organized a series of conferences at the *Musee de l'Homme* devoted to a comparative study of the media coverage of different groups, bringing together people from all over the world in Paris, including anthropologists, filmmakers, television executives, video artists, amateur movie makers, as well as people from the societies being viewed, to begin to see how different media agendas, as well as the culture/nationality and gender of producers, shape the images produced. According to Ginsburg (1995), the juxtaposing of these different kinds of films and their producers and subjects together to jointly contemplate the images that they had created of a culture is precisely what the parallax effect is meant to describe. In my work, all of the discussions I instigated around what to film, how to film it, and who could be allowed to be audiencing were catalyzed by the use of the video camera and smartphone. I had to develop sensibilities to understand and practice visibility and concealment. Interfacing with informants via experimental collaborations and using digital and image-making technologies to produce (moving) images has been one of my strategies in striving for a parallax effect.

Working in the medium of (smartphone) video was a radical break in terms of media used in my research, and I conceive of this parallax movement as *harakat*, a movement trick. I have, literally, attempted to "do a *harakat*" on Orientalism (Said 1978). I have sought to pay attention to the applied tools and methods and how they enter into and configure the knowledge-making. I argue that the video camera affords "unconscious optics" (Benjamin 1986) in zooming in on micro-moments: filming made it possible to revisit moments via the footage, as a form of sensuous audiovisual notes to be analyzed in the editing processes of cutting up, enlarging, speeding up and down, and combining elements in montage form—paying more attention to what I thought I knew and what I thought I was able to see. These analytical moves allowed me to rephrase questions, or rather to shift registers, as I tried to answer them and provide better ones. A new iteration of analysis is possible through the sensory immediacy of images and the systematic use of feedback, elicitation, and parallax effects. In many cases, the digital dimension *is* increasingly peopled with fieldwork partners, collaborators, colleagues, and everything in-between. This points to how the analytic modality "at the desk" is radically changing with smartphones and new technologies. We confer with informants; we are continuously presented and updated on developments from the intimate micro to the macro. This challenges our initial understanding of a given phenomenon and adds layers to it. Our representations of people, their environment, and the phenomena that they are invested in potentially reach them, as well as other stakeholders in their lives, immediately (Waltorp, In press).

A film cut or a draft paper or an article is a tentative analysis to be presented. In this format, one can receive feedback on it from various audiences or publics.

I have worked extensively with having informants give feedback on paper drafts, as described above—either face to face (filmed or not), over the phone or via the Viber app or FaceTime. In the endeavor to include feedback in my ongoing analysis, (moving) images and exhibition making is important, as this format allows for communication in registers beyond the scholarly articulated discourse. The smartphone and social media make up part of an infrastructure for conversations, where informal feedback and analysis take place in new ways.

Generative relationships in fieldwork are predicated on mutual usefulness—on stakes and mutual appropriations for different purposes (Rabinow et al. 2008:66). The purposes of my informants and me in engaging with each other are bound to differ. My take on the collaborative method grows from the idea of "joining with another" through the metaphor of fieldwork as interface, facilitated in specific ways through the smartphone and video camera (Waltorp 2018a). This understanding of the collaborative method is a critical part of how I conceive of knowledge-making. I intervened by my sheer presence, my questions, my filming, and my continual requests for participation and feedback. In the experimental ethnographic film (see images) I portray two of the young women I worked with, who had been best friends since they attended the local public school, Blaagaarden school: a young Sunni Muslim woman of Palestinian origin whose parents migrated from Jordan to Denmark and a young Shi'a Muslim whose parents came from Iran. The latter travels from Blaagaarden to Dubai to meet her love and to Iran to visit family. The other young woman's daughter is kidnapped, and through images she shares in social media of her visits to her daughter in Jordan, the film moves with her there. The form of the film mirrors the need to be able to leave things unclear, partly concealed and ambiguous—so as for the women not to be "caught" in something too directly that could impact in a negative way on their name and reputation, should someone see it who would want to judge the person. The film is in its form a *harakat* move.

The experimental ethnographic film portrays body language and interactions; the camera follows the moving in and out of specific (private/public/intimate) places and traces the layers of makeup, clothes, veils, and (in the digital sphere) "filters" that are added as the individual women move from one to the other room, context, audience, and corresponding role. It focuses on revealing/concealing and invites the audience into images of women doing their hair and putting on makeup in front of the mirror: is there one "true" person *behind* the veil or the makeup or without the filters in social media apps? All of these performances and surfaces are equally true and real and contextual—as aspects of the person and the interaction. I denote it an experimental ethnographic film, yet the only voice-over used in the piece is in the opening scene, which states, "This is *not* a film, this is not a mirror image, this is movement—harakat" (Waltorp 2017b). The material is filmed on a Canon xf100 video camera and with various smartphones and flip cameras. In an attempt to "conjugate the ambiguity and provocations of art with documentary attachment to the immediate flux of lived experience" (Castaing-Taylor 2016:149), material from Denmark, Jordan, the United Arab Emirates, and Iran is juxtaposed seamlessly without letting the viewer know the exact location, breaking with documentary conventions of establishing shots. For privacy reasons of the women portrayed, the film cannot be shown to a broader audience or widely circulated but has been screened at universities and ethnographic conferences and film festivals. This might—hopefully—change with time, but for the moment it is a "moral pause" (MacDougall 2019). In addition to the women in the film, the smartphone is a main protagonist. It is in quite a few scenes, sending snaps, writing text, talking on the phone, showing images to the video camera, and finally—doing selfies.

It is possible to access interesting information without entering into a relation with people. Online you can access limitless information without mutuality;[5] yet, it is the multitude of surfaces, self-representations, and performances across the digital and physical spheres that I find interesting. To get at these various performances, and versions of selves, the anthropologist has to collaborate in ways that are negotiated continuously. Giving time and attention to each other—the relation made visible in the text, images, and videos exchanged—is paramount. This dynamic included me as anthropologist. The fact that you can follow someone's open profile on Instagram or on Facebook without befriending them might give a sense of having access to someone's life and self-representation; yet, these platforms have private functions and spaces for interaction that presuppose mutuality, and these are not freely accessible (Waltorp 2016). The widely used Snapchat app is a poignant case in point. I was allowed by informants to take screenshots of the snaps they sent me, and in that sense, I went against the ephemeral nature of the app because of my need to go back to the snaps and analyze them in juxtaposition with other material. The photo-messaging application allows users to take so-called snaps: photos or short videos, onto which they can add text and drawings and send them to a controlled list of recipients immediately. The users of Snapchat "chat" using "snapshots" from their lives. The snap is automatically deleted after a set time limit of up to 10 seconds. You can make a selection of "snaps," compiled into "MyStory," which all of your contacts can see for a limited time, or you can send snaps individually. The focus is not on editing, filtering, and framing things, as with other platforms such as Instagram. As the snap is only seen once, the ephemeral feel is the framing. A snap cannot be saved and sent at a later point in time: it is for sharing the fleeting moment you are in with persons you choose. Should the receiver choose to take a screenshot of the snap, and thus save it, the sender will be notified of this.

The young Muslim women I worked with engage in experimentation with self-representations and the possibilities of identification on a daily basis in various media platforms. As already demonstrated, they carve out distinct private spaces for themselves within what are otherwise very "public" platforms, which they modify, censor, or make revealing, depending on audience and context (Waltorp 2015). Snapchat works particularly well for this purpose as it can be controlled (or at least feels as though it can, as everything digital can be hacked potentially). Creative experimentation takes place within the confines of various (opposing) dominant sociocultural conceptions of "the virtuous woman," "the free, modern woman," etc.; (a critique of) these notions and their supposed opposition will be expanded on below (cf. Hirschkind 2006; Mahmood 2012). Because of the ephemeral nature of the images, Snapchat offers a particular feel of immediacy and intimacy between those sending and receiving, an intimacy that is lost in other mediums. Not all of my informants wear a hijab or veil, but most of them do. They will not have their hair covered, though, in the privacy of their homes, in the company of other women or men of the immediate family (*mahrams*), and it is often in the private sphere of the home that they use Snapchat. Any social media image and text and its "encoding" and "decoding" of meaning (Hall 1980) are fundamentally dependent on the platform. A format that is "reified," sharable, and where a picture and text can be viewed publicly over time is opposed to appearing in a private online space such as Snapchat for up to only 10 seconds.

What a person shares with an anthropologist is not necessarily what they wish to disclose to other project participants or their own "followers" or "friends" online. If the anthropologist then shares this information in an increasingly technologically mediated and hyperlinked world, it most likely reaches the everyday realm of the informants. When participating in an anthropologist's study, people discern what they want to disclose to the anthropologist. They are in charge of what to inform (cf. Strathern 1999:7), but this demands ethics and sensibilities in terms of visibility, vulnerability, and differing notions of public, private, and who has the rights/access to knowledge. It has consequences for our informants how they, and issues of concern to them, are made public. How to communicate intimate and visual aspects without revealing and exposing informants has been a continuous challenge across text and visual work. Working visually across social media and video has prompted reflection on representation, as well as on the public imperative and the variously configured and historically contingent understandings of visibility and concealment in (gendered) public and private spaces (Waltorp 2015, 2018b). Knowledge in different registers—intimate, embodied, tacit, verbalized, and formal—can be shared differently, courtesy of social media.

The ongoing discussion of reciprocity in ethics is integral to making knowledge that is active in the world we share with our informants. Ethics are never isolated or detached from practice. The young women I worked with created and used digital imagery, shared it with each other and with me in various online platforms, each with their own sets of privacy policies. I was also allowed to film intimate moments and to save intimate photos shared in the Snapchat platform that were not intended for public scrutiny. How to share knowledge emerging from these encounters across digital and physical domains? What can be revealed to different audiences, and how to control its circulation in this day and age? Nothing can be kept "secret" once shared in digital media. So what should be concealed from the viewpoint of my informants, knowing this to be the case? What should remain ambiguous, so as to not point equivocally back to the person involved? I cannot show the footage in any straightforward way, as it would be haram (forbidden) to be seen by men if one is not dressed modestly and acting in a way that would be appropriate—the same rules applying as if the woman was in a physical public space.

The conversations that emerge from these shared fieldwork situations are very intimate, private, and personal. In some situations, I have been relieved about the camera in my hands, giving me something to focus on, during what I experienced as intimate or intense moments. I filmed many women, knowing that much of the footage could never be shared unaltered. I needed filmic strategies resonating with other ways of inhabiting public and private spaces, strategies of partial concealment and particulars of disclosure of ambiences and moods (see Waltorp 2018b). I discussed many alternative filmic strategies with informants. They were mostly discussed in terms of appropriate revealing, concealing, and sharing. Among my informants, one woman wished she had the courage to start wearing the *hijab*, as she said. But she was too put off by the reactions she was expecting to get from coworkers at the pharmacy where she worked. Another woman would rather not wear it but felt that her peers would look down on her if she did not. One informant stopped wearing the hijab during my fieldwork, and another started wearing it. The latter was a Danish woman who had converted. Most said they were happy to wear it, stating the relation between themselves and their God as the most important factor, pointing out that it had to be their own choice; if not it would not make sense (this is expanded on in Chapter c). The knowledge I gain, as an anthropologist, is through the reactions in my own body and mind to other habitual and habituated ways of going from public to private to intimate, beyond, and back again. Knowledge is the mutual reflections and discussions on this between my informants and myself, not least in the tacit bodily knowledge and interaction. My own clumsiness and challenges when trying to shift "frames," navigate interfaces, and perform appropriately also constitute important knowledge pieces. My informants share some of my frustrations, accommodating—inhabiting—components from various traditions of ideas of public/private and also freedom/control, religious/ secular, male/female, which sometime clash, sometime complement each other, which is also a source of insight and ties into the notion of a composite person.

Hannah Arendt ascribed modern meanings of public and private spaces to the ancient Greek contrasting of the public space of the town *Polis* (the place of equality and personal freedom) to the home (*oikiri*) and the family (represented by biological and natural need and characterized by hierarchy) (1998). She sees the distinction between public and private as that between things that have to be *shown* and things that have to be *hidden* (1998:58–59). I argue that this "modern" understanding of public/private, as mirroring the shown/hidden distinction, becomes blurred with the various gendered private spaces that are enacted and inhabited by my informants and by their use of social media with its many intermediate spaces. The borders between the private, public, and intimate, and the various cultural understandings, all intersect with each other. The introduction of audiovisual media such as the smartphone further complicates and informs the way these intersections occur. Filming my informants' interactions across intimate, private, and public spaces made it clear to me that social media are radically challenging the boundaries between private and public. Hijab (covering/concealing parts of yourself) is about what is appropriate, in what situations, and with whom. It is about borders and about the appropriate (kinship) relations and the interfaces between intimate, public and private. The smartphone and social media form a key part of the way the young women explore issues such as what is appropriate in intimate settings and in public domains to them in their everyday lives. Inspired by Gibson, I see person and place as mirroring each other—as habitus and habitat in my investigation of how a person comes to move in a skilled way in the environment, to move in a *harakat* way in the case of Blaagaarden. What Gibson's ecological approach and the notion of affordances point to is exactly how "perceiving gets wider and finer and longer and richer and fuller as the observer explores the environment. Being 'in touch with' or 'aware of' means being able to guide one's activity to formulate goals and accomplish them" (2015:xxiii). I explore this in empirically and conceptually tracing how personhood is constituted in new ways through the smartphone via the concept of "composite habitus"—for this specific group of women, in this specific place. In the next chapter, I move to Blaagaarden.

Hanan al-Noerrebro: Affections for the Neighborhood

An urban habitat—a typical blaagaarden girl

A summer day in 2014, I was pushing the stroller with my youngest son, next to Fatmeh who was pushing her youngest daughter in a pram. Fatmeh was a 27-year-old woman who had lived in the Blaagaarden area for 6 years. She was born in Denmark to Palestinian parents who had arrived in Denmark from Jordan. We had left the "mother group" meeting[1] we were both attending close to Blaagaarden, and we were walking along the lakes in central Copenhagen. We were discussing my work and the subject of what smartphones mean to young Muslim women in Blaagaarden. She loved to help and give feedback yet warned me time and again that I might not be able to use her opinion "as she was not really a typical Blaagaarden girl." On one occasion I invited her to define "a typical Blaagaarden girl," and though she clearly did not feel comfortable admitting her opinion about this, pressed on the issue she distinguished herself on grounds of being well educated—her husband too—and she pointed to not having grown up in the area: "I would never have agreed to move into an apartment here if I had grown up here," she stated. The gossip in the area, according to her, affected her less than others. She did not have her whole family network in the area and was not "as big a part of people" there, as she formulated it. "There's too much gossip, people keep an eye on what everyone else is doing and everybody knows each other. 'Is someone wearing too much makeup?' or 'why is this one going out in the company of these people'? You know ...." While Fatmeh lived in Blaagaarden with her husband and children, her extended family lived in a more upmarket Copenhagen neighborhood, and she considered herself spared in terms of the pressure of the local gossip. Many of my informants commented on their frustration with the gossip and close-knit networks in the area, using the formulation: "det *er* hovedpine" (literally "it *is* headache"). Education, family background, income level, and the people she associated with in the area distinguished Fatmeh from other women in the area. Few of my informants were as highly educated as Fatmeh. Some of my informants were studying, some were unemployed, and some had no training or education after lower secondary school (Folkeskolen). Those in employment were in the service sector: kindergarten, social work, care of the elderly, or working in retail as shop assistants, in cafés or bakeries. I spent time with them on their way to work at times, talking in the metro or bus, or at their workplace, where I would entertain them when there were no customers in the café or shop, or I would help sweep floors and lock up at night.

Blaagaarden is an old working-class neighborhood. Residents today are mostly immigrants and second-generation immigrants, ethnic Danish working-class families, and students. The social housing area is centrally located and close to the lakes in Copenhagen in the vibrant inner-city neighborhood of Noerrebro, the most ethnically diverse neighborhood in Denmark. Hanan al-Noerrebro means affection, care, sympathy, or fondness in Arabic and is borrowed from Laura Marks's book title *Hanan al-Cinema*, affections for the moving image (2015). The feelings of affection are mine, shared with the women I worked with, toward the neighborhood of Noerrebro. Lining the streets, filled with people at most times of the day, are cafés, shawarma restaurants, music playing, and shops selling everything from furniture to hipster health food, and from sexy lingerie to Islamic fashion for women—and then there are the ubiquitous phone shops. In the eighteenth century the neighborhood of Noerrebro was way out in the countryside. The area outside of the city bulwark had very few built structures—a few bars, places where people could bleach cloth, and some industry and crafts. The inhabitants were craftsmen, workers, millers, gardeners, and brewers. By the mid-1800s, the population within the old city had become so large and living conditions so poor that Copenhagen's magistrate gave permission for the establishment of housing outside the existing boundaries of the city, the demarcation line, in 1852. This instigated a major building boom in the second half of the nineteenth century.

Noerrebro grew as people moved out from the crowded old city, and people living in the countryside migrated to the capital to find work and a better livelihood. It became a workers' neighborhood with very small workers' apartments. In the 1970s the area went through a process of urban renewal, and in the decades to follow it became known for its varied and vibrant cultural life and activist spirit. A large portion of Denmark's Muslim inhabitants arrived during the economic boom in the 1960s and 1970s as invited work migrants from

Turkey, Pakistan, the Middle East, and North Africa. They were denoted "guest worker" and many took jobs in the service industry. In the 1980s and 1990s groups of refugees from conflicts in the Middle East, Africa, and the Balkans arrived in Denmark, and many settled in the larger Copenhagen area, mostly in the area of Noerrebro. As the years went by, the guest workers who had arrived in the 1960s and 1970s had applied for family reunification and been permitted to bring their families to Denmark. This unification saw spouses and children arrive after the so-called "immigrant-stop" in 1973 (Rytter and Pedersen 2014; Simonsen 1990, 2006, 2012).

In the beginning of fieldwork, I would often suggest to meet informants in a café in the main street Blaagaardsgade, but I quickly realized that there was a preference among most of the women, I worked with, to meet *away* from Blaagaarden, especially if we were to discuss something they did not want others to gossip about. When not meeting with the women inside of an apartment, they would instead propose cafés or the coffee chain Baresso in the Center of Copenhagen (where no alcohol is served) as meeting places. It could also be the Main Library or in a park. I realized after a while that the only one perfectly comfortable with meeting in Blaagaardsgade was Fatmeh, the "non-typical" Blaagaarden girl.

The ghetto, the square, behind the curtain

On "Sankt Hans Eve" Midsummer Celebration 2014, I had expected to meet up with informants at a concert held at the Blaagaarden Square, with big names featured and a large turnout. But this held no interest to them. A few women who were hanging out together in an apartment invited me to join them. I wondered why they would find it more exciting to be in an apartment than in the square with the event happening. The square, Blaagaarden Square, is where people meet and chat, go to concerts, and gather for demonstrations; there is ice-skating in winter and football in summer. The name Blaagaarden—which translates as the "Blue Estate"—comes from the name of a prominent estate located where the square is today, originally built in 1697 by Prince Carl. The estate's blue-black glazed roof tiles inspired its name.

In 1828 the main building of Blaagaarden estate was made into a theater and the land was sold off, some of it to Heegaard's Iron foundry, and it was finally turned into a public square by the City of Copenhagen in 1898. Surrounding Blaagaards Square is a community house, a church, a public library, and a pathway leading to the local sports facilities at "Korsgadehallen." Close by is "People's Park" (Folkets Park), known as the home and hangout of recently arrived undocumented migrants and homeless people, as well as pushers selling marijuana, cocaine and other narcotics. When I would walk in the vicinity of Blaagaards Square with informants, surrounded by eleven identical blocks of flats on all sides, I would notice myself mirroring my informants and becoming more and more careful about what I said out loud in conversation the closer we got to the square, not to be overhead and leading to gossip. Near the square—the heart of Blaagaarden—I would limit myself to certain topics that would in no way be intimate or controversial. On a subconscious level, it seemed as if the "courtyard" spaces of Blaagaarden functioned as a loudspeaker, augmenting the volume of our conversations. Furthermore, as in a kind of urban "panopticon" (Foucault 1975), one can be seen from each and every window in the court: there is always potentially an audience, including the groups of young men at their usual hangout, as one enters the inner court of the building. The inner court is known locally as "the entrance to hell" (Helvedes forgård). The young women in the area are acutely aware of this, just as they know exactly who are dealing drugs and who is affiliated with whom. My informants do not contemplate or discuss it much, though, considering one informant's brother was arrested and incarcerated during my fieldwork, as was another informant's husband, and another informant's brother-in-law used to be involved in the local street gang and engage in criminal activities but had reformed.

On the Sankt Hans Midsummer Celebration, we were not in the square with the crowd. For the women I worked with, the most intense and exciting sociality oftentimes took place behind the curtain in an apartment building, where music turned on, cigarettes and perhaps a water pipe would add to the "hygge" (cosiness). This kind of behavior they could not engage in, in the square. On this late afternoon, Jasmin moves her hips in a sensuous way. The video camera is "on," recording her every move, her facial expression as she dances, tossing her long black hair in the air and singing along. The R&B tune has succeeded the Arabic tune that she was belly-dancing to a minute earlier, wearing a full-length skirt and a belt decorated with coins tied around her waist. The music is turned up high, the bass distorted, and her moves change into a dancing style of the kind you would see in R&B or rap music videos on YouTube. She dances over in the direction of where Pernille is sitting in the sofa. Pernille is a close friend, a young Danish woman who has converted to Islam. She jokingly and playfully "takes on the role" and as Jasmin shakes her ass in front of Pernille, she whistles and laughs while slapping Jasmin with the one hand, cigarette in the other. Jasmin returns to the middle of the floor, while a Beyoncé hit-song plays from the iPad connected to the loudspeakers (see Playlist). I am filming with a camera and I zoom in on Pernille who inhales, tilts her head, and smiles, singing along:

> Cigars on ice, cigars on ice
> Feeling like an animal with these cameras all in my grill
> Flashing lights, flashing lights
> You got me faded, faded, faded
> Baby, I want you, na na
> Can't keep your eyes off my fatty
> Daddy, I want you, na na
> Drunk in love, I want *you*

Pernille goes over to the iPad to fix the distorted bass, all the while Jasmin slips out of the full-length skirt, wearing hot pants underneath. She adjusts her clothes and turns to the camera smiling: "Can I wear it like this?" She stops for a moment, grabs the iPad, all the while Pernille sits on the floor answering a text message on her smartphone. The room is dimly lit, and the light from the screens illuminates their faces. "Is there space on the phone, honey?" Jasmin asks Pernille. "Yeah," Pernille answers. "Ok, then I'd like to just record with this song playing, ok? Shouldn't I wear the stilettos?" Jasmin dances in impressively high Michael Kors stilettos, which she bought recently on sale and that she sent me a picture of as a "Snap." I am filming, feeling shy. Pernille is also filming the dancing with a smartphone from the other end of the comfortable corner sofa that I share with her. Only young women are in the house. Yet through the video camera, and smartphones, other latent gazes are present in the room with us, adding to the atmosphere. Pernille's recording is sent as a Snap video to Jasmin's secret boyfriend. I worry whether he will treat the video of his sexy, dancing girlfriend with discretion; what would be the consequences if other people saw Jasmin without the hijab she is normally wearing when leaving the house? What if her family found out (Waltorp 2018b)? He would not take a screen shot though; if he did the Snapchat app would notify the sender of the snap of this— an inbuilt safety in the app to remain exclusively and intimately in the moment (since my fieldwork, replays have later become possible as a feature in the app).

My informants do not frequent clubs, and they would never dance like this in the Blaagaarden Square for people to see and gossip about. They would risk getting the reputation of a "whore" immediately. In nightclubs, there is alcohol, and genders mix, which they agree is *haram*. The women dance only for each other (and some potentially for their fiancé or secret boyfriend through the social media as in the example above), as they do at weddings with only other women present. In the dark living room that night, behind the curtains, we were giving compliments to Jasmin dancing, admiring and envying her slender body. We all listened to her dreams of becoming a belly-dancing teacher and giving classes—something which her family would most likely not agree to, I thought. A very intimate sociality was going on inside, which could never play out in the Blaagaarden Square and never in a club or other semi-public places with mixed gender.

Facebook flirt: The stabbing of Taher

I worked on a participatory photo project in Blaagaarden with a group of young men and women between the ages of 16 and 25[2] in the years 2010–2011. I lived with my family across the street in Noerrebrogade, and we had previously lived in the Islamic Republic of Mauretania, which seemed to give the women an indication that I "would understand" them to some extent, having lived with my family in a majority Muslim country. I heard this trajectory of mine repeated when informants introduced me to others, as well as the fact that I had done film and photo projects in areas dubbed ghettos in Paris and Cape Town. That I lived in Noerrebrogade was mentioned most often as *the* point of connection between us. The photo project that I carried out in Blaagaarden, Paris, and Cape Town was impacted by the conservative-liberal government's (VKO) announcement in October 2010 of Blaagaarden and twenty-eight other urban areas as officially ghettos. The project developed into a multimedia exhibition with the collaboratively chosen title "Ghetto NO Ghetto," which the participants felt quite strongly about in light of the new ghetto stamp. The stamp fixing place and ethnic identity becomes a shared experience: In 2017, 66.5 percent of all non-Western immigrants in Denmark lived in "ghettos," and according to the Housing Ministry, the majority of these are Muslim. "Ghetto No Ghetto" was exhibited at the Noerrebro Theatre in the area, as well as in the local sports and community center Korsgadehallen, behind Blaagaard Square. During the work on the project, which focused on disposable cameras and analogue photography, I observed the importance of the smartphone in the lives of the women living in this area and its importance for image-making and "keeping record"[3] (Waltorp 2018a). This project also caused me to become intimately aware of many of the issues the women living in the area were facing. One of these issues concerns "image" and the daily impact of not feeling in control of your own image/images.

The fact that you face stereotypes as a Muslim woman, and as a resident in Blaagaarden, a so-called ghetto, you face stereotypes. In this situation, feeling in control of the images you circulate of yourself is of crucial importance.

One of the participants in the collaborative photo project I carried out in the area was Taher, locally known as Taha or "Switch." I had kept in contact with him since 2010 and was shocked when he was stabbed to death at the Forum Metro Station in the area of Frederiksberg, adjacent to Noerrebro in 2013. Confident that he had not been involved in the local street gang (Blaagaard Square Group-cum-Loyal to Familia), I was confused as to why he had been targeted. As it turned out, Taher, Tunesian-Moroccan and born in Denmark, was stabbed to death at only 18 years of age. The assailant was a 19-year-old man, Danish with Iranian parents, who accused him of having flirted with his girlfriend on Facebook. The women I worked with had different stories and opinions about the event and the rumors surrounding it. The different stories I was told by the women I worked with depended on their broader network. Those with Iranian background defended the assailant as they had heard the versions that underscored how he had only approached Taher with the intention of scaring him and teaching him a lesson with the knife. Now his life was ruined at the age of 19 and that of his family as well. As for Taher's family, one of my informants, Fatima of Pakistani background who lived in the block adjacent to the apartment of Taher's parents in Blaagaarden, told me how she could hear Taher's father crying every night. Everyone's hearts were broken for the family of Taher, she said. Taher was popular in the local area and beyond. Hundreds came to his funeral and attended a memorial event at Forum Metro Station where the stabbing had happened. Most were other young people from his school, Niels Brock High School, while others came from the local area. I attended the women's function for his mother in the communal space of the Housing Association in Baggesensgade in Blaagaarden. We waited and waited with the tables filled to the brim with soda, dates, nuts, and dried fruits. She did not show up the whole day. She couldn't.

This tragic event gave another dimension to (flirty) behavior online and how indiscretion can, indeed, be a question of life and death. It is with this in mind that navigating expectations and sets of norms and values on- and offline should be read. Blaagaarden is the "habitat" of these young Muslim women, whose families have either fled or migrated from Middle Eastern or North African countries, who were born and grew up in a Scandinavian welfare state, in a specific urban environment, at a time where the technological development has made it possible to live parts of your life through the smartphone. The term *harakat*, which I introduced above, has specific meanings in the context of these women's lives in this neighborhood—in this "habitat." In this particular environment, the term describes how the young women I worked with move in a skilled way, conscious of how to behave and how to move to preserve their safety. The habitus forming in this habitat is highly dependent on *harakat*. It is a challenging environment that informants navigate, where both young men and women might feel inclined to associate or affiliate with certain people to feel safe.[4] Crime, violence, conflict, "social control," coercion, and threats were an intimate part of the area. Inevitably, the presence of crime in this area—and also the broader, and frequently false, perceptions that became associated with it—intersected with larger national policy issues that also notably impacted the area and the lives of my informants.

In 2004, 10 years prior to my fieldwork, Noerrebro and other parts of Copenhagen were deemed "visitation zones" (visitationszoner). These zones allowed police to "stop and frisk" (search) anyone they wanted to for weapons and were part of a broader "securitization policy" introduced in the prior years. Various preemptive measures in this "security/integration response" intensified at the beginning of the new millennium when Denmark became actively involved in the US-led coalition in Iraq and Afghanistan. The Muslim population was cast as the "usual suspects," affecting the everyday lives of ordinary Danish Muslims in an increasingly harsh national media discourse toward immigrants and refugees, which intersected with a securitization policy inward and outward (Rytter and Pedersen 2011, 2014). Young men of other ethnic origin than Danish were targeted continuously, including many young men who had not broken the law and had no intention of breaking the law; they were stopped over and over and made objects of suspicion (see Henkel 2010; Kublitz 2015). In daily parlance, the area of Blaagaarden is just called the Square (*pladsen*), and it is acknowledged that "everybody answers when 'the Square' calls." The violent conflicts between Blaagaards Square Group (later to be known under the name Loyal to Familia) and other street gangs and biker gangs (notably Hells Angels, the largest in Denmark) are about territory, the drug market, honor, and personal vendettas. The Blaagaards Square Group (BGP) feels rejected by Danish society, as a member argued in an interview with Danish TV2:

> Hells Angels have started three wars now. They opened the war with Bullshit, they opened the war with Bandidos, and now they did it again. Even so, the whole of Denmark, the media and politicians, they talk as if it is Noerrebro, immigrants and Blaagaards Square that is the problem. (Braagard 2015)

The then Minister of Justice, Brian Mikkelsen from the Conservative party, is quoted as saying "they" should leave the country, referring to the street gangs only,[5] and not the biker gangs:

The group positions itself in a victim role … the Blaagaards Square group members are hard-core criminals. They have been convicted of murder attempts, violence, threats and drug dealing. They threaten and destroy others people's lives. I am well aware that the bikers are equally raw and callous. But that does not change that we have a right to defend our country against foreigners (udlændinge) carrying loaded guns. I know this sounds very nationalist, but I say "out of our country"! (Braagard 2015)

The above rhetoric from politicians, the media, and MPs affect everyone in the area, not just the thirty-five to forty-five young men involved in the gang (a number estimated by the Gang Intelligence Unit). How these events are handled in the press, by police and politicians, has the effect of making young Muslim people in the area feel excluded, as informants pointed out (see also Henkel 2014; Hervik 2011; Kublitz 2015). The stereotype about the place and the people there is something they navigated constantly—a stereotype forming at the intersection of ethnicity, religion, and class/residence. The explicit implication—that not all should be treated equal by law—has since been developed further in an attempt by the center-right government to target so-called parallel societies in ghettos. A part in this is a new package of Danish assimilation laws for immigrants, including plans to separate toddlers from families to teach them national values (25 hours per week from the age of 1). If people fail to comply with the measures their welfare payments are discontinued. Other punitive measures proposed (not passed yet) include the doubling of criminal sentences for crimes committed in twenty-five ghetto neighborhoods (as defined by the government, see above) and a 4-year prison sentence to parents sending their children back to their country of origin for extended periods of time (on re-educational trips). The UN's Human Rights Commissioner has condemned the new package and warned that the measures will only increase "racial discrimination against people of migrant origin" (Økonomi- og Indenrigsministeriet 2018, UN Human Rights July 3, 2018).

The "Migrant Bill" (L87) was approved by parliament (as of January 26, 2016), implementing measures against letting refugees and other immigrants into Denmark and bringing their families. This added to a growing feeling among some of my Muslim informants of being unwanted in the country where they were born and grew up. They had similar reaction to the ghetto package and policies targeting "ghetto areas" and the "Anti-Mask Law" of May 31, 2018 (the

General Civil Penal Code §134b), the latter going under the popular name "The Burka Ban." My informants formulated a wish to counter the stereotypes that they experienced in Denmark toward immigrants and Muslims, most importantly the stereotype of young Muslim women wearing the veil as being subdued. They were all upset about being reduced to a binary stereotype, whereby you can be perceived as either free (from Islam) or subdued (by Islam), other nuances or combinations not available in dominant public and media discourse (see Ahmad and Waltorp 2019). Add to this the so-called Paradigm shift in 2019, where the government changed the policy in terms of refugees from one of integration to one of "sending back home" (*hjemsendelse*).

A working paper from the Danish Centre for Social Research (SFI) from 2012 stated that "the lives and opinions of the less visible majority of Muslims more or less vanished in the Media coverage. In this way, the newspapers constructed a distorted and negative picture of Muslims and their religion, and thereby contributed to a general climate of intolerance and discrimination against Muslim minorities" (Jacobsen et al. 2012:1). However, the conversations I had with the women about minority-majority relations, Islamophobia, and stereotypes in the media occurred almost exclusively at the beginning of my fieldwork, before I got to know the women better. Later in the fieldwork, we only had these discussions when I initiated them, or when new policies were introduced and the media focus soared, leaving them feeling targeted and associated with radical Islam and the threat of terror.

As the women whom I worked with navigated all of the social complexities of their lives as young Muslim women born to immigrants living in Denmark, a key tool for them in this *harakat* movement was the smartphone. Nearly every element of their lives intersected with it, including the way they communicated with their family and friends, and it influenced how they responded to the stereotypes and other forms of social pressure. The smartphone and social media have a central place in the women's environment—habitat—in which they move and dwell and in which their habitus is formed. A focus on the smartphone as a constituent part of this emerging place is in following with the conceptualization of an assemblage constituted of the material, digital, and mental spaces, as well as the real and imagined, the perceived, conceived, and lived.[6] The young women in Blaagaarden use the smartphone to invest in relations—with places, with people, and with futures. They shape and are shaped by their environment, and in an increasingly interconnected, mediated, mobile world, with "outside" forces shaping any "local place."

Combinations of smells, sights, sounds, tastes, and textures continuously impress themselves onto the nervous system, but at the very same time a person transforms and modifies the environment through their thoughts, movements, and actions. As such, both the perceiving organism and inhabited environment are in a process of constant change and adaptation through which life and personhood is individuated and expressed.
(Irving 2017:14)

b

What's in a Field?

Enacting hybridity

The built environment, the mobile devices, the social media, the young women, and their imaginaries—all make up the assemblage I sought to interrogate. Over the course of my fieldwork, Blaagaarden and Noerrebro became several places to me—a slightly schizophrenic feeling, unsettling and rewarding at the same time. It became obvious to me that what one is capable of is afforded by place, and consequently it changes when one moves to a new place or when one spends time in the same place in the company of another group of people (cf. Corsín-Jimenez 2003). Over time spent with my informants in their lived environments, I felt my own capacities change as a result of being in that place, and I felt the capacities of the place change as well. This is interesting as the physical place was Noerrebro where I had been living for years with my family. A growing uneasiness made me aware of how I was constantly, albeit often subconsciously, negotiating with myself about how to behave: what behavior was possible and appropriate for me as seen from various other's perspective? Or rather, what was possible for me in this place—what did the place make possible after I started to move and dwell in the place in the company of the young Muslim women I worked with? Could I still sit with friends and drink a beer in a café on the sidewalk of Blaagaards street while being fully aware that I might meet a husband, parent, uncle, aunt, or acquaintance of my informants? Could I wear short skirts and still feel comfortable? My informants all maintained that I should not worry about "immodest" dress, as I was not judged by the same criteria as them, and thus their association with me would not reflect negatively on them due to my immodesty. Several of the women I worked with visited me at home, met my husband, and introduced me to theirs, as well as to other family members. Their rationale was that this is "natural" to do as a respectful insight for one's husband as to whom one is spending time with. I noticed how other Muslim people *saw* me or saw me in a different way. I became visible or relevant in a way that I hadn't been previously now that I was moving in the company of young Muslim women: someone now *part of* persons who were known in the Muslim immigrant "community," and because I was seen with people, as part of people, in different connections—in the street, at home, at weddings, and so forth.

I myself started to perceive the urban environment differently, perceived different affordances (Gibson 2015), as I saw connections that I had not heretofore: who "owned" different places, for example, and who was affiliated with whom. I encountered webs of connections and slowly learned an additional set of norms, including how to greet people in a specific way and learning phrases in Arabic and Persian, as well as orienting myself to the women's sociality, not the Muslim men's, for example. I knew, and felt in my body, that I did not live up to the appropriate ways of behaving. It was a source of conflict to me that I failed to live up to criteria of what was considered modest behavior and dress, as they clashed with my habitual way of comporting myself as well as ideals to stand by—and simultaneously I experienced inner conflicts about feeling that way. It was unsettling to feel that *part of me* felt uncomfortable in my normal summer outfit in "my own" neighborhood. My informants also experienced discomfort, not identical, but parallel conflicts between different sets of norms around how to dress and how to behave. Different "others" demanded and awarded different versions of them. "Be modest and respect yourself!" some would urge them; others would demand of them: "Be 'free' and respect yourself." The young women navigated and negotiated these conflicts in various ways. One way was to show—or live out—versions of oneself in social media, as I discuss in more detail in the next chapters in relation to their use of smartphones. This embodied experience of my transformation in my own "physical" environment made me even more interested in the relation between people and places: where do we feel we belong and how does attachment to place and community occur? How are people bound to their material environment? How are we differently connected to the same material environments? And how are digital and imaginal realms entwined in the material environment?

Shaun Moores (2015) considers people's everyday use of media as place-making, focusing on movement, dwelling, wayfaring, and habitation (see also Ingold 2000). One dwells in one's habitat and familiarity comes over time; one develops skills in moving about in that environment (Gibson 2015; Gupta and Ferguson 1997; Ingold 2000).[1] It is through engagement over time, in a physical place or an online space, that one gains "inhabitant knowledge." It thus connotes the idea of habitus and an ecological approach that considers a human being as embodied and embedded in her environment: "People find their way about media settings or environments just as they know, in the course of their bodily movements, how to get around, say, in a room, a building, a street, a neighbourhood or a city … finding a way about is fundamental for dwelling or habitation" (Moores 2015:18). Place is constituted when a "habit field" is formed, in other words, when routine activity gives rise to attachments (Moores 2015:19). Inasmuch as a place contains sources of "nurture and identity," Yu-Fi Tuan argues, so, too, does a painting, photograph, poem, novel, motion picture, dance, or piece of music (Tuan 2004). My informants would encounter all of these—paintings, photographs, poems, novels, motion pictures, dances, or pieces of music—through the smartphone (as well as physically in print, on the radio, and on flow TV). By assembling relations and places, the smartphone affords significant new ways of constituting places and personhood; the person emerges as a microcosm of her social world. New technologies radically affect the environment—the habitat—and consequently the habitus of the people inhabiting the environment. So what is in a field today?

> "The field" can now exist down the block; it can be accessed by a computer interface; it can unfold in surreal montage rather than in neatly bounded realist narrative. In some respects, the epistemic horizons of anthropology have never been wider. Yet what remains crucial is that one reports from an environment that is not entirely one's own, that one mediates or translates between X and Y.
> (Boyer and Howe 2015:16)

I do not mediate or translate between X or Y but insist on the Z, the *thirdness* that emerges from studying with others (cf. Elhaik 2013; Narayan 1993). My field did exist down the block, though, as Boyer and Howe point to in the above quote, and my field was accessed by a smartphone interface; it unfolded and was later also edited into experimental montage. My field was my neighborhood—but it was also a place that was different from it. It was a place where new layers of social events and experiences created new routes and familiarity over time: taking the bus together, the s-train, walking together, riding together in the car with the windows rolled down, and honking the horn while singing along to the car radio playing Mohammed Assaf and whirling a scarf and driii'ing. As I followed my informants around the areas of Blaagaarden and Noerrebro on foot (see de Certeau 1984; Lee and Ingold 2006; Pink 2007), by car, and by bus, I also followed them in social media. Our trips in the physical area of Blaagaarden made me realize how different their routes were as compared to my previous use of the area. Whereas I would walk down the main street in Blaagaarden and the other larger side streets lined with cafés and shops, they would avoid all the gazes and gossip that Blaagaarden street meant to them. I, for my part, followed my informants' leads into media platforms that I had not previously used, such as Snapchat and Viber, as well as learning different ways of using the "back alleys" in the platforms I already used prior to fieldwork, such as Facebook. I also followed my informants physically on travels to Dubai and to Tehran and Esfahan as the opportunities presented themselves. As mentioned, I regretted not being able to join women who participated in the research to trips to Pakistan and Jordan. Time constraints and economic constraint made me prioritize more time spent in Blaagaarden.

As Ghassan Hage has discussed in "A not so multi-sited ethnography in a not so imagined community" (2005) in the study of migrants sharing a unifying culture across a number of global locations, multi-sitedness is less helpful than a notion of a single geographically discontinuous site (2005). Yet the culture, as I experienced it, was not "unifying" as such, as the women born and raised in Denmark, giving birth to their children in Denmark, were changing it—changing the culture. This is not to say that I do not agree with Abdelmalek Sayad, that emigration and immigration are two sides of the same coin, that one cannot study without taking both sides into account (2004), both sides are *in* the person. Sayad's work is deeply historical and integrates temporality as fundamental; immigration is considered as a continuing process that begins with emigration and not simply as a mode of adaptation to the host society. As he shows in "Les enfants illégitimes" (1979)—the Illegitimate Children—the (Algerian) immigrants' children born in France suffer a double estrangement with respect to both the immigrant generation of their parents and the society into which they are born. Sayad elaborates on an extended interview with the young woman Zahouda, who was born in France to Algerian parents. In the interview, she keeps returning to her experience of feeling almost like an illegitimate child, as her own parents do not recognize themselves in her. She, along with those of her siblings who were also born in France, had become too French according to their parents. Zahouda describes her experiences of visiting Algeria and how she was unable to fit in and understand the codes, the tacit knowledge of how to move, talk, and behave. Yet, in France, as she says, she would be seen as Algerian. This experience mirrors that of several of my informants; below is Hadia of Palestinian-Jordanian origin:

You can be born in Denmark, grow up here, but you're not Danish (in the eyes of ethnic Danes)—and the minute you set foot in Jordan, they know that you're not from there: Then, you're suddenly Danish. They see it right away: the way we dress, the way we move, simply the way we look at them! We have a different way of looking, I've been told.

Especially when visiting the parents' country of origin, the differences become all the more obvious in the stories told of visiting "home" by the women I worked with, as well as the experience of traveling with two of the women to Iran. A number of my informants have married and settled in their parents' country of origin or other Arab countries, and most of them have sisters or girlfriends who have done so. Dubai, one of the "related sites" that I visited with an informant, is a popular place, according to my informants, because "it is like a European city, but at the same time it is a Muslim and Arab city." Copenhagen remains the preferred place to live, however. This is where they felt at home and had a network, history, and a future. And the most important site in this present study was the area of Blaagaarden and the smartphone tying this place together with the other important sites. With the increasingly "restrictive foreigner policies" in Denmark, the future that one sees for oneself is impacted. On June 19, 2015, the day after the national elections, I was with two informants, Hadia and Bita. There was a lot of joking in the face of the exclusionary politics, and I felt uneasy in my position as Dane in the joke, although they knew that I did not agree with the Danish National Party that had grown to become the country's second largest with thirty-seven mandates, and the "Blue" block (liberal-conservative coalition) winning with ninety mandates, exactly the needed number to form a government. Carl, my son, yelled from the apartment into the courtyard in the Blaagaarden apartment if he could come down and play with Hadia's daughter. As he left, Bita joked: "Tell him he promised to be my boyfriend when he's older! Karen, don't you have a good friend who can marry me—so I can stay in the country, ha ha." We talked about how we didn't think it would come to this and were surprised about the election results.

Harakat and composite habitus

One reason the main streets of Blaagaarden are avoided by the young women I worked with is because local people gossip so much, "er hovedpine" (literally *are* headache—the grammar is on the awkward side, staying true to the slang in the area). On the other hand, the young women feel they are likely to be gossiped about by majority Danes for wearing the veil and not acting like young Danish women when they are *outside* of the local area. The navigating of different sets of expectations, and stereotypes, trying to "keep cool and stay virtuous" (Waltorp 2015) is what I allude to as *harakat* movement. As mentioned in the introduction, *harakat* is an Arabic term signifying movement. In the local slang of young Muslim people in Noerrebro, however, *harakat* means to "make a move" and to "play a trick" on someone in a cunning, smart, or charming way—the term is used by young people and relates to the category of being young. I use the term to denote a specific skilled mode of moving in one's environment, counting here both the online and the physical realms. *Harakat* is a necessary skilled way of moving in an insecure environment in which one is not in a power position to make the rules; it finds parallels in Michel de Certeau's conceptual pairing of the "strategy" used by those in power to the "tactics" used by the weak (1984, see also Vigh 2006, 2009; Vium 2016). Julie Archambault draws on Vigh and de Certeau in her analysis of how her informants in Inhambane, Mozambique, cruise their uncertain everyday environment, noting the new range of possibilities to do so via the cell phone (2013, 2017). The smartphone and social media represent an interesting set of affordances in this place to this group of young women. Situational revealing and concealing is a challenge and an opportunity in the habitat in which they move. In describing my informants' skilled and challenging navigation of "keeping cool and staying virtuous" I coined the term *composite habitus* (Waltorp 2015), drawing from Marcel Mauss's Techniques du Corps (1936)[2] and particularly Pierre Bourdieu's theoretical development of the habitus concept (1977, 1990, 1999, 2000). My empirical material seemed to push at the limits of or overflow the notion which Bourdieu developed and championed through many years of research and writing, though.

The young women I worked with are not only in between two different cultures—the culture of their parents' country of origin which they inherit and that of the Danish culture into which they were born and are living. Rather, their habitus is formed at the conjunction of the country of origin, the receiving country, religious prescriptions and norms, the subculture of the social housing project, socioeconomic class, and the specific mix of other migrants, descendants, and Danes in the area in this specific historical time: the assemblage that I have described above. The young women in Blaagaarden used the smartphone as a very tangible technological device, a particular instrument, or tool that affords specific forms of networking or relationship building and maintenance on multiple levels in time and across space. Over the course of my research, I have come to understand the smartphone as a particular kind of relational device that aggregates relations and places that are valuable to the young women in my study. According to Bourdieu, migration entails a rupture in that "practices are always liable to incur negative sanctions when the environment with which they are actually confronted is too distant from that to which they are objectively fitted" (Bourdieu 1977:78). Intergenerational conflicts solicit not age classes separated by natural properties but forms of habitus that have been produced by different modes of generations, as in the case of the families migrating from Algeria to France, with the younger children born and socialized in France: "By conditions of existence which, in imposing different definitions of the impossible, the possible, and the probable, cause one group to experience as natural or reasonable, practices or aspirations which another group finds unthinkable or scandalous" (Bourdieu 1977). These conflicts between the impossible and possible are indicative of the intergenerational relations among the Muslim families of my informants. The term *composite habitus* points to the ways in which these young women, as most people in the modern, globalized world, are informed and formed by *multiple fields* and *multiple forces* during their life trajectory. The notion of a composite habitus builds on Bourdieu's writings late in his career on the split habitus (*habitus clivée*).[3]

The term *split habitus* also points in the direction of a less unitary understanding of the habitus (Bourdieu 1999), but I take this further, arguing that the young second-generation immigrant Muslim women inhabit not only a split but a complex, composite habitus which affords a range of possible strategies. This does *not* imply that any of the composite parts of the habitus can easily be disregarded or applied in a conscious and flexible manner. This is also what the concept of habitus, implying sedimentation over time, offers; a composite habitus is not "roles" one can choose freely and consciously to shift between as convenient. On the one hand, young women use smartphones and social media to reproduce moral norms, since they do not publicly question or challenge what should be considered private and what can be public, what is acceptable and not. Yet, on the other hand, their actions signify how the range of possible strategies (Zigon 2009:254) has opened up through their use of social media through which they can conceive of possible ways to challenge norms, which thereby become open to them. This paradox of following yet challenging moral norms may also be understood with reference to the composite habitus. As written in the foreword to a popular book in Danish on *Virginity in Fashion* (Mødom på Mode), focusing on modesty and stories about marriage, the authors Aaman and Uddin write:

There are invisible pioneers, who pick their battles carefully so as to not place their family in a bad light. Their voices drown in the loud, shrill voices insisting on the upholding of tradition from the countries of origin, where the woman is the family's "security" in a good reputation, and where the woman's body and sexuality is not her own. Not seldom, both voices are represented in one and the same person. (Aaman and Uddin 2007:8, my translation)

Even though I do not agree with the approach of Aaman and Uddin, I was struck by how precise the description of the opposing voices represented in one and the same person is.

It is rather *multiple predispositions* that inform the preferences, opinions, and choices of my informants than dual opposing identities, or split habitus, as Bourdieu has it. Habitus is a principle of repetition and conservation and he, in fact, started working with the concept to understand the mismatches he experienced in Algeria in the 1960s between objective structures and incorporated structures (2000:159). In situations of rapid social change or geographical mobility, the mismatch is felt intensely. Bourdieu proposes that there is an inertia in the habitus, or a hysteresis effect, in which "dispositions are out of line with the field ... habitus has its 'blips', critical moments when it misfires or is out of phase" (2000:160, 162). In his later work, he opened up to the idea of habitus being split or "clivé," which he also terms a double bind. This double bind/split habitus term is applied in his analysis in *The Weight of the World* (1999) to denote groups of people in which there is a great variation and at times contradiction between experiences and expectations in their families, on the one hand, and those of the educational system and broader society, on the other hand (1999:383, 507). When the "structuring of habitus" happens across partially overlapping fields, the tension between them can result in a split, or fragmented, habitus (Bourdieu and Waquant 2009:112–113). This resonates with the work with first- and second-generation Algerian migrants to France that Bourdieu's associate Abdelmalek Sayad, mentioned above, worked with (1979, 2004) as it does the specific situation of young Muslim women, descendants of immigrants, in my study. What could be considered as being "at home," where there is an unquestioned fit between habitus and field? I propose that feelings of belonging and feeling connected are mediated by social media in new ways for this group of young Muslim women in Denmark. A difference from Sayad's study of Algerian immigrants in France in the 1960s, 1970s, and 1980s and of particular interest to the argument I put forward here is that, at the time he was conducting his research, smartphones and social media were not available. Hence, the ways in which these technologies afford opportunities to negotiate one's place in the world were not present among his informants, as it is today.

Bateson's double bind theory (2000:94, 96) inspired Bourdieu's "split habitus." What is important to my discussion and forwarding of the composite habitus rather than the split habitus is that to Bateson, the double bind did not necessarily imply a pathological condition but could be associated with the potential creativity embedded in learning to deal with the transcontextual "condition," which he regretted was overlooked in people's use of the double bind theory. Bateson was discussing this on the level of the individual and the family (2000:278), but the creativity of the transcontextual condition is important for the notion of the composite habitus here. It is, in particular, Bourdieu's take on a less unitary habitus in which several dispositions are embodied and act simultaneously as durable dispositions that inspire my analysis, emphasizing the transcontextual creative potentiality. The term *composite habitus* puts stress on these aspects of the habitus.

Perceiving affordances

The question of how we perceive the surrounding world was discussed in the 1950s by psychologist James J. Gibson, as discussed above in relation to Ibn al-Haytham's theory of perception. Gibson rejected his own—and other's— theories of vision building on the retinal images and based a new theory on what he termed "the ambient optic array" and argued that we use the head and eyes to look around (ambient vision) and we use the body to get up and walk around (ambulatory vision) to see all the way around at a given point of observation and to take different points of observation (parallax). This he contrasted with snapshot vision and pictorial depth perception (Gibson 2015:xiv). I find his theories to be illuminating in terms of the mutual formation of the environment and people that inhabit it, or in a different terminology—habitat and habitus. "When vision is thought of as a perceptual system instead of as a channel for inputs to the brain, a new theory of perception considered as information pickup becomes possible. Perceiving is an act, not a response, an act of attention, not a triggered impression, an achievement, not a reflex" (Gibson 2015:141).[4] Even though Gibson's terminology is quite technical and presupposes a range of interrelated terms, what he is pointing to is significant for the exploration that I attempt here: to understand "what's in a field," what's in the field of Blaagaarden,

Noerrebro—conceptualized as a habitat, an environment also composing the online (and imaginal) realms. A very useful term, that Gibson coined, to explain this entwinement of person and environment and which sheds light on the habitus-habitat relation in an environment emerging across on- and offline is the term *affordances*:

> The affordances of the environment are what it offers the animal, what it provides or furnishes, either for good or ill. The verb to afford is found in the dictionary, but the noun affordance is not. I have made it up. I mean by it something that refers to both the environment and the animal in a way that no existing term does. It implies the complementarity of the animal and the environment (Gibson 2015:128).

The term has been appropriated by the field of design, where the meaning of it has changed fundamentally. It has found its way back to social science with this meaning, which differs from the original usage, which is what I am building on here. The term points two ways: to the environment and to the subject perceiving it. The environment, other persons and beings, as well as "detached objects" (tools, utensils, weapons) afford special types of behavior on the part of the perceiving subject in this understanding (Gibson 2015, see also Knappett 2004).

Gibson points to how "behaviour affords behaviour, and the whole subject matter of psychology and of the social sciences can be thought of as an elaboration of this basic fact: Sexual behaviour, nurturing behaviour, fighting behaviour, cooperative behaviour, economic behaviour, political behaviour—all depend on the perceiving of what another person or other persons afford, or sometimes of the misperceiving of it" (2015:127). The environment is not the same as the physical world, if one means by that the world described by physics. The environment of animals and men is what they perceive, but as the above quote points to—so much in the environment, and particularly in other persons, are there to be perceived and sometimes misperceived. Andrew Irving considers in relation to a place namely this:

> The content and character of any given neighbourhood in a particular moment needs to be understood as incorporating the simultaneous co-presence of many different qualities of inner expression, dialogue and memory that range from the ordinary to the extraordinary and on occasion encompass both. Some of these may be recurrent and ongoing to the extent that they define a sense of personal or collective experience and understanding, while others are destined to remain inconsequential and unarticulated or even unarticulatable. (Irving 2016:451)

The richest and most elaborate affordances of the environment are provided by other animals and, for us, other people, Gibson writes (Gibson 2015:126):

> There has been endless debate among philosophers and psychologists as to whether values are physical or phenomenal, in the world of matter or only in the world of the mind. For affordances as distinguished from values, the debate does not apply. Affordances are neither in the one world or the other inasmuch as the theory of the two worlds is rejected. There is only one environment, although it contains many observers with limitless opportunities for them to live in it (Gibson 2015:129).

Gibson did not agree on any separation between cultural and natural world, or natural and "artificial" for that matter, and does not discern between an artificial environment and the natural environment—but sees it as "the same old environment modified by man" (Gibson 2015:122).

> It is a mistake to separate the natural from the artificial as if there were two environments; artefacts have to be manufactured from natural substances. It is also a mistake to separate the cultural environment from the natural environment, as if there were a world of mental products distinct from the world of material products. There is only one world, however diverse, and all animals live in it, although we human animals have altered it to suit ourselves. (2015:131)

The technologically mediated is part of the neighborhood and part of the environment of the young women I worked with—it is *real* virtuality, rather than virtual reality.

C

Hijab, Desire, Social Control

Entanglements of free speech and veiled women

On February 14, 2015, a fatal shooting occurred at the event "Art, Blasphemy, and Freedom of Speech" at "Krudttønden" in Copenhagen. A young man Omar Abdel Hamid El-Hussein, 22, shot and killed filmmaker Finn Nørgaard, who was in the audience at the event. Subsequently, a guard at the Jewish Synagogue, Dan Utzon, was shot dead by El-Hussein, who was himself killed the following morning by police. The event at Krudttønden was a debate about the infamous cartoon drawings of the Prophet Mohammed printed in daily newspaper *Jyllands-Posten* 2005. The so-called cartoon crisis in 2005–2006 saw caricatures of the Prophet Mohammad moving from the pages of the Danish newspaper to the entire world, offending many Muslims (Henkel 2011; Khan 2010; Kublitz 2015; Mahmood 2009). Bearing in mind that "an image has the power of synthesis: it condenses whole realms of possible ideas and interpretations and allows complex relationships to be perceived and grasped in an instant" (Wagner 2012:535),[1] the cartoon crisis can be approached from this perspective. In the context of Muslims in Denmark, Naveeda Khans's analysis of the reactions to the images of the Danish cartoons points to the specific importance of the image in Islam. Rather than seeing the modalities of relating to images as a minor tendency within the Islamic tradition, they may be thought of as the practice of imagination that has as strong a claim upon Muslim pursuits of religiosity as sense perceptions, intellectual cognition, even ardent faith, she suggests (Khan 2010).

Many ethnic Danes, though, for their part, felt offended that Muslims who had been welcomed into Denmark would disregard one of the principles held highest in the country: the freedom of speech. They saw the protests against drawings of the Prophet in a newspaper (demonstrations, burning of flags in front of Danish embassies, boycotting of Danish commodities) as inhibiting people's democratic freedom to openly criticize and voice their opinions, something so central as to be almost approached as sacred in the Danish context (see Mchangama and Stjernfelt 2016).

I had heard about the shooting of the filmmaker Finn Nørgaard via national media, social media, and directly from informants. Some shared alternative explanations with me that what they had heard, as to what had happened that night and morning, did not align with the official media's version. One version circulating had it that it could not have been Omar, as people had seen him at another place at the time of shooting. According to another version, it was indeed El-Hussein, although not on his own account but set up and paid by PET, the Danish intelligence service. The day after the shooting, I picked up a copy of the free newspaper *Metro Express*, available in the metro and buses. The headline read: "Muslim group ready to arrest people: Danish women have a new secret hotline." The article started with the word *vigilantism* (*selvtægt*) in capital letters. Muslim women who are attacked—verbally or corporeally—can opt for calling a group of Muslims who will serve as an alternative to Danish police, the article reported. The spokesperson of the group was quoted saying: "We're not a gang, or thugs. We're peaceful Muslims, that wish harm to no-one, regardless of their beliefs. If the police are not able to do their job, then we have to help them." Inside the paper was more on the secret hotline. An ethnic Danish man had attacked 21-year-old student Aooa Alomari of Iraqi descent, born and raised in Denmark. He had grabbed her jacket so hard she fell all the way down the stairs and started crying. She called the hotline, and within 10 minutes, four men of other ethnic backgrounds (than Danish) were on the spot, ready to protect her. She felt safer calling the group than calling the police. She was quoted in *Metro Express* saying: "I don't dare go out the door without somebody accompanying me, *and I don't even wear the veil*." Conspicuously, the newspaper had chosen a large photograph to go with the text showing four women in Niqab (full body and face coverage), only their brown eyes showing from under the dark covers, even though the article was about Aooa who did not even wear the hijab. Islam, the hijab, and notions of freedom are interlinked in specific, intricate ways in the Danish context.

As I moved away from Noerrebro in Copenhagen to the second largest city in Denmark, Aarhus, to take up a position at the university there, I would visit my informants' homes once or twice a month for 2–3 days at a time. I would sleep over at the family homes of my informants during these stays. Moving away from the neighborhood intensified our interaction in social media platforms. The stay-overs that commenced after I moved away from Noerrebro in the fall of

2014 gave me an insight into the dynamics of the families in a slightly different way, from when I was a visitor returning to my own home and family in an apartment up Noerrebro street. It made me appreciate the rhythms of day and night, weekdays and weekends, the duties of different family members, visits from extended family members, nighttime sociality, prayer time, etc. And not least, what happened when going out the door or opening it to let others in—how dress and behavior changed accordingly and appropriately, as mentioned. The same space is multiple, in the sense that it changes in terms of being more or less private or public, with the hijab off or on, depending on who buzzes the doorbell. A look through the door spy will determine if it's *marhram* to the woman wearing it, family dropping by, or the next-door neighbor woman or her kid with a plate of food from his mom, or if it is someone who makes it necessary to put on a veil. These stay-overs also revealed very clearly that at no time does the smartphone necessarily rest: being in bed at night can easily be the most private moment of the day when living many people together in a small apartment, and it can conveniently be used for communicating with others and creating a space of one's own with earphones in and attention devoted to the conversation one is engaging in through the smartphone, or attuned to the music one is listening to, series one is watching, or images or news bits one is scrolling through. The smartphone has the affordance of making the privacy of one's home more public through posting images, but then one's attire would also be carefully adapted accordingly and matched to the audience addressed, mediated by the smartphone.

At times it placed me in awkward situations to stay over—such as when combining a social event with friends in Copenhagen with fieldwork and living with a family in Blaagaarden: leaving dressed up for a big party and returning early in the morning, a little drunk, while the mother in the house was up, performing the morning prayer (*fajr*) as I snuck into the room, where I was sleeping, feeling disrespectful. The mother in the family did not mention this with a word, instead saying that I had looked beautiful in the dress I had worn for the party. She prayed five times a day, veiled, and fasted during Ramadan. Her oldest daughter reflected on this:

> My mom, she believes it says it is written in the Qur'an, that you should wear the headscarf—I don't know actually, it's her religion! But she has given us the choice to freely decide to wear it or take it off. I obviously did not wear it like this before (loose, Persian style/Pakistani style), I wore it very closed and jilbab and all, but that's not me. And I feel very bad, I feel—I get a really bad conscience, when people ask, why do you wear it then. I don't get upset with people, they have a

right to ask. I get angry with myself, because there are billions, that believe in it, that don it, and that respect it. I feel disgusting (ulækker) when I wear it like this, as I feel I'm playing with it. But I also don't feel like taking it off, and then donning it again, so I'm waiting for the right moment.

The Qur'an, and the life of the Prophet Muhammad as put forth in the *Hadith* (the collected sayings and exemplary doings of the Prophet), provides a set of fundamental guidelines for navigating everyday life for Muslims. But understanding and implementing these guidelines in the Danish context—an effort which requires negotiations with oneself, face to face with others and in social media—engender complex reflections and practices around autonomy, sexuality, and modesty. The positions taken on this issue by my informants are manifold, and they are all influenced from different family, ethnic, national, class, and religious (sectarian) backgrounds (see also Simonsen for the very varied lifestyles and background of Muslims in Denmark 1990, 2006, 2012).

The passages from the Qur'an[2] below are from a post on Facebook page, April 23, 2014, where many discussions unfolded concerning the issue of veiling and modest dress; the page is called "Når Dk er et frit land bør tørklæder også være et frit valg" (When Denmark is a free country, veiling ought to be a free choice):

> And tell the believing women to cast down their glances and guard their private parts and not expose their adornment except that which [necessarily] appears thereof and to wrap [a portion of] their headcovers over their chests and not expose their adornment except to their husbands, their fathers, their husbands' fathers, their sons, their husbands' sons, their brothers, their brothers' sons, their sisters' sons, their women, that which their right hands possess, or those male attendants having no physical desire, or children who are not yet aware of the private aspects of women. (Qur'an 24:31)

> O Prophet! Say to your wives, your daughters, and the women of the believers that: they should let down upon themselves their jalabib. (Qur'an 33:59)

The above verses point to the virtuous intentions of veiling, which helps the individual's striving toward virtuousness *through* veiling. In the Merriam-Webster Online Dictionary, *immodesty* is defined as "not modest; *specifically*: not conforming to the sexual mores of a particular time or place." For the young women I worked with in Copenhagen "sexual mores of a particular time or place" is a multiple phenomenon. According to the Qur'an a woman ought only allow for her physical "natural" beauty (bosom, head) to be seen by her husband, father, father-in-law, sons, husband's sons, their brothers, nephews, female relatives, and female slaves (a reminder of the historical context of the verses!), men related to the family and who, due to age or sickness, assumedly do not feel *sexual desire*, as well as children not yet sexually conscious (mature). Persons in this category are the *marhram*: those whom a woman could never marry because of gender, affinal, or conjugal relations.

In nonsexual terms, God is desired, and oneness with God is desired by some, while for others this is "hovmod" believing that oneness with God is possible. Submission to his will is sometimes underscored by calling one's occupation "slave of Allah," in one's Facebook profile in the settings "about." Desire in sexual terms is seen as positive and celebrated within marriage—it is prescribed, *halal*, in Islam. An informant alerted me to the fact that if you do not have sex in 6 months, that grounds for divorce—for the man as well as for the woman, this is a right for a healthy adult human being.[3] Sex before—and outside of—marriage is on the other hand sinful and prohibited in Islam. In this sense, virginity and sexual activity outside of marriage are not an issue for the individual (woman) alone, but reflecting on the whole family—something which the young Muslim women I worked with feel responsible for.

During my fieldwork, a video circulated on Facebook, pointing to the danger of sexual desire and contact with the opposite gender in the context of social media. It warned against the misfortunes befalling a girl who is lured into contact with a young man through Facebook. In this video, an exchange between the girl and young man starts very innocently but ends up with actual meetings in a park, where pictures are taken that are later used by the young man to pressure the girl to meet him again, even as she is about to marry another man. She is caught in this dilemma and ends up taking her own life in order not to cast shame on her family. The video ends by advising strongly that parents and brothers look out for their sisters' well-being by being alert to what can take place in social media so that they do not end up in such an unfortunate situation. It is the family that must guard the young woman. Failing to do that would mean diminishing her chances of marrying well and living with the stigma of not being virtuous—"not conforming to the sexual mores of a specific time or place."

One night, during a late-night socializing in a Blaagaarden apartment, it struck that four of the six women in the company had fresh haircuts and their hair newly colored (no men were present). As I took part in complimenting their beautiful hairdos, I asked whether they did not feel *in some ways* like it was a shame that they did not have the possibility to "show it to the world." No one confirmed feeling that way. On the contrary, as many times before, several of them expressed that they enjoyed the modest clothing they wore in public.

In the beginning of fieldwork, I could not help but find it contradictory that a woman sitting in a super-tight, short skirt and top would purport to be happy in Islamic dress in the street. I did not fully appreciate that there are numerous spaces in which to show oneself. As one of the women, Amira, pointed out jokingly: "You Danes will just show yourself looking good to everyone in public, in the street and so ... but we, we save that for our husband at home. He knows he's special that he's the only man allowed to see us like this. He knows we did all this for him!"

Among the young Muslim women I worked with, as well as the specific group we were gathered that evening, the opinions on veiling varied. Samira told me, in a hushed voice, that she actually felt like taking off the hijab and going to the beach and feeling the wind in her hair. Her fiancé wanted to do that together with her, once they were married, but without other people knowing about it. At the opposite end of the spectrum, Jamila, who did not use a veil, said she wished she had the courage to start wearing it (as some of her sisters did) in a conversation over lunch. I was struck by how she put it: "I wish I had the courage to put on the hijab," since previously I had found her quite courageous in not donning the veil when her sister and mother did. She expanded on this: "If I start wearing the hijab now, everyone I've studied with, my colleagues and so on, will wonder; they're bound to have an opinion about it—and quite frankly I can't really deal with that kind of attention and speculation—not right now at least. Perhaps I'll find the courage, inch'Allah (God willing)." Two Danish-Pakistani sisters, friends of an informant, also chose differently in this regard and were supportive of each other. The one sister would regularly post texts on Facebook in which she urged all Muslim women to wear the hijab. The other sister, who did not wear a hijab herself, would "like" all these Facebook posts by her hijab-wearing sister.

Another woman, Hadia, in a different vein shared with me that people would be quick to judge someone as a "luder" (a whore) if they stopped wearing the veil—wearing it actually gave some leeway in other areas. Most informants, wearing a hijab or scarf Iranian or Pakistani style had experienced harassment for wearing the hijab by everyone from schoolteachers to people in the street. From comments that "no one can know what's hidden underneath that veil," to people asking whether one sympathizes with Islamic State (DAESH), to simply frowning or exclaiming "yikes" to their face. When discussing the breadth of experiences pertaining to veiling and the notion of "social control," the experiences of two Danish (non-Muslim) women whom I met through informants are informative. I was acquainted with the two women because they were in the same circle of friends as some of my main informants. Both young women had veiled for fun at an occasion with some of our mutual Muslim women friends, who recounted the unfolding of events for me. The Danish women had posted pictures on social media platforms together, wearing the veil. The older brother of one of the women told her on that occasion that it would have severe consequences should she choose to ever do something that "fucking gross" (*klamt*) again. In this instance, the young Danish (atheist) woman was confronted with a direct sanction by her older brother. This kind of controlling reaction from an older brother toward a sister is often mentioned as endemic to ethnic minority families in a generalizing fashion. Danish forms of "social control" are usually not considered *as* social control, but making young women (and men) conform to socially acceptable norms of dress and behavior in subtle ways, understood as raising young people to become responsible adults, making safe and sound choices—and here a brother looking out for his sister, knowing how she might be perceived by others if wearing the veil in social media.

When I went to Iran with two informants, Zara and Neda, and their mother to live with their family, I was forced by law to use a veil in public spaces; it was odd yet ambivalent to have an embodied experience of veiling. This experience was obviously brief and largely void of the significance and content that the Islamic head coverage is infused with in differing ways to my informants, as I am not religious.[4] In Iran, women who appear in public without the veil risk being arrested—as happened to one of my informants during my fieldwork. The *gaz*, translated as "modesty police," walk the streets in *chadors* (fully covering, loose garment) looking for women not living up to the so-called modesty laws. We had just left Tehran from the Meher Abad Airport and arrived in Isfahan, our small company counting one middle-aged Khala (aunt), the two women, whom I worked with, and a cousin, a teenage boy nearing 15. He would retreat to a quiet corner every chance he had and listen to Danish-Iranian artist S!VAS (see Playlist), his smartphone his solace when missing Denmark, and his home environment and friends terribly. A stern-looking middle-aged woman dressed in *chador* came up to one of the young women, Zara, asking her about her dress (why so tight), her makeup (why so much, why even use makeup, and for whom?), her veil (why not closed around her face, covering her hair properly). Zara started arguing that she lived up to all formal requirements and was taken to the police in the airport, where the woman quickly gave an account in Farsi to the two officers in the office and left us there. The older woman started apologizing and pleading with them, while Zara defended herself in no uncertain terms and raising her voice. Neda told her in Danish, "Honestly, this is not Denmark, you do *not* have freedom of speech, you do *not* have a right to an opinion on this—what is it that you don't get?" Neda, the other sister, was also questioned as to why her style was so tomboyish, and she immediately wore a larger, long cardigan that she found in her aunt's luggage, on top of her loose baggy jeans. After hours in the office, we were free to go. Zara was devastated; she had had to give her fingerprints to the police and was afraid this would be interpreted as her having behaved like "a slut," as she had been arrested due to immodest dress. Others would approach us out of the blue—always men—telling the older women that they should not let the tomboy look get out of control (we were never outside in public space without men from the family or older women accompanying us). They worried less about the feminine sartorial choices of the one sister and much more about the gender codes being challenged by the tomboy, street-style of the other sister—regardless of the fact that she wore her hijab in a style where not a single straw of hair showed, neither neck or ears, and also did not wear makeup. Zara once remarked in the park, after the entourage being stopped by worried men in the public space, "It's her own fault, people are staring at her here (for dressing like a tomboy)." Her stylistic choices were never an issue in Blaagaarden.

"Playing with the scarf is playing with our religion"

Zara, 27, an Iranian-Kurdish woman introduced above, was in her mid-20s and lived in Blaagaarden. She donned the *hijab* and also used to wear the *jilbab*, full-length outer garment, but had changed her mind. She did not wear jilbab anymore but still a loose scarf in "Iranian style," which does not hide the hair around the forehead and ears as a hijab does. She had become undecided as to whether she actually wanted to wear the scarf or not. Zara had also been sharing pictures with girlfriends in Snaps and WhatsApp messages without the veil. This is common practice, but some of these were taken in a café in the city, not within the privacy of a home, something which spurred discussion, and Zara's decisions regarding the veil were debated among her girlfriends (when she was not present). They somewhat paradoxically "accept her for who she is" *but* point to the general sentiment in the local Muslim immigrant community, "You should choose either to wear the veil properly or not at all": "Playing with the scarf is playing with our religion."

Yet another Danish woman—who had one Danish parent and one Iranian—decided to stop wearing the hijab. It was a process that entailed her group of friends to become reconfigured—not necessarily because her decisions were condemned or opposed directly but sociality had become somewhat more difficult within those previous social configurations. It was frowned upon by those of her closest friends dressing like this. They went from socializing on a daily basis to spending less and less time together. With other friends it was easier to reconcile her new choice. She did not stop being a Muslim but changed how she interpreted this, and accordingly, what social events she would partake in. This was mirrored in her profile on Instagram. She chose to close down her former profile, showcasing mostly her and friends about town (often in a car), memes of affirmative feminist quotes with attitude and religious quotes that she related to, and her own poetry written with the typewriter font. She opened a new profile, post-hijab. Her own poetry did not feature anymore, but the memes alluded to states of mind, such as "Don't ever let anyone feel bad about doing what makes you happy" and images of a dying plant, slowly getting back to life and blossoming with the words on the pots: "just," "keep," "trying," graffiti with "Hate doesn't come from religion, it comes from fear," and a personal favorite of mine: an image of a full-size mirror with a sticker in the corner reading "WARNING: Reflections in this mirror may be distorted by socially constructed ideas of 'beauty'." Many friends continued liking her posts on this new profile, including hijabis commenting, "I love your hair." There is an idea that if you stop (bodily) performing religiosity and submission, other (haram) behavior might follow. And some friends did point out that she had changed in the sort of company she was in, and the places in Copenhagen she would go to hang out at late hours, not drinking herself but in the company of people who did. Of the groups of friends I spent time with, all of them counted women wearing the hijab and women who did not. But it was also the case that if someone chose to wear it and then, at a later stage, decided to stop, some of the women would take this as a rejection of their choice to wear it, while—again—others did not.

Bita, 24, of Iranian origin, initiated a relationship on Facebook with a young Iranian man living in Dubai. They had been in a relationship for 2 years. Her mother knew about it, as did a select few of her trusted friends. She and her boyfriend had never met "irl" (in real life), but their relation evolved from a Facebook romance into communication within a more intimate media sphere and to using FaceTime or Viber daily, through which they could see each other while talking. She only ever sent him pictures with her veil off. He would not find wearing the veil "cool," as she said; it would imply that she was boring and old-fashioned, wearing the veil in a European city where nobody forced her to (as mentioned, hijab is compulsory in Iran). He asked her to close down her Facebook account. He was on Facebook himself, but since other young men might contact her on Facebook, he felt uncomfortable with her being visible in that way. In response to her boyfriend's demands, Bita closed down her "old" account and established a new fake account (an alias profile) on Facebook without his knowledge and managed to acquire over 300 "friends" in common with him. She monitored him closely, all the while he was (or thought he was) controlling her visibility. Officially, she complied, but, through the smartphone and social media, she made her own rules in the relationship.

One evening at a popular restaurant owned by Muslim immigrants, I witnessed a man tear off Bita's veil from behind, saying in a stern voice, "What is this? On or off with it!" I was shocked when I saw this, but Bita played it cool, covering her hair and laughingly responded, "So, which do you prefer, if it was up to you?" Effectively, Bita is doing a *harakat*. She is skilled in balancing and navigating people's expectations and demands on her and her appearance and finds ways of asserting herself. Humor, tact, and a street-smart attitude are necessary. *Harakat* movement entails turning preconceptions and prejudice on its head by playing along or having the situation somehow turned to one's advance. If it can amuse the company of girl friends at the same time, it proves one's prowess. The young Muslim women with whom I worked occupy a complex position in moral terms: how to lead a good and desirable life and be recognized as both virtuous women and "cool" persons. They have to negotiate the often conflicting expectations from family, friends they grew up with in Denmark, and the broader Danish society (Waltorp 2015). *Harakat* movement is born of this and navigating in this way—smartphone in hand—allows them to live with the paradoxes, if not reconcile them, of other people's diverging expectations and demands, as well as their own.

This condition of needing to navigate different "roles" or versions of oneself is not only specific to the young women I worked with, but it is arguably more radical for them. It is a composite habitus, pointing back to both split habitus and double bind, which—pace Bateson—is not pathological per se but a place from where creativity is born (Bateson 2000:278; Bateson 2018). In the everyday use of smartphones, the women perform, and experiment with, different versions of themselves. Regardless of their background, they all have pictures and a host of selfies in their photo stream showing themselves without a hijab, with elaborate hairdos, and with makeup and dress. I often asked if they were not afraid that a man could come into the room when they were not present, take the smartphone, and look through their (private) pictures. But this was not the case and no one worried too much about that. Or rather, they were not naïve to the possibility of this happening, but they felt this would be the responsibility of the transgressing man—and God would be a witness to that, as he is to all actions and intentions. In a Facebook group, the image of a voluptuous hijabi with sunglasses, expensive very tight-fitting jeans, T-shirt, and high heels was posted. Members of the page urged the person who posted it to both stop judging others and remove the image on the following grounds: Yes she "receives sins" (*modtager synder*) by dressing in this fashion, but so do the men who look at her on the image in Facebook as well as the person posting and sharing it. In the Qur'an verse that is often quoted to argue both for and against the idea that women should wear hijab, as mentioned, there is an equal focus put on the man's responsibility to cast his eyes down and not look at what he ought not see:

> Tell the believing men to cast down their glances and guard their private parts.
> That is purer for them. Indeed, Allah is [well] acquainted with what they do.
> (Qur'an 24:30)

During a discussion about hair removal at a beauty salon, I was told that men are required to cover everything from the navel to the knees. The Arab women denoted this "*awra*" (the area between the navel and the knee) and pointed to how it was relevant in the same measure for men and women in terms of modesty. Some thought it more appropriate that a professional (woman) should be the one to remove hair in that area, rather than a neighbor (woman), even if the neighbor might be really good at the technique of "threading" (hair removal with threads). This is fine with hair removal on the upper lip, under arms or legs, or for shaping eyebrows. But the intimate area (bikini waxing), they all contended, should not be done by a neighbor or friend, but by oneself or a professional. In sum, the fact that a woman veils in the public space in no way indicates that she does not dedicate time, attention, and money to her appearance.

The Danish spoken-word artist and singer Mazen, originally from Lebanon, released a music video where the romantic, intimate interplay between himself and a beautiful young woman with long brown hair is at the center. They are newlyweds in the video and depicted indoors in their love bubble, until the end of the video where he kisses her goodbye in the doorway and she smilingly goes out into the world, into the public sphere with a hijab on (see Playlist). Mazen wanted to show that hijabi women also have all of those aspects in their lives; only under the gaze of the public this is hidden. He expressed in an article in daily newspaper *Information* how he had been shocked by the very overwhelming responses to the video. The article was entitled "I took part in the debate about the scarf and was threatened on my life" (Jeg kastede mig ind i tørklædedebatten- og blev truet på livet). Many women had privately let him know that they appreciated the video—while right-wing males *and* Muslim men in quite large numbers had critiqued him, some with arguments, others with actual threats. As he summed up, "the debate about the scarf is dominated by men. The two opposing wings have nothing in common—and yet they are strikingly similar. The rhetoric they use is violent, and they could not care less about the opinions of the women who wear the scarf" (my translation from Danish).

The reactions that you might meet on the street in Denmark are difficult to imagine. Feeling the rejection in people's behavior and attitude toward you arguably enters the nervous system. An evening, visiting the newly built Imam Ali Mosque in outer Noerrebro, I was joining the Shi'a Muslim family that I had traveled to Iran with. We were spending time in Blaagaarden in their apartment, and everyone had veiled, knowing that we were going to the mosque—also those family members who did not veil normally. I was veiled as well as I needed to be, to visit the mosque with them. As I was in their company, in the bus and walking the last stretch there on foot—"in the bubble" so to speak—I forgot that I was wearing the veil. When we left the mosque it was dark outside and filled with people in the street. We were at the corner of the main road, close to the s-train station, Noerrebro Station, waiting for the green light to cross the street. People were serving mint tea and snacks in the street because of the opening of the mosque, and there was cozy commotion and crowding. Unaware I was blocking a Danish ethnic man pushing his wife's wheelchair. He spoke to me in English, in no uncertain terms telling me to get out of the way so he could pass—surprised I quickly turned, moved, and looked at him with an apologetic smile. I met his eyes and saw that he did not see *me* as I am used to being seen; there was cognitive dissonance when meeting his gaze. It took me a few seconds to realize that in the dark evening with only streetlamps, he saw a woman with a headscarf who he thought would not necessarily understand English and who was in his way. I felt it in my body, the nonrecognition.

Social control, modesty and desire

In a discussion about social control in a WhatsApp group with two informants and a mutual friend, the main themes that emerged from their responses were irritation at being uniformly represented by mainstream media as subdued Muslim women with "tørklæde" (headscarves) on the one hand and simultaneously discontent about having less control over their own affairs than they wished for, on the other hand. A questioning around freedom, secularism, and religion, and what this entailed for each of us, followed (Waltorp 2018a:126–127). Samah, 26, who had written a long message about social control, called me up: "Do you have a minute," she asked. "You know, the things you mention in your message (WhatsApp thread): dress, sex before marriage, alcohol and so on—what it's about is honour. For us it's a duty to get married, you know. And when a family approaches, the first thing that'll be asked is, whether the girl is 'pure' (clean), if she's a good girl. You know, if you smoke, drink, go out with boys, go out at night at bars—then you're not." I asked what the situation is if for example you go out at night, but don't smoke (publicly) and challenged that you can go out without any intentions of what would be deemed bad behavior. Samah explained that it would in itself be bad behavior to be out "in the streets" at that hour:

> It says something bad about you: Why would you do it? To get attention from the boys? We (Muslim girls) want that too ... but then we might go somewhere like a hookah café. And you know, you're going to get attention, and eye contact and all of that. Well, my family would say: Why are you going there, what for ... All the hookah cafés in Copenhagen have become a bit too ... But the family does it for your own sake (Samah shifts in between first and third person in her explanation). If a girl has been with guys, when the man (suitor) comes ....

Samah leaves the sentence unfinished. I finished it for her: "Then it's hard to get a good man?" She confirms and sums it up:

> It's about honour, about family. Immigrants (*indvandrere*) are so hung up on that. For Danes it's not like that! Sometimes I feel like just disappearing somewhere where no one knows me and just start fresh, with the weight of it all, I mean, just do what makes *me* happy, what *I* feel like. I mean I love my family, you know I do (Samah is unmarried) but—sometimes I feel like everything I do is for everyone else *but* me.

Social media play a significant role for Samah as for many of the women in trying to strike a balance, in navigating desire and virtuousness, individual wants, and concern for the family. With regard to their parents and grandparents, I can only guess what practices were in place, respectfully concealed from the public eye, when they were young. Abu-Lughod (1986) writes about practices of veiling and relations between the genders in Islam. As mentioned above, the Awlad 'Ali Bedouin women she worked with in Egypt use poetry (*ghinnawa*) as a means to express (non-virtuous) sentiments that would never be talked about in public.

This is analogous to how some young women communicate (secret) messages layered with multiple meanings and sentiments in social media (Waltorp 2015). Concealment and subtlety is key here. No one I knew or heard of were using actual dating apps, such as Tinder. That would signal a clear intention to others and oneself.

Samah's messages and arguments remind me of another young woman, Manal, and her use of popular songs to help describe the longing, desire, and frustration of social obligation. Late one day in spring of 2015, we sat close together on a bench in a courtyard with one headphone each looking at the YouTube video on her iPhone screen. Manal showed me a video by (ethnic) Danish artist Xander (see Playlist). She was friends with him on Facebook and she told me that he lived across the street "on the other side" of Noerrebrogade (more upscale). "He mostly hangs with 'indvandrere' and his partners have been 'indvandrerpiger' (immigrants and immigrant girls; here meant as second generation also)." She showed me the video which had been filmed across Noerrebro and locations in Iraq. In the video he and his girlfriend, a Danish-Iraqi woman, cross the bridge, Queen Louise's Bridge, leading from the center of Copenhagen to the main street of Noerrebro, Noerrebrogade. She gives him a quick goodnight kiss and enters an apartment in Blaagaarden. She does not wear the hijhab, but it is clear from the conversation that she does not drink. Her father is waiting up and confronts her as she sneaks in. She is yelled at by her father and the conversation ends in the father's decision to send her "back home" to learn manners—and not least to meet her cousin, who her dad says is "a real man." Manal adds while we look at the iPhone screen, "That's what people do, you know—send off the women to the home country and marry them off." She tells the story of her cousin, who has more or less "given up on things," as Manal puts it. "She's lazy now in her life and just wants to stay home. It's because she wasn't allowed to be with the guy she loved—he was also from Noerrebro, also Arab." They had been in love since they were both 16, Manal confided. All of the other cousins and sisters know him, as they were always used as cover story for the two to meet. As Manal's cousin's father died, it was suddenly decided whom she should marry: someone from the family, a cousin. That marriage had not been very happy, and Manal's cousin and the man she loved did not give up on each other for many years. "It happened to her as in the video," Manal says, "she was sent 'back home.'" After many years she had "settled into" the marriage she was in, with two children. The young man she had loved had not married. Xander's song expresses the struggle of finding love in a way that can be reconciled with expectation from the family, as Manal puts it, "the family who wants what's best for you, but who have really no idea what you go through." We watched the rest of the video on the bench in the courtyard, sun in our faces:

Xander:

> *If I can't be allowed to see you anymore*
> *I don't wanna se anyone*
> *Night fall, yeah, but it's burning like the sun in me*

Nadia:

> *I know we could reach each other*
> *But a girl like me, cannot hang with a guy like you*
> *So we're gliding under water—both of us, by ourselves*
> *At open sea*

Both:

> *All or nothing*
> *I've never felt like this before*
> *I'll do everything*
> *Tell them, if they close their eyes, they'll hear*
> *My heart is burning, ohh, my heart is burning*
> *My heart is burning, ohh. My heart is burning*
> *If you feel the same way, then let all the world know*
> *My heart is burning (repeat)*
> ...
> *We've talked about everything, while we walked through fire and water*
> *But you're living life "halfway" in open waters*
> ...

Xander:

> *I walk through the city, to knock on your door*
> *I couldn't help it*
> *Your father says you're not at home*
> *But I know that you are*
> *And you're calling*

Nadia:

> *I'm calling*
> *Your name*

Both:

But the whole world is against us
I wish they understood us
So the two of us didn't need to live apart
My heart is burning …

Individual wishes and desires often run counter to the knowledge that "immoral" behavior reflects directly on their family. For some women, having a secret online (nonphysical) romantic "affair" with someone is an experiment—it represents steps toward another possible life in a semi-parallel yet overlapping universe that might be actualized at some point. But the experiment is risky and may fail completely. However, the experimenting seems imperative, regardless of the risks involved. Engagement with social media is a contested practice and has the potential to make these young women appear immoral if secret, discreet behavior is suddenly revealed. A disclosure of such clandestine activities would be shameful and the consequences unbearable, including a loss of social status for both the woman and her family and, potentially, also exclusion from the family and community. The fear of social exclusion and of being categorized a "whore" (luder) in the eyes of others represents a particularly feared sanction. This has consequences for marriage opportunities, not just for oneself but, potentially, for one's siblings, too. This is one reason sisters keep an eye on each other, making sure that no one acts indiscreetly or in ways that are detrimental to the family's honor. The social media platforms, thus, accommodate explicit debates and facilitate concrete actions when pursuing love, as I will discuss in the following.

For those of my informants who were married, the paths they had taken were quite varied. Most women were intricately involved as driving forces in their own marriage, while others had little say in the matter. Still others fall in between these two poles, some finding love and working patiently toward actualizing the union in a respectable, accepted way. Some married couples have been through years of proposals, rejections by the family, and finally acceptance. Some of my informants have, or have had, intimate relations with young men. Some of these relationships take place solely online; others develop and include meetings in person, and yet others transform into morally sanctioned marriages, that is, if the young woman plays her hand well. Playing your hand well involves letting parents take over at the appropriate time and to proceed according to the tradition of a number of official meetings between the parents. One informant met her future husband while she was studying. After slowly getting to know each other (albeit not physically), and falling in love, they introduced the idea of future marriage to their parents, who then took over from there. Arranged marriages occurred among my informants, but only one example where the woman had very little say in her marriage—a marriage that did not last. She was taken out of eighth grade by her parents and married off at the age of 16 to a cousin, 12 years her senior. This was not the kind of process that any of my informants, married of unmarried, agreed with, supported, or wished for anyone.

Several of my unmarried informants received marriage proposals or requests to begin conversations toward that end via their parents, who were contacted by the parents of a suitor. None of them lived alone or with friends or a partner before marriage. All of my informants and the Muslim women I talked to from the area lived at home with parents and siblings (some in female-headed households) until they married. Marriage thus implies a change of status and residence more radical than in the case of their Danish peers, who would often have lived alone and with other partners or housemates before marriage. Several marriages were celebrated during my fieldwork. In one of the couples, both people had been born in Denmark, also settling there, though both partners were of Palestinian-Jordanian origin. Another couple—where the bride was born in Denmark and of Syrian origin, and her spouse was from Syria—settled in Dubai. One couple married in Pakistan, another married in Denmark—the couple celebrating both her Pakistani traditions and his Turkish traditions—and the Danish influence from both having been brought up in Denmark. I had the pleasure of participating in a number of weddings and followed how people kept in contact after their living arrangements changed, the smartphone and social media central in their lives after relocation. Some of the women settled in Denmark; some moved to their parents' country of origin. My informants kept in daily contact with girlfriends, sisters, and also other more distant relatives and contacts via social media. The smartphone and social media impact on the questions of where to settle and with whom. The main affordance of the smartphone, in this case, is that a young woman, to a larger extent than before the advent of social media, can "bring" her social life with her "in her pocket." This is something that is explicitly stated by friends in Facebook threads congratulating young women who are newly married—"we'll miss you, but we'll be in contact all the time." The smartphone and the image-sharing are also important during the various phases and elements in the wedding preparations and the wedding, with the process being different depending on family background and traditions. The Muslim wedding—nikah—is shared by all: The exchanging of the vows and the acceptance of marriage by both the bride and the groom take place. "I do," said thrice by each of them, and they sign the marriage contract containing the terms and conditions agreed by both sides which they have to adhere to. The fathers of bride and groom and other family will stand as witnesses. The dynamic in each family was different concerning marriage and negotiations around expenses and what the bride's and groom's side of the family were expected to pay toward the wedding expenses and as something which is for the woman herself to keep—*mahr* or dowry (and for Iranians there is also the *Mehriyeh*, a gift the groom promises to the bride in "gold coins," along with things that the groom's family buys for the bride, among these a mirror, which represents immortality).

Some of the young women simply turned down suitors. There are various traditions when it comes to asking for a woman's hand in marriage. Most often, the family of the groom will call the parents of the young woman and ask if they can come over and have tea. Many times it comes only to the call; sometimes the parents will say, "Please do come over, we do not have any daughters ready for marriage as of yet, but you're our honoured guests." At other times, the visit will transpire, and the daughter will be called in to say hello to the potential future-in-law. In the case of young woman, Mona, she and her suitor were meeting on Skype after their families had held initial Skype meetings. She did feel that she came to a point where she felt that she had an impression of him which was good, and she was willing to proceed. The family arrived from Jordan, but unfortunately the families did not reach an agreement on the *mahr*, which was disappointing after investing feelings and future imaginings in this union. If the process is successful until this point, then follows the henna, *nikah*, registration, reception, and honeymoon. But before the couple will take the seats at their wedding—which usually is on a stage with two luxurious, comfortable seats or a sofa in front of the guests in one of the big banquet halls in Copenhagen—a lot of shopping for the dress(es), jewelry, booking of appointment with hairdresser and makeup artist, and preparatory sociality transpire. This is oftentimes with people living abroad involve via images shared in WhatsApp.

When it comes to reception, it can either be mixed or segregated. More religious or traditional families might opt for a wedding reception that has separate sections for men and women. This will allow the practicing women to throw off their hijabs and enjoy the party in sophisticated evening gowns. The groom is the only male who is allowed to make an appearance in the female section (but also the fathers of bride and groom and the brothers). They will walk into the reception together, with music playing and guests on both sides, until they reach the stage. They will later greet their guests and have their first dance. The groom then leaves the women to go on with the party.

The pictures were an important and integral part of these stages of the event—as was the wedding video. Images were circulated widely, different images for different audiences. No less than three informants made a small business as wedding videographers or photographers. I helped one of them pick out the best shots and thus had a view into many more marriages than the ones I attended. I was given permission to film some of the wedding albums that I was shown in Iran as well. Not to be shared as this was segregated weddings, and thus only women could see the albums. An informant, Fatima, was sharing images from her sister's wedding in Pakistan with family there; I only attended through the images shared in a WhatsApp group and understood only little of the ceremonies. It all lasted quite a while, almost a week counting everything, the "departing ceremony" for the bride following the arrival of the groom in a procession to take her away. This event is held and organized by the bride's family. The most important part of the *baraat* is the *Rukhsati*. It can rather be a sad moment for the family of the bride and the bride herself. *Baraats* can be rather stressful occasions for the bride and her family. This is because it is a kind of goodbye between them. Also stress gets built up from all past preparations and events, which adds to it. Slow music is usually played on *baraats*. More focus is made on the décor and presentation of the event. Such is done because a lot of pictures are to be taken on *baraat* day. At a surprise birthday party I had a chance to discuss the events around that departing with two young Pakistani women, who had married Danish-Pakistani men and left their family with thousands of kilometers in-between them.

> Like you know, when we came here it was all different for us because we don't know the atmosphere here, we don't know the society over here—and the most important part: the language. So it's like a totally different atmosphere for us. So you can say for us, we depend on them (their respective in-laws). A mother-in-law is not like your own mother, I'm not going to lie, but she is a good mother-in-law, she's not that harsh, as a proper ... ha ha ... as an in-law, like, in our culture.

This was underscored by a Yemeni-British woman, who overheard the conversation and who had also migrated to Denmark because of her marriage to a man here: "Belonging is about the language—when you know the language, you know your future is here. It's when you're able to shut somebody up that you know you belong, really!"

All of my unmarried informants, without exception, wanted to marry a Muslim man who had grown up in Europe, preferably from the same background (country, ethnicity), but religion was the most important aspect.

Having the same religion and having grown up in Europe to them represented a fundamental understanding of expectations between man and wife and "we will agree on how to bring up our kids" was often mentioned, and "it is the whole family that you marry, so it is easier if there is an understanding." Most would be open to a Danish guy as a suitor if he was the right one and if he converted. Several others, however, pointed to how such marriages did not always work out. Some of the conflicts and divergent wishes regarding marriage and romantic love can be traced to the fact that the concepts of love and marriage seem to be quite different between the younger and older generation. Is marriage about securing the larger family, building a strong foundation, and securing a viable liaison for your offspring? Or is it about finding the one and only, that significant other to whom you are attracted and with whom you fall in love, someone who makes you feel special and with whom you want to start a family and spend the rest of your life? The older generation expresses—and is perceived as having—clearer ideas regarding marriage as being about more practical matters than "just" romance between two individuals (even though they might have experienced similar dilemmas). The romantic love is celebrated in songs, poetry, and memories, but not necessarily understood as relating to the figure of the husband. That is an institution carrying so much more than romantic feelings experienced between two people. The fact that a marriage to some represents an opportunity to give a family member a life in a European country also makes it a larger family decision. (Some women used the expression "she gave him his residency" about this dynamic.) It was a top priority for them that the man had grown up with a similar understanding of "what you can expect between a woman and a man." They did not wish for a suitor they could not understand:

> There was one girl from the other apartment building, she was completely covered, and was married to an imam, that she was pressured into marrying. Now she's divorced, and she's a Christian, does not even speak with her family. She, honestly, dresses in clothes with, like, a plunging neckline. Why? Because it's like a bird: You keep that bird in a cage for years, you do not give it the food it wants. You're giving it the same all of the time. That's it.

On a spring evening we were sitting in a small living room in Blaagaarden with the curtains drawn and the sound of children's voices playing in the courtyard through the window. Besides my children and Mariam's son, a friend of Mariam was present: a Danish woman who had converted to Islam. The children wanted to go to the courtyard and play and Mariam's son looked after my children. Her Danish friend joined the discussion on morals, which very soon turns into a discussion on moral and gender roles. She mentioned what she saw as double standards—men treating women poorly and demanding of them to have high morals and not living according to those same moral standards themselves. She said very coolly that it's hypocrisy and "all cultural." It has nothing to do with Islam (she gestures with her hands to show how men and women are equal). Then she adds, "It's easier for me, as I wasn't born into a family where it is like this." This dynamic—whereby converted women strive for, and position themselves to have access to, a purer Islam that is free from the tradition and culture—is often laughed off by women born into long-standing Islamic traditions. Other times it becomes a source of conflict. Whether it is religion or culture or tradition (applied in a reified sense) which is seen as the cause of the "unfreedom" of the immigrant "other" in Denmark, it seems that there is a widespread prejudice toward Muslims that centers on the nexus of freedom and gender. What the immigrants from the Middle East lack due to tradition or culture in the opinion of Mariam's converted Danish friend is a specific form of equality between men and women. This is interesting as it seems to be the nexus of freedom, gender, and most importantly Islam that is most often problematized by Danish (right-wing) politicians, almost always in connection to veiled women who are presumed to be subdued and "unfree." This is understood to be "social control" which the state seeks to counter through measures of state control, such as the law prohibiting face covering (L219), discussed above.

Her happiness became a restless creature
Flapping its wings inside of her
As if only looking for an
Opportunity
To fly away
(Snap received from an informant)

Orientalism, Freedom, State Control

Smartphone as valve or part-revolution?

The previous chapter pointed to the notions of "freedom" vs. "social control" in ways that indicate that in Denmark there is freedom: freedom of speech and freedom from social control. The young women whom I have spent time with experience constant negotiation and self-conflict around values, as they are caught between collectivity and individuality. This is an existential, human condition. But few people are asked to constantly choose between alternatives presented as mutually opposing or clearly state their position on matters in the way these women are on a daily basis: "Be independent and prove that you are free," my informants are challenged—and at the same time they are expected to prove that they are not "too Danish" by significant others. The middle ground is nowhere in sight. The women navigate the transcontextual condition everyday— via *harakat*, via obviating paradoxes, via the smartphone.

> Are the smartphone and social media merely a valve for young Muslim women's various desires for expressing themselves and forging relations, while not actually changing the status quo, enacting "part-revolutions," as Bourdieu calls it (2001:119)? Or do ideals about morality and modesty and gender and generational relations become dramatically reconfigured through the ways in which young women use the smartphone and social media to *navigate* their everyday contested and monitored lives? (Waltorp 2015:65)

The question above concerns ideals about morality and modesty, as well as relations between genders and generations. My informants experiment, and push boundaries, continually extending their range of possibilities (Zigon 2009) through the use of social media, "keeping cool while staying virtuous": "Engaging in the field of social media might allow for negotiating paradoxes and navigating between conflicting desires and expectations in everyday life, if not resolving or dissolving these conflicts and paradoxes. This is not to imply that another set of challenges and risks is not introduced as part of these new practices" (Waltorp 2015:65). This way of answering the question remains within the same register in which the question is posed. From my empirical material, I would argue that it is not simply a question of the younger generation needing or wanting to revolt against the older generation in any clear-cut way, nor simply that the women need or want to revolt against the men—though some might want to do exactly that. The point is that another way to approach the question is by reconfiguring it and asking the question differently. A fundamental part of ethnographic fieldwork and anthropological conceptualization is to constantly search for better questions to ask. This becomes possible only along the way as the assemblage one interrogates stabilizes (DeLanda 2002:177), and "problems have the solutions they deserve depending on the terms in which they are stated … stating the problem is not simply uncovering, it is inventing" (Deleuze 1991:15–16).

Something the empirical material led me to question was the idea inherent in the formulation of the question—that the young Muslim women are necessarily to be viewed as agents vis-à-vis a set of structures and norms that they would want to get rid of or expand their possibility for negotiating within. Bateson urges a consideration of the *levels of abstraction* of the questions asked: "What circumstances promote that specific habitual phrasing of the universe which we call 'free will'?" (2000:163). Free will, freedom, social control, and the relation between the individual and society are central to my inquiry. And it seems to be at the center of conflicts around values and Western ideals in the encounter with Muslim immigrants and descendants in Denmark in ways where the lines are rather sharply drawn. The above question would first imply answers to a new set of (potential) sub-questions: What are their desires for "expressing themselves?" What is desire? What is expression? What relations do they (wish to) forge? And why? What is the status quo? From who's point of view? Who/what is the revolution against? Defined by whom? What are the ideals about morality and modesty that the different genders and generations hold? And how are they reconfigured from the viewpoint of my informants? I contend that their everyday lives are contested and monitored, often such as family members and close friends as well as by majority Danes: the politicians, the press, and the public (Waltorp 2013b, 2015). How do they navigate this and what do social media and smartphones afford in this regard, in their navigation?

All of the questions above can be approached at various scales, starting by zooming in on how many internal differences there exist among my informants and their families. For example, a discussion of the form that "desire" takes could be addressed in relation to a submission to God (which can be experienced as ecstatic) or to the good of the family, which can fulfill a desire for belonging and for being recognized as a good daughter or sister or as a good, loyal friend—"augmenting her social being." Desire could also be discussed in the more sexually oriented or individual sense of being "free" to put your own (sexual) wants, needs, and desires first. It could also be a desire to express one's opinions on various political matters or a desire to express forms of creative practice without feeling constrained. A "desire to express oneself" depends. Crucial to repeatedly return to was whether the (sub)questions in the above question were approached from the lived experience of the women I worked with or from the notions about freedom, desires, expression, and individualism that I culturally take for granted. As indicated in the subtitle of this book, this cannot be disentangled, but the entanglements can be teased out and addressed critically in a way that may shed light on how the women I worked with draw on the same cultural ideas and values as I do and at the *same time* hold other values dear as well. In an essay critically examining her own earlier work, Lila Abu-Lughod writes that in order to describe the specific forms that acts of resistance take, they need to be located within fields of power rather than outside of them and avoid ascribing "feminist consciousness" to those for whom this is not a meaningful category (1990:47). Her analysis of the Awlad 'Ali women's poetry, mentioned above, casts it as a socially legitimate, semi-public practice which was to be understood as an expression of women's resistance and protest against strict norms of male domination (1986). But later she contends that we should not look for "resisters" but let people's "practices teach us about complex interworkings of historically changing structures of power" (1990:53). In her *Politics of Piety*, Saba Mahmood (2012 [2004]) quotes this and invites for pushing further, beyond the term "resistance," which might "impose a teleology of progressive politics on the analytics of power—a teleology that makes it hard for us to see and understand forms of being and action that are not necessarily encapsulated by the narrative of subversion and reinscription of norms" (2012:9). She considers the distinction that liberal theorists make between negative freedom (absence of external obstacles and constraints imposed by state, corporations, or individuals) and positive freedom (the capacity to realize an autonomous will, capacity for self-mastery and government) and focuses on the concept of individual autonomy in relation to coercion and consent, what she calls the "topography of freedom" (Mahmood 2012:11), suggesting that liberal presuppositions have become naturalized in the scholarship on gender (Mahmood 2012:13). Others have challenged this for at least three to four decades including Latin American,

Afro-American, and Indigenous (feminist) thinkers, as well as later queer and LGBTQ activists and theoreticians. Native and African-American feminists on their part have been arguing that intersectional considerations of class, race, and ethnicity should be central in any rethinking of "individual autonomy," with freedom being the ability to form families (after slavery and genocide had made this difficult), rather than dismantle the nuclear family as an oppressive norm (Mahmood 2012:13, see also Crenshaw 1991; Lorde 1983), though it is exactly an oppressive gender and family norm that others are fighting to dismantle as the only acceptable configuration. In short, the binary model of subordination and subversion might not be helpful in understanding the lived lives and future aspirations of women everywhere, nor for the women I worked with in Copenhagen (see Ahmad and Waltorp 2019). The notions of freedom and its relation to "choice" are central to this discussion.

Freedom/choice

In the Danish context, Muslim women wearing a hijab must defend their choice within an understanding of individual freedom: a freedom of choice that arbitrates and decides between two given things is what Hannah Arendt calls *liberum arbitrium* (1993). Such freedom is not inaugural but by definition restricted to "what exists"—to what can be heard and recognized. Arendt is highly critical of the notion of freedom as a phenomenon of the will inherited from the Western philosophical and political tradition (based on Man in the singular) and she conceives of the political as action:

> Since the whole problem of freedom arises for us in the horizon of Christian tradition on one hand and of an originally anti-political philosophic tradition on the other, we find it difficult to realize that there may exist a freedom which is not an attribute of the will but an accessory of doing and acting. (Arendt 1993:165)

Adeline Masquelier contextualizes norms and available choices around (un) dress, purity, and dirt historically, pointing to how dress is implicated in complex and far-reaching ways in the fashioning of bodies and persons (2005:6): "The Judeo-Christian tradition of associating nakedness with shame has a long and complex history … Christian theologians advocated modesty and concealment at times to the point of obsession—in some European Catholic families, children until World War I wore gowns while bathing, lest they engage in the sinful contemplation of their nudity" (2005:2). Masquelier further argues that in the West it has been a common assumption that nakedness exposes the essential self. This assumption has long guided the Western search for knowledge: to know is to lay an object entirely bare ... it becomes the "naked" truth. From Francis Bacon onward, scientific discourses were thus permeated by the vision of a veiled female nature being unclothed by male science ... Such a gendered metaphysics of power and knowledge is a productive point of departure for exploring questions of bodily transgressions in their diverse sociomoral ramifications. (2005)

The above quote situates the discussion about the hijab—what does it say about the women wearing it, depending on whom interprets it? As the previous chapter pointed to, it is often defined by those who do not wear it—men as well as women who wish to "free" the Muslim women from wearing it.

The fact that modesty and concealment as well as nakedness and truth are related in intricate ways is not new. But it is worth mentioning this in situating the discussion and focus on the headscarf. In the words of Alia Al-Saji, the veil has become metonymic in the Western world not just for Islam, but for Islam as a perceived patriarchal oppressive system (2010). It is about boundaries and matters and behavior out of place, as Mary Douglas pointed to in her analysis of Leviticus (Douglas 1966, 1991), when prescription and prohibition is at stake—and it is often the concern with women's bodies first and foremost (Butler 1990). The linking between what is perceived as a "dirty" person or the opposite, a person with moral worth, is in my material discussed with this exact word—no matter whether it is the body or the "behavior" that is perceived as being "dirty." The phrases used are being pure/being dirty (*ren/beskidt*), a dirty whore (*beskidt luder*), dirty people (*beskidte mennesker*), or to be in the gutter (smidt på gaden, kastet væk; someone who's lost their social standing, the family have turned their back). A lot of time was spent in beauty salons, hairdressers, and in people's apartments where they had set up shop "after hours," investing in the equipment to be able to treat clients and acquaintances at home. This was then a different experience than being at a salon. There were greetings, tea served, and family members who were politely talking for a bit before leaving the beautician in the family to her work. The work was anything in-between removing hair with threading, upper lips, eyebrows, underarms, etc., to doing full facials.

According to Bita: "Iran is no. 1 for plastic surgery." "Everyone can become a princess there," she claims. She herself had her nose "fixed." Her full lips she was born with, but many insist that she "had her lips done, too." The dividing lines are not always including and excluding who one might suspect. A burqa-wearing woman was spoken about in private as "klam" (disgusting). She was wearing gloves "as if we're not clean enough for her," and at the opposite end of the scale, an ethnic Danish woman riding the typical Christiania bike, with dreadlocks and armpit hair showing, is thought of as "klam" (disgusting). I defended the choices of the style of dreadlocks and less frequent showers, "hippie" style, with the argument that it is better for the planet as well as healthier for the skin and hair not be washed too often, which brought about a raised eyebrow, a scoff, and laughter and a "yikes, honestly" (*ærligt!*). The tension in fashion between individual freedom or choices and the social dimension of emulation is also pointed to by Emma Tarlo and Annelies Moors: "The wider sphere of relationships women find themselves in—with family, husbands, friends, colleagues, and God—affect and are affected by veiling practices as is evident in the narratives Muslim women produce about why they dress the way they do" (Tarlo and Moors 2013). Wearing the hijab can attract what it is supposed to defect: the male gaze and unwanted attention, the emulation and performativity are of the essence (cf. Mahmood 2012:9, 27, 157, 162).

My informants and I share taken-for-granted assumptions about individual freedom guaranteed by the state. They also have paradoxical ways of relating to specific dilemmas pertaining to what is framed within a discourse of "free choice" or, as they say, "doing what *I* feel like." Simultaneously my informants express an appreciation of strong family ties, and that one's husband (or parents if unmarried) looks after one, at times by preventing one from partaking in activities that would be seen as *haram* by others, or that would impact negatively on one's reputation through gossip. This is done, the young women explain, from a position of care and responsibility. They are acutely aware that this is seen as problematic, unfree, and as social control by majority Danish society. At times, they disagree with the constraints they feel are imposed on them by parents, siblings, or their husband. In these instances, those in the family in a position of authority and responsibility are described as being "*for stramme*" (literally "too tight," constraining). The nuances and the relational dynamics in their everyday lives fall uneasily within a framework of "freedom" and "individual autonomy." In other words, the question of "free will" as individual and autonomous is particularly complex in a situation where the young women both share in the (liberal) discourse on "free will" and have experiences that are not encompassed by the freedom/control dichotomy. As pointed out by two of my informants, Amal and Sana, both of Palestinian-Jordanian origin in their 20s, they "do not lie directly" to their Danish girlfriends; they just "make up alternative explanations or excuses." They give excuses for not being able to meet and partake in different activities that are in *haram* places, such as where people drink alcohol and where men and women mix at late hours or when they cannot join planned trips abroad with their friends. They do not want to explain that their husbands do not approve, because "Danes don't understand" and "we know what they're going to think: that we are subdued and that 'these veiled girls are suppressed by their husbands, and their husbands are assholes.'"

My informants Amal and Sana do not want to be judged by their Danish peers as "subdued" and "controlled." At times, my informants expressed disagreement with norms around husbands, parents, or older brothers surveilling their whereabouts, company, and the time they spent away from the home. At other times, they would draw attention to the aspects of care that also formed part of such surveillance. They have grown up with the discourse of (individual) "freedom," which they share as a value with their Danish girlfriends. They simultaneously understand "freedom" and "submission" in ways that they know fully well they cannot expect their Danish counterparts to understand. The word *Islam* from the root *s-l-m* means "submission" or "entrusting one's wholeness to another" (God). The word "Muslim" literally translates into "one who submits." When friends of my informants post on Facebook that their "occupation" is "Slave of Allah (swt)," it is a freely chosen identification, to the extent that any act can be said to be free from socialization and influence from the surroundings. It is an *entrusting*: a submission to God and his will. This submission is at the root of Islam, metaphorically and literally speaking. But when one has not been introduced to its various aspects, it may have a ring of "un-free," and young women like Sana and Amal are fully aware of this. It is registers such as this one they navigate in different social contexts across the on- and offline. It is entailed in the composite habitus that you know how to leave out certain things, depending on what company you are in. It would reflect negatively on them to start talking about submission with Danish peers, so they avoid that.

Returning to the question of *liberum arbitrarium*, Mayanthi Fernando (2013, 2014), who did fieldwork with "Muslim French" informants, argues how the debate about the "French Islamic revival," and the veil specifically, posited her informants in situations where they could only answer in terms of "forced to veil" vs. "it was *my* personal choice" as the discourse "depends on and reproduces a series of oppositions between choice and constraint, personal autonomy and religious authority, and self-realization and external norms … [whereby] secular assumptions about freedom, authority, choice, and obligation make Muslim French religiosity unintelligible in law and public discourse" (Fernando 2014:146–147). Fernando demonstrates how her informants challenge these dominant binaries by conceptualizing practices like veiling, praying, and fasting both as modes of personal freedom and as authoritatively prescribed acts necessary to become a proper Muslim subject (Fernando 2014:147). Politically, the wearing of the hijab plays into complex dynamics on both sides of, and alongside, a continuum of conservative and progressive forces. Some in Denmark argue that it is a concrete manifestation of patriarchal oppression—observing "from the outside"—not realizing that veiling has a long and complex history and has also been embraced by many women, both as an affirmation of cultural identity and as a feminist statement (see Abu-Lughod 1986, 2002; Al-Saji 2010; El Guindi 1999; Fernando 2014; Ismail 2015; Mahmood 2005; Masquelier 2005; Moor and Tarlo 2007; Scott 2010; Tarlo 2005, 2007, 2010; Tarlo and Moors 2013).

Traveling to Iran with informants and living with their family summer of 2015 allowed me to experience the dynamics around the compulsory hijab. In Iran the law prescribes that all women in public should wear the hijab and dress modestly. Under the rule of Reza Shah (Shah of Iran until 1941) it was on the contrary illegal to wear any kind of head-covering. In July 2018, attention in Iran became focused on the use of smartphones and social media as headlines appeared about the arrest of the 17-year-old Maede Hojabri for uploading videos of herself dancing in her bedroom without the hijab required in public—a testimony to how the smartphone and social media reconfigure the interfaces between public, private, and intimate space. A number of other people were arrested for posting videos on Instagram as well. Hojabri has since appeared on a state television program with other detainees in which she and other activists gave what appeared to be forced confessions. State TV showed a young woman, her face blurred, crying and shaking while describing her motivation for producing the videos. "It wasn't for attracting attention," she said. "I had some followers and these videos were for them. I did not have any intention to encourage others doing the same" (Dehghan 2018).[1] Instagram could be blocked due to these cases, even though it has remained one of the few unblocked Western apps, while Facebook and Twitter are filtered (censored). Snapchat does not work at all in Iran—to the daily frustration of my informants who were used to the app as a means of keeping an ongoing dialogue in images and videos with friends. The result was that they could not check what other people sent them and could not reply to it. In the same vein, fashion designers are negotiating their way around state prescriptions on dress, and the Islamic dress being obligatory in public space. The "*gaz*," or modesty police, also called the moral police, arrested the women I was traveling with, as I mentioned. This might be attributed to the fine line, which is impossible to "have a feel for" habitually when only visiting.

Small changes in-between each visit, which could be many years in-between, made the women living in Denmark out of tune and unable to balance the interplay of social status and related attitude. Knowledge of theses limits made it possible for a friend of them to wear her hijab so low on the back of her head so as to almost forfeit its purpose, fashionable flowy materials in layers, and quite heavy makeup. She lived in the upper-class 1st arrondissement of Tehran. She was not arrested.

As Janet Bauer writes, for Iranian women whether living in Iran or abroad, external appearances are central to the protection of a virtuous selfhood—as signs of purity, piety, and even penetration can be reconfigured at will, thanks to fashion and plastic surgery (hymen reconstruction), policing the boundaries between chaste and tainted bodies has at times meant rethinking the aesthetic grammar of bathing, clothing, and manners that traditionally guaranteed the integrity of selves—personal and communal. The strategies they elaborate to "fit in" while also maintaining their ties to the Iranian community become ways of disguising the self through a complicated dynamics of concealment and revelation which must be continually reinvented (Bauer 2005). Exiled Iranian journalist and writer Masih Alinejad, initiator of the movement *My Stealthy Freedom*, has said that she is not opposed to women veiling but believes it should be a matter of personal choice (Dehghan 2015). The movement she began works against the *compulsory* hijab and sees women post pictures in social media without the *hijab*—and men in solidarity posting pictures where they wear the hijab.

In May 2015, *Vogue Arabia* featured Alinejad in Altuzzara designer shirt, chequered trousers, and her big, curly hair almost forming a halo around her head. When featuring US Congresswoman Ilhan Omar in their April 2019 issue wearing a black hijab and a broad smile with burgundy lips, Alinejad posted it on Twitter and on Instagram next to a repost of herself, critiquing that "leftists" had problematized her being featured then but supported Vogue being pro-hijab now. The debates following in social media such as Twitter, Instagram, etc., show how different positions and lived experiences people speak from, and the very strong emotions evoked. The discussion is framed sharply within the notion of "free choice" vs. "coercion": "No one puts a scarf on my head but me. It's my choice—one protected by the First Amendment," Ilhan Omar responded to the many comments on her wearing the hijab. She took her seat in parliament donning a hijab (Yaeger, vogue.com, January 3, 2019). The Danish hijabi and model Amina Adan was featured on the cover of *Vogue Arabia* with the headline on the cover reading: "My Choice." She was the first Dane wearing a hijab to be signed to the modeling agency "Unique Models."[2] A diversity of interpretations for Muslim dress is visible in Denmark. Decisions about what clothing to wear are not only taken out of considerations of devotion; they are also informed by local and global, social, religious, and political forces, as well as by personal aesthetics, fashion, peer groups, and, obviously, faith (Al-Saji 2010; Ismail 2015; Moors and Tarlo 2007; Tarlo 2010; Tarlo and Moors 2013).

Interpretations of the headscarf among Muslim women who were born and grew up in Denmark as a religious practice differ from theological ones (Ismail 2015:108). It is often pointed out among my informants that God is the one who witnesses and the only one, ultimately, to judge. This is voiced in situations of gossip in the area and in the sphere of social media (circulated as "meme," for example). The notion that some people are "fake" and perform and dress over-virtuously without having the pure and virtuous intentions that ought to accompany it is shared among informants (see also Tarlo and Moors 2013)—and so is the knowledge that God sees and knows all actions as well as intentions. It is even the chorus of one of the hit rap songs from the artist Gilli: "Only one can judge me—and that's God" (kun én kan dømme mig og dét Gud) (see Playlist). It is also a defense against other Muslims who will judge them as less pious and perhaps as being too much of "muhajababes" (see Ismail 2015), and that concern and preoccupation with fashionable and beautiful looks runs contrary to the intended effect of veiling. The notion that God will know your intention is alluded to often, as Moors and Tarlo point out in the introduction to a special issue of Muslim dress in the journal *Fashion Theory*: "The idea that dress is a visible indicator of the piety and moral worth of the wearer is constantly undermined by the suggestion that the wearing of particular forms of covered dress is insufficient if done with the wrong intent and if the wearer cannot live up to the moral expectations linked to particular garments" (2007:136). The rich diversity of styles favored by Muslim women contradicts the assumption that by being religious a person is by definition unconcerned with fashion or that by following fashion a person cannot really be truly religious—what counts as Islamic and Islamic fashion is a matter of considerable debate among Muslims (2007:133–134). In Blaagaarden the women know that there will be those ready to judge them and gossip if they find that they are wearing too much makeup, or the dress is not living up to standard be being too "made-up": that is a reason to go via one's own routes through back-alleys and courtyards. Social conventions are always dependent on time and place, and at this specific conjunction, the Muslim woman's headscarf is perceived by some as metonymic not just with Islam but with Islam as patriarchal subduing system (Al-Saji 2010:880), with laws to ban the burqa in 2018 and ongoing discussion about the veil (tørklæde).

In 2018 the Danish National Party ran a campaign with posters on bus sheds with the words: "Loose the scarf and become part of Denmark." Mursal Khosrawi, part of a current research project I am engaged in with collaborative filmmaking with Danish-Afghan women, "went viral" after she confronted the spokesperson of the Danish People's Party Martin Henriksen on National Television. She called Henriksen "cute" (*nuttet*) in thinking that he ought to legislate what women could wear and not: "My mother fled Afghanistan because men wanted to decide what women must wear, now you want to also decide." (Danish National Broadcasting Channel, May 10, 2017). Calling Henriksen cute is a *harakat*, subverting by using an infantilizing description on him—as he is infantilizing women by telling them what to wear. As Masquelier points out, stripping

> has been variously used by wilful disrobers as a catalyst of ritual transformation …
> a tool of resistance, or conversely, as a way of reinforcing the status quo … has
> vastly different implications when those who are denuded do not control the
> process—and this is true regardless of what portion of the body is being stripped
> or what is considered "proper" dress in the first place. (2005:2)

In a conversation on the topic with Hadia and Nour, Nour stressed,

> They (majority Danes) do not *know* who girls with headscarves (tørklædepiger)
> are! We (her and Hadia) are a good example of that. We started HF (education
> on the level of High School), and we were met with "Watch out, here comes
> the bandits from the square (Blaagaarden Square), from Noerrebro". This was
> teachers saying this. Obviously, the whole class get a bad impression of us right
> away. They haven't met—or communicated with—immigrants, but what they
> see on the news…. what they really need to see, is that no matter if you live in
> Noerrebro or abroad, it doesn't matter, it's about the human being.

Hadia added: "Yeah, that one teacher was joking about the headscarf, that you cannot know really what's hidden underneath, if it's a bomb." While there is agreement that "counting people's sins does not make you a saint," there is constant boundary work going on among informants to define who is "not-us"—not proper Muslim. But this boundary work—which includes a focus on other people's behavior—also results in the young women not always following their own advice about not judging purity of heart from outward behavior. Women of Muslim immigrant parents who either frequent nightclubs, drink, date, and do not veil or wear modest dress belong in the "not-us" category: "They've sold their religion," as some informants put it. There are many positions to speak from, and "tradition," "culture," and "true Islam" are invoked in a multitude of ways. The converted Danish women, especially, talk about "pure Islam" in ways that cause the women with origins in the Middle East to roll their eyes—sometimes suggesting jokingly that the person move to Saudi Arabia if they think this is how to act—as if the world revolves around you, strangely echoing right-wing Danes: "This is Denmark—if you want to act like that, then how can you live here?"

Do Muslim women need saving?

In entering a small shop, on a cold winter day, filled to the brim with all kinds of beauty products on display, I felt immediately awkward and then stupid about my assumptions that Muslim women would be more bashful in certain situations of nudity. Jamila started chatting away with the beautician right away, as it turned out they had a mutual acquaintance. We went up the three stairs to the back room while talking, and the beautician held the curtain aside, so we could enter. One thing led to the next, and I ended up lying down stripped from the waist down, and the beautician performed a Brazilian wax on me (a style of waxing of a woman's pubic hair in which almost all the hair is removed, with only a very small central strip remaining), all the while Jamila and a mutual girlfriend, Amira, sat next to me in a chair chatting. They had just gone through the same, painful, procedure with me sitting in the chair, chatting.

This social situation was intimate, and I continuously found myself in similar situations where my ideas of what would be (im)modest, private, intimate, shared, discussed, and in which ways, among my informants, were proven wrong. Confronted with other spaces and other gendered ways of relating than I am used to, I was led to question taken-for-granted notions—a classic situation for the fieldworker. My self-image of being a liberal Scandinavian woman did not hold outside of the confines of social and cultural practices and spaces with which I am familiar. Most of the women I worked with would cover their hair with a veil in the public sphere, as mentioned, and when in the presence of people of the opposite sex, unless those people were her *mahrams*. Notions of modesty and virtue as practiced among my informants are centered on gender relations in ways that appear to be a provocation in Danish society and more broadly in the United States and North European context.

In "Do Muslim Women Really Need Saving? Anthropological Reflections on Cultural Relativism and Its Others" (Abu-Lughod 2002, 2013) Lila Abu-Lughod has sought to debunk the myth of the need for "foreign intervention to save Muslim women" and questions commonly held normative assumptions about Muslim women in the Euro-American context. In her "Writing against Culture" (1991) she discusses the notions of equality, freedom, and rights and proposes that rather than pursuing superior, ethnocentric, and violent ideas about "saving" the Muslim woman, a better way to proceed would be working together in situations subject to historical transformation and to consider larger responsibilities and the nexus of politics and global injustice that are powerful shapers of everyday lived realities. Women's bodies have historically provided a fertile terrain for imagining, reasserting, or contesting the porous boundaries of moral worlds:

> The sexualization of power relations and the erotics of conquest—often represented as the male penetration of a veiled female interior—have proven remarkably resilient, judging from the recent decision by French government to ban Islamic head-scarves in public schools and the equally recent U.S. campaign, spearheaded by Laura Bush, to liberate Afghan women from both Taliban control and the tyranny of the burqa. (Masquelier 2005:4)

The process of unveiling has remained to this day a justification for colonial interventions and promoting the "liberation" of countless Muslim women from symbolic shackles (Masquelier 2005; Fanon 1967) as well as in the case of Iran under the rule of Reza Shah, the "modernization" of the country's women. Today in Iran it is the other way around with forced veiling, and no recognition of other ways of expressing one's choices and/or one's faith. As Joan Scott argues for the European context:

> We cannot take at face value the simple oppositions offered by those who would ban it (headscarf ed.): traditional versus modern, fundamentalism versus secularism, church versus state, private versus public, particular versus universal, group versus individual, cultural pluralism versus national unity, identity versus equality. These dichotomies do not capture the complexities of either Islam or "the West." Rather, they are polemics that in fact create their own reality: incompatible cultures, a clash of civilizations. (Scott 2010:5)

Edward Said (1978) describes Orientalism as a dynamic exchange between individual authors and the large political concerns shaped by the three great empires—British, French, American—in whose intellectual and imaginative territory the writing was produced. A study of the way in which the West has represented the Orient as a reflection of how the Occident wanted to imagine itself—through colonial encounters, politics, and representations of its culture. From culture to religion, the West created a discourse to deal with the "otherness" of eastern society, customs, and beliefs. This chapter has sought to perform a tactical movement vis-à-vis the Orientalism in anthropological mirroring: to "do a *harakat*," as the women I worked with would phrase it. What I have sought to show is how these issues play out in Denmark in the lives of my informants and to also "look into the mirror." In the words of Alia Al-Saji, the argument is that

> western perceptions and representations of veiled Muslim women are not simply about Muslim women themselves. Rather than representing Muslim women, these images fulfil a different function: they provide the negative mirror in which western constructions of identity and gender can be positively reflected. It is by means of the projection of gender oppression onto Islam, and its naturalization to the bodies of veiled women, that such mirroring takes place. (Al-Saji 2010:875)

The Danish Foreign Ministry (the department for gender equality) ordered a report on young people in Denmark between 16 and 20 years old and their attitudes to sex, sexting, and social media. The results clearly show that Danish young men are celebrated for sexual activity, whereas young women must be careful not to be seen as "cheap" when engaging in erotic and sexual relations with young men—on- and offline (Dahl et al. 2018). This points to the widely held notion that Danish women (and men) are "free" from social control and dynamics of shaming to engage in whatever sexual liaison they want without repercussions or to dress as they please without social repercussions. The ideas of how a free woman in Denmark ought to dress are largely taken for granted in Denmark. As a result, those ideas are not understood to be a variant of social control upholding a specific set of moral codes. A miniskirt hiding *too little* is seen as problematic in the context of young women—possibly "trafficked"—hanging around Istedgade—a street in the red-light district adjacent to the central railway station in Copenhagen (Plambech 2016). Wearing *too much* clothes, on the other hand, as some Muslim immigrant women are seen to do, can be similarly perceived as problematic (and unlawful in the case of burqa and niqab as of the anti-mask law of 2018). Discussions on the borders of the female body play out across social media platforms.

George Herbert Mead puts the dynamic of "social control" in the classical sociological sense in the foreground:

> The "me" is a conventional, habitual individual. It is always there. It has to have those habits, those responses which everybody has; otherwise the individual could not be a member of the community. But an individual is constantly reacting to such an organized community in the way of expressing himself,

not necessarily asserting himself in the offensive sense but expressing himself, being himself in such a co-operative process as belongs to any community. The attitudes involved are gathered from the group, but the individual in whom they are organized has the opportunity of giving them expression which perhaps has never taken place before. (Mead 1962:197–198)

"Social control is the expression of the 'me' over against the expression of the 'I'. It sets the limits, it gives the determination that enables the 'I', so to speak, to use the 'me' as the means of carrying out what is the undertaking that all are interested in" (Mead 1962:210–211). This is Mead's explanation of the dynamic of social control as a socialized individual controlling him—or herself according to the social situation in which he or she finds themselves in. In the situation of my informants this is not so straightforward. What is the social situation they find themselves in—and what is "the undertaking that all are interested in?" They navigate multiple social situations that are overlapping and at times opposing.

A lot of skillful navigating is demanded for the "I" to use the "me" (for my informants) to behave in ways that all the various social actors around them agree with. The point being that the various other social actors, family, friends, coworkers, politicians, etc., might have very different ideas about how they should behave. The women want to live their lives, have fun, pursue careers, be good daughters, wives, mothers, and good Muslims. They feel constrained to varying degrees by family expectations on them—not always easily reconcilable with life as a young adult in Denmark, where they grew up. In some cases, the expectations weigh so heavy that it goes beyond social control as a general dynamic of all groups, and it is experienced as negative social control. At the same time, the Danish state wants to "save" Muslim women from social control and from men who are those who cared for them in their upbringing—fathers and brothers—in ways that stereotype *Muslim men. A lot of focus is given to social control—as it should—but unfortunately it is being collapsed with horrible (very rare) offenses such as honor killings, as well as violence toward partners or children. All criminal offenses fall under the criminal justice system and should be treated as such—not as an "ethnic problem."

As mentioned above, the Danish state also outlaws certain practices of dressing (L219 'Tildækningsforbud) and demands that Muslim women in areas categorized as ghettos, such as Blaagaarden, must send their children in institutions 25 hours a week from the age of 1—and in this, treats them differently than other citizens in Denmark. What does "individual autonomy" look and feel like in the cross-pressures of state control and social control? Mead's explanation of the "self" above is added to by Bateson in his discussion of the double bind theory:

What is a person? What do I mean when I say "I?" Perhaps what each of us mean by the "self" is in fact an aggregate of habits of perception and adaptive action ... If somebody attacks the habits and immanent states which characterize me at the given moment of dealing with that somebody—that is, if they attack the very habits and immanent states which have been called into being as part of my relationship to them at that moment—they are negating me. If I care deeply about that other person, the negation of me will be still more painful. (Bateson 2000:247)

The term *double bind* refers to a pattern of perceived impossibility produced by cross-contextual limitations. The term was introduced, as mentioned, by Bateson and a team of researchers to describe the conditions for schizophrenia. However, as pointed out by both Bateson himself (2000:227, 276–278), and since then by his daughter Nora Bateson, the pattern was never intended to be concretized as a cause for any particular pathology. "An organism can learn only that which it is taught by the circumstances of living and the experiences of exchanging messages with those around him. He cannot learn at random, but only to be like or unlike those around him. We have, therefore, the necessary task of looking at the experiential setting of schizophrenia" (2000:239), Bateson insisted.

Central to the theory of the double bind is the idea that any structured context also occurs within a wider context—a meta-context—and there may be incongruence or conflict between context and meta-context. The person is then faced with the dilemma either of being wrong in the primary context or of being right for the wrong reasons or in a wrong way. This is the so-called double bind[3] (2000:250). This is helpful in an understanding of the cross-pressures of (negative) social control and state control experienced by the women I worked with. The burden is on *them* to demonstrate continually that they are not "victims" of the social control on the part of their family or "home context" or they risk state control in ways which potentially entails a negation of their self. Bateson insisted the double bind was a "learning theory," a description of a pattern of interaction producing both the trap from which all options appear blocked and the possibility of escape which comes with finding another level of perception. And in terms of methodology he noted that "the observer must be included within the focus of observation, and what can be studied is always a relationship or an infinite regress of relationships. Never a 'thing'" (Bateson 2000:251). The double focus of this book is a step toward being accountable for the ways in which the relationships and the contexts in which knowledge emerges entail the knower herself (even if the regress of relationships is infinite and it is an illusion to fully account for them).

According to Nora Bateson,

> Double Bind theory is similar to what is sometimes called a "Catch 22" in that there is a high-stakes problem in which multiple contexts overlap and eliminate any strategic solution. The experience is one of being stuck from multiple directions, and usually contains the additional aspect of there being no way to express this multiple stuckness. ... the double bind is not only a pattern creating stuckness across contexts, but is also a pattern that permits release from that stuckness. The release requires that the stuck ones find the capacity to perceive their contextual circumstances in a new way ... The ability to identify the double bind patterns is a step toward at least recognizing that the way the problem is being described is part of the problem. A new description will open otherwise unseen possibilities. (Bateson 2018)

To successfully navigate the "transcontextual" situation, the women I worked with find themselves in, in their everyday life, a lot of *harakat* moves are needed—and the smartphone comes in handy in this. Different aspects of the selves and slightly different performances can be kept apart, and behavior adjusted via the smartphone: who does one mirror oneself in? The habitus of the young Muslim woman "of the second generation" is a "composite habitus" born of this historic situation and specific subject position. It is a skillful, painful—*and* a resourceful and creative—movement. Is *harakat* tactics—with and without the smartphone—merely a valve and half revolution? The "experiential setting" of the young Muslim women in Blaagaarden has been described here—they impact and navigate it—they learn how to do that by *being in* the environment. The habitat forming them, and forming their habitus, is also the media ecology. The stereotypic representation of them in Danish national media, politics, and public discourse is painful. When one *is* also Danish, it is hurtful to experience that without even qualifying in the eyes of some politicians and fellow Danes as Danish; one might also be sanctioned for being "too Danish" by others.

D

The Flow of (Mirror) Images and Future-Making

The kidnapping

In 2014 the 8-year-old daughter of Amal, one of my close informants, was kidnapped by the child's father and taken to Jordan.[1] The girl's father, Talal, insinuated that Amal was "too Danish" and bringing up their daughter in a way too "free"—letting her wear dresses, watch Disney Channel series with dancing and romances going on, etc. This event demonstrated, in the most disconcerting way, where divergent ideas about modesty and immodesty, virtuousness, and expectations between man and wife can lead. Prior to the kidnapping, the marriage had already been an unhappy one. One night, Amal told me, she had asked God for help in her endeavor to improve the marriage by making a *du'a* (prayer)[2] before going to sleep. Several times that night, she woke up bathed in sweat from horrible nightmares. She told me about this the following day over the phone, very affected by what she saw as a bad sign for the future.

Among my informants, it is very common to operate with signs in dreams: When unsure as to the correct action to take in life choices—such as whether to marry or, as in this case, to find a way to stay in an unhappy marriage—people frequently ask God to send them a sign. They then pray and go to sleep. With the Islamic belief of God as all-seeing, all-knowing, and unbound by time and place, the proposition that a dream can be a realm in which the future is present and not ahead of us in a linear sense is sensible, imaginable, and intelligible. A close friend of Amal's had experienced bad dreams about Amal during the period leading up to the kidnapping, and the dreams had left her friend very upset. Apparently, the friend had seen Amal's daughter Isra in her dreams being caught under something and crying out for help. For Amal and her friend, looking back on what happened, the dream took on an ominous meaning.

One week after the kidnapping, I met with Amal in Copenhagen: We kissed each other on the cheeks and hugged. Longer than usual. Amal lit a cigarette and updated me on the events that had taken place since the kidnapping, and her struggle to act in the situation in a way that would bring about a future with her daughter. Amal had had no direct contact with Talal after he left Denmark with Isra. She talked to Isra regularly, but she was not sure as to whether she could trust her daughter when she said she was happy. While Isra talked to Amal on her iPad in the Viber app, Amal overheard her father-in-law tell Isra to sit down next to him. When Amal would pose Isra a question in Danish, she would watch Isra on screen look up behind the iPad, and the answers to Amal's questions would come hesitantly. Soon Isra declared that she did not remember how to speak Danish anymore and preferred to only speak in Arabic.

> We'll speak our language, I told Isra when we Facetimed the first time. I didn't
> say the word Danish, just called it 'our language' … and she told me in Danish
> that she had known she was leaving with her father, but that Talal made her not
> say anything about it to me or to anyone else. When we talked, she repeated "I'm
> fine, mama, I'm with my cousins and having a fun time, you don't need to call all
> the time, I'm on vacation"—I've asked her to call and text me, and she normally
> Snaps all the time, but I don't hear a word from her, and I know she has her iPad
> with her. I live with my parents now. They want me to [live with them], and also,
> I cannot stand being in the apartment when she isn't there.

Was Isra just on vacation, after all, as she insisted? Was this a kidnapping, or could it be re-negotiated? Interpreting actions is invariably predicated on the time that passes, and in light of other events, past and future, that re-signify the "original" event. Amal confided: "Karen—Talal's Boss didn't know anything about him leaving, and he said Talal is going to lose his job if he isn't back within 48 hours," clinging on to that sign that he might come back with their daughter. Amal tried to stay open to what was happening as a way of staying optimistic that her daughter might still be returned to her. But she also forced herself to act in ways that recognized the possibility that Talal might intend to keep their daughter with him in Jordan. In the days, weeks, and months following the kidnapping, the uncles in Amman discussed the matter over the telephone with Amal's father in Copenhagen. After many talks back and forth, it was agreed that Isra would be returned to Amal and the family in Denmark before the beginning of the new school year. A few months after the kidnapping, I met with Amal and Mariam, a friend of Amal's, at a café in Copenhagen. Mariam analyzed the situation of the kidnapping of Isra in light of her own experience as a child in

Denmark, trying to do the right thing toward both her mother and father, whose marriage was at times difficult. She spoke in rather blunt terms:

I feel sorry for Isra. You have to have been through something like that to really understand it. If … I hope, by God, that Talal will be punished for what he's done. I tried the same thing with my mom and dad. To get your dad to leave your mom alone, and not end in 'argument-argument', you do everything you can to make your dad happy. But I should just have let them divorce, that would've been better.… A father loves his daughter—and he doesn't know what he's doing to her.

We went back to discussing the legal aspects of the situation. Amal and Mariam disagreed on whether it was national legislation or *Sharia* (Islamic law), in Jordan that would guide how the family there would solve the situation. Some also mentioned 7 years as the age where the father automatically is given custody of the child in case of divorce. As we sat down at a table in the corner of the café, Amal spoke, close to tears:

I looked more into it, and according to Shariah, the child belongs with the mother until the age of 12, or until a girl starts menstruating. After that, the child belongs (equally) with both parents … I was told that this is what it's like in Jordan too. Still I don't want Isra to worry. I just take away her worries and say: "have a nice time, I've told the school that you are on vacation"—because she is worried about that—but I can feel that she isn't happy … she isn't happy. I feel it.

Amal's husband had arrived in Denmark a few months after their marriage. Although he was her cousin, he was a stranger to her. She taught him to speak Danish, but he did not make any Danish friends. He asked me one night in their apartment what my husband thought of me spending so much time with Muslims? Was he not racist? It was asked in the most straightforward manner, and it made me wonder what encounters he had had in Denmark, what media stories informed his views, since he would assume that. Maybe he never got to the point of investing in his life here, and so finally he wanted to invest his and his daughter's future in what he believed was the best scenario: back home in Jordan. August, after the summer holiday, Amal's father-in-law, who is also her paternal uncle, let the family in Copenhagen know that they would not bring Isra back for the new school semester as agreed on earlier. He added that his son still loved Amal, and the family hoped that she would come to Jordan too and live with them:

I heard my uncle asking my father on the phone whether I wasn't coming …
I was listening by the door. 'Excuse me? After what he did', my dad answered

them. It is also a sign of disrespect towards my father, that Talal did not come to him first, before acting like this.

Amal could not move to Jordan and live under the roof of her parents-in-law, after what had happened, yet she described her insistence on going to Jordan to visit Isra and confront the situation, her head held high. She had been portrayed—via Talal's version of the events leading up to his departure from Copenhagen—as someone acting unmotherly, as a bad wife, and a bad Muslim, leading a life where she went out with girlfriends and prioritized socializing with them over being at home cooking and making a happy home. She felt this was unfair as the couple had devised a situation together where they each worked shifts, so that they spent very little time together, their marriage difficult, and the love for their daughter the only thing they had in common. She had thought it part of their deal, and how they had agreed to compose their family life, so how could he expect her to be home spending time cooking, when he was not there to enjoy a meal with her anyway? She was happy to notice over time that the family in Jordan did seem to change their attitude. She kept visiting, she kept circulating images in social media, and she openly said that she was prepared to sit before Talal and talk face-to-face. He did not wish that however. But it seemed to have made an impact on the family that she "held her head high," as she put it. She appreciated her father's support most of all, she confided. "And finally, I don't have to explain anything to nobody, I don't fear anyone, the only one I fear—is God! And God has witnessed everything of what has happened, he knows."

Moral/laws

In August, her daughter still not returned to her, Amal contacted the police again. She went to the police station accompanied by one of her sisters for moral support this time. They interviewed her, rather superficially she felt. "Is there nothing you can do to help me get my daughter back, what am I to do?" Amal had asked the police officer who interviewed her. "There's nothing we can do—you can try to kidnap her back, that's what I would do, I guess" was his response. There was apparently nothing they could do to help Amal get her daughter back. Talal had violated Danish law by taking the daughter without her consent. She was in fact the sole custodian, as it turned out, and the couple was now divorced on Talal's initiative. He intended to remarry. In practice, this meant that Danish police could arrest Talal, if he came to the border of a European country, but nothing could be done from their side in terms of getting to him, save returning Isra, while they were in Jordan. The only thing that ensued from the police interview was that Amal was, retrospectively, categorized as not having had a daughter to provide for since the Sunday night where she found the apartment empty and called the police. As a consequence, she was asked to pay back child support and housing subsidies for the 8 months that had passed since the day the initial case was registered, when she called the police to say her daughter was missing. The unfortunate turn of events where the uncle refused to return Isra to Denmark made time loop back on itself, as it were. The official categorization with retrospective effect threw Amal off. For 8 months, Amal had put aside the child support she received from the Danish state. She bought clothes and presents for Isra that she had brought to Amman on her first visit there. In Denmark, she lived in a room in her parent's apartment, that she shared with her sister, while trying to find a smaller apartment for her and Isra for *when* she would come back. She hoped and planned for the future return of her daughter. That line of argument, however, did not correspond to any categories in the bureaucratic system. According to the now-updated file, the daughter had been out of the country and out of the system since the kidnapping.

Amal tried everything she could to get her daughter returned to her by her former husband. She sought to create and disseminate images of herself with relational and future-making power on various social media platforms. She sent out images of food prepared for family gatherings at home, old pictures of her daughter, and new pictures and texts of herself in sorrow, missing her daughter, as well as from the mosques and holy places she visited on her travel to Mecca (on *umra*, the "lesser" pilgrimage as compared to the *hajj*, which constitutes one of the five pillars of the Islamic faith). She shared images of herself being a good Muslim woman and mother, who endured hardships, while cultivating and enacting *sab'r* (patience). Simultaneously, she contacted all the relevant legal authorities who could potentially help her and her daughter to be reunited. Dreaming, praying, lobbying with family members, and circulating images in social media were forms of action that ran parallel to approaching the Danish authorities pleading to help her. She found the contact number for a Danish lawyer on the Internet who offered help in cases of kidnapped children—free of charge—contacted him, and went to see him accompanied by her father. The father was relieved that the lawyer was willing to help and "not create trouble for our family." The lobbying with family members in the immediate and extended family was what secured her continued ability to visit her daughter twice a year and to stay in contact in social media. The pink iPad that had been lying all over in the Copenhagen apartment was now the portal for Isra to see her mother, aunts, grandparents, cousins, and friends in Denmark. Isra's room, now without the pink iPad and without Isra, was left the same way as when she left: the white walls with posters over the white bed with the pillow formed as Hello Kitty, with Minnie & Mickey Mouse posters, girl band posters on the wall and stickers, glimmer, and toys on the shelves.

More than a year after that ominous day, I was driving around Copenhagen in a car with Amal and another friend during a cold night in December 2015. Amal recounted a recent dream:

> I don't know what it's a sign of. It was so unpleasant, or I don't know if it was … unpleasant. But she was hurt and she cried soo much, she cried so much. Like, it came from the heart. We were in a Tivoli. Or maybe it was a Zoo, Zoo-like. There was a horse or elephant in front of us, and there were lots of people and she was like that (showing with her hands how Isra and her were positioned at a distance from each other), in front there, and the train came—like a Tivoli train—and she was hit. She hurt herself on the knee, and she, like, fell down, twice. And she cried soo much and it really came from the heart, from inside, like she was really unhappy. I ran there, but I wasn't in time to help it. But I comforted her, and she cried and I said: Do you love me "mama," and she said "yes."

Tears came to her eyes as she told the dream, and she was crying silently. Isra was happy in the dream because they were together in this fun place—she was not aware that the train was headed directly toward her. Amal called out to Isra, who could not hear her. Amal tried to go toward her, but she was unable to reach her because of all the people gathered around whom she had to move through. The approaching train caused Isra to fall and Amal hurried to help her on her feet again. People were laughing in the dream, Amal remembered, and Isra was embarrassed, but not hurt physically. In the dream, Isra blamed her, she said, asking her "You're not helping me—why didn't you help me?"

The (bodily) practices of *du'a*—as well as the dreaming and negotiating with oneself and others about what meaning the dream holds—impact on the future. Dreaming is a realm, or an experience, that defies a linear time sequence, and allows for forms of apprehension and intervention. In my material, the significance of dreams encountered emerges as an amalgam of divine or spiritual intervention, the practices of *du'a* (prayer), the nightly dreaming, and the negotiating with oneself and others about what meaning the dream holds. Amal worked with different vague, tentative future scenarios that she did not concretize when I pressured her on the matter. She sometimes struggled with the feeling of having *no* horizon at all, with not feeling like getting up in the morning and carrying on. She oscillated between different states of mind. I sensed this in both telephone conversations and text messages. I was the one pressuring and driving the conversation to the point of: What is the status? What will happen? However, she wanted to talk about the small developments—had Isra reacted to something said in Danish even though she purported not to speak the language anymore, had she seemed to be asking a lot about her friends or school—and not foreclose anything. My questions, infused with impatience and a wish to know what would happen, and what to do next, were met with unfinished sentences, silences, diversions, or "I don't know Karen, Inch'Allah" (God willing). Amal did not resign in her efforts to get help through the official routes: She kept contacting whoever she knew in her network and searched the Internet for someone who could help her. She had me engage lawyers in my family to check up on family law and contact a former social worker in the local area. She contacted the Copenhagen Legal Aid (Gratis Retshjælp) after finding their site on the Internet. She would arrange to meet me in a café and read through e-mail answers on the screen of her white smartphone when she succeeded in having lawyers contact the Swedish and Norwegian embassies in Amman. She did not want to miss anything in the formulations that were in a very formalistic language. These answers from the official stakeholders were polite, but it was to no avail. They could not—and would not—interfere in such a matter.

Sab'r enacted and shared in social media

Amal was a very active agent and practiced patience at the same time. Sometimes I had trouble understanding that her *inaction* was an action. How can she let time pass and not *do* something, I thought. While in fact, she *was* doing something: practicing patience for her family in Amman and everyone else to witness, both directly and mediated through gossip and by sharing pictures on various social media platforms. The Islamic virtue of *Sab'r* (patience) is highly valued and helps a person bear the tests that God presents you with in *Dunya* (this world) before meeting the Last Day, or Day of Judgment in the most exemplary way possible, and hopefully reach *Jannah* (heaven). Within this framework, the way to get Isra back was not for Amal to go to Jordan and fetch her, but to go to Mecca and Medina with her father, drawing closer to God. Three months after the kidnapping, Amal had traveled to Saudi Arabia with her father, as mentioned. She visited Mecca, the birthplace of the Prophet Muhammad and the holiest city in Islam, and Medina, Mohammad's burial place and the second holiest city after Mecca. It was not a *hajj*, but an *umra*, the non-mandatory lesser pilgrimage made by Muslims to Mecca, which may be performed at any time of the year. At the time of their travels I found it difficult to see why Amal would invest time and money going there instead of flying directly to Amman to fetch her daughter. Amal had friends who supported the idea of kidnapping Isra back. I did not know how she would do that without a passport or someone to help her. The various potential interventions would possibly ruin what Amal was trying to build up slowly, and which held a different future scenario. According to Islam, the return for *sab'r* is blessings, mercy, and guidance of God. Demonstrating herself to be a pious person worthy of respect might be a more likely way to get her daughter back, with a future that entailed a family and social network.

As a Sunni, Amal believes in divine destiny: God wrote down all that has happened and will happen, which will come to pass as written, in the so-called Preserved Tablet. According to this belief, a person's actions are not caused by what is written in the Preserved Tablet but, rather, the action is written as God already knows all occurrences beyond—or rather *without* the restrictions of time. God is without any bond in terms of these phenomena. It is only humans, who are limited in—and by—time and space. An individual has power to choose, but since God created time and space he knows what will happen. Therefore, the saying *Inch'Allah* (God willing) is widely used—because everything that happens is literally God willing. This makes for a temporal framework of a kind in which the future can also be anticipated, even (fore-)experienced through dreams and impacted though prayer and magic.[3] In Amal's friend Mariam's' personal take on the question of *qadar* (foreordainment in Islam) and free will, "there is a God, and Allah is great, but God also gave us a brain so that we could think for ourselves!", as she puts it.

Amal lived through the trials put on her. She would show in her actions over the year following the kidnapping that she was patient (*sab'r*) and a good person, a good mother, and a good Muslim. She aligned herself with God and the ultimate long-term anticipation, while simultaneously hoping for— and keeping open—the short(er)-term return of her daughter. She visited her daughter in Amman again, also accompanied by her father this time. Throughout, the smartphone was part of the setup as a relational device and a means of ordering and making sense of the emotions. I received Snaps with "selfies" of Amal looking worried with accompanying texts that underlined she was nervous and excited. While in Jordan, her Snapchat "MyStory"—a medley of snaps which all her contacts can view—was updated every day with pictures and videos of Isra, her father, and herself having fun: at the pool, at fun fairs, and out and about in Amman. There are snaps with mother and daughter posing together in identical pyjamas and looking happy. There are pictures from restaurants and at home in a garden, sharing food with family members: uncles, aunts, cousins, and her ex-mother-in-law. Then I received a Snap of her sad face and the text stating that she did not want to "leave the apple of my eye," "my one and only love, forever," her beloved Isra. A little while later, a snap of a plane in the airport at night and an accompanying text was updated: "goodbye Isra" with a "smiley" emoticon that did not smile but had a tear down the cheek. I was on the telephone with Amal the day after she had arrived back in Copenhagen. It was only 2 PM, but I could hear Amal and her mother preparing the dinner already in the background, the noise of chopping onions and scrambling with pots and pans. Several of Amal's sisters and their husbands were coming for dinner and there would be a lot of people gathered. It was hard visiting Isra in Jordan, Amal confided over the telephone. But she pulled herself together and made sure that they made the most of their time together. I was curious as to what happened before she left her daughter again. What was said, or agreed on, concerning the future?

> Amal: I told her: 'you know you just call me, and if you want to come to me, you know where I am'. 'yes, mom, I know', she said. She can call me and tell me to come anytime, and I will find a way, but I do not want to put more stress on her. She is very concerned with not upsetting her father, and says that she is happy in Amman, but she's very afraid of upsetting him, Karen, I know.
>
> Karen: I'm beginning to understand, not completely still … You remember when I told you that time at the café that I think I would be standing in the street screaming, if it happened to me? I didn't get the idea of having to show patience, and all that.
>
> Amal: Yeah, what good would that have done. It would not help in getting her back. My dad has played a really big role in helping me understand that it's better to go there and show them that I have nothing to be ashamed of, I hold my head high. Going to Amman and making problems would just make it much harder to get her back. He has really been supporting me … Now I feel good, Karen, that I at least know I'm doing everything I can. You know I'm not overtly religious, you know me, but still when you believe and you let God into your life, it's such a *warm* feeling inside I don't know when I will get her back, I hope I will—if it doesn't happen in this life.

Amal kept visiting with her daughter. All of the images that she shared in social media with girlfriends, sisters (and me) would increase before and after a visit, hopeful and excited before; snaps of all the presents she was buying for her, letters and drawings from Isra's classmates to bring to Jordan. Afterward would follow the disappointment that the family in Jordan would not let Isra wear the clothes Amal had bought for her, because they were too tight, not covering enough, or not in good style according to them. While she was visiting she would share snaps of the two of them in matching pairs of pyjama and the Snapchat filters that make you look soft, doll-like, snaps with puppy ears and nose. There was one short video of Isra laughing so hard; she almost couldn't catch her breath. Amal's one hand was in the image tickling her, the other hand out of the picture, holding the phone filming. After she left, she would receive messages from Isra; one snap showed her in a video-selfie, kissing the screen, and the filter made it seem like the screen splintered like glass when Isra kissed the screen. Amal had taken a screenshot and saved Isra in time, in her photo-stream to look at. Her profile images in Instagram showed her and Isra. The photo on her phone screen was an image of each of them and a zigzag line—as in a broken heart—separating the two images. I told her I admired her patience, that she kept going to Jordan and showing Isra that she was not giving up, showing her in messages, phone calls, and visits that she is there for her, doing everything she can. She told me that God tries people, one must endure and keep faith, keep going. Also she added "if I didn't continue and put my trust in God, where would I be now—in the psych ward?."

The house of my love is empty. Birds flying in it ... I feel oppressed, confined, anguished, exasperated ... At the moment of Impasse, then, an overflowing, and a passage to another scene: hâj khâtrî, my mind, thoughts, and desires rise and overflow, like water is moved by the wind. They spill out and depart from my body, from my narrow and confining present, and journey away. They migrate back to my blâd, the land from which I am separated, for the intemporal and atopical journey of a "saying." The kelma, the poem, is an impossible return. However much I cry I can't reach: my wings are broken ... Yet the broken wings of the body, the powerlessness in the real world, liberates the wings of the imaginary.
(Pandolfo 1997:268–269)

d

Images and Mirrors

The imaginal realm and virtuality

In this last chapter, I return to what I have termed "the composite habitus" and the transcontextual situation. I discuss how working with young Muslim women in Blaagaarden with a focus on smartphones and the circulation and flow of images in the digital realm has opened up for insights about *harakat* movement in an environment that *demands* it. By adopting the concept of *al-harakat* in my thinking about personhood and environment, habitus and habitat, in this particular setting, I hope to unsettle what Trinh T. Minh-ha has described as "pure origin" and "true self" (Trinh 1989). In *Woman, Native, Other*, she writes: "The differences made between entities comprehended as absolute presences— hence the notion of *pure origin* and *true* self—are an outgrowth of a dualistic system of thought … 'I' is, itself, infinite layers" (Trinh 1989:94). To explore these infinite layers of the self, I start with the dreams of Amal and her friends as recounted in Chapter D. With *sab'r* and *du'a* foregrounded, it might be patience, silent forbearance, and "leaving it in the hands of God" that seem to be the attitude of Amal in the preceding chapter. At the same time, as Kaveri Qureshi points out from her study with Pakistani migrant women in Britain, there are inherent tensions between self-sublimation and self-assertion in the practice of sab'r. She suggests to understand sab'r as an agential capacity rather than passive acceptance and fatalism (Quereshi 2013).

Amal jumps in between all available registers and different ways and modes of reacting. She is struggling along, staying afloat, trying to *make* the future how she wishes it. In her situation, praying to God is experienced as powerful. When I discussed my understanding of her reaction and sab'r specifically, with Amal on the phone, she pointed out that I had understood those aspects correctly, but overlooked that she was "acting very Danish" also. By this she was alluding to her efforts at searching out all the different bureaucratic possibilities, the authorities, etc. I was so fascinated with her register of religiosity and responding to an unbearable situation, and she pointed me back in the direction of drawing on all that she is and knows: Yes, she put her faith in God—he witnesses all—and "If not, where would I be now? In the psych ward (den lukkede)?" At the same time, she acted "as a Dane" who grew up in this society, "knowing the system."

Dream images and digitally circulated images inform anticipations of the future, and actions in the present. Images, accessed in a sleeping state, are understood to be signs for the future; and through digital technologies, images are shared and circulated in social media, as tactics for impacting on the future. In this disconcerting situation—the kidnapping of Isra—a conflict played out between spouses of different generations in the Bourdieusian sense, as mentioned above: "by conditions of existence which, in imposing different definitions of the impossible, the possible, and the probable, cause one group to experience as natural or reasonable, practices or aspirations which another group finds unthinkable or scandalous" (Bourdieu 1977:78). These conflicts between the impossible and possible are indicative of the intergenerational relations among the families of my informants and they are also in some marriages, such as that between Amal and Talal, not separated by age, but conditions of existence that make them perceive each other's behavior as unthinkable or even scandalous. Amal and Talal grew up in very different environments, different habitats that helped form them, and condition how they navigate.

The fact that the majority of the young unmarried women I worked with, of very different national, ethnic, and class background, wished to marry a Muslim man who had *grown up* in Denmark (or Europe) makes sense. They point to a shared set of values, ideals related to the Muslim faith, as well as sharing an idea of relations between spouses, what a man and woman can expect of each other informed by the place where they grow up, as well as sharing an understanding of what it means to "grow up minority." What they share, and expect to share with that kind of ideal and preferred spouse, is the feeling of being estranged from their parents' country of origin as well as their embodied habitus and worldviews from these countries of origin. At the same time, the women share many values, ideas, and habits with their *parents*. They tacitly embody and share values with their parents *and* pose questions and hold other values and beliefs that appear contradictory. While most people lead lives full of contradictions and paradoxes, few are expected to be able to solve in absolute terms or choose between the contradictory and guiding norms in their lives on a daily basis. This is the case for my informants.

Conflict within the family can be sparked by the fear that the younger generation (Isra) will be influenced by what is perceived by one parent (Talal) to be amoral behavior by the other parent (Amal), not living up to the ideals he had for a Muslim mother and wife. The kidnapping also represented a permanent departure for Talal from a country where he felt rejected and never found a home. For his wife, Amal, this *is* her home—her habitat, to which her habitus is fitted—and where she moves with more ease. It is fair to assume that Talal did what he felt he needed to do, to secure a future for himself and their daughter, in his understanding of what was best, but with devastating effects for Amal—not to think of how it must impact Isra. Amal had dreamed this before it happened: She had received images of her world being turned upside-down. In my fieldwork, informants' dreams were a means for them of relating to the future, most intensely in times of crisis, as for Amal in this situation. Iain Edgar proposes that paying attention to night dreams can be a technique of ethnographically researching the future (Edgar 2004). He argues that the images of ourselves and the images that we portray to the world when rehearsing future action explore imaginative resources and reveal implicit knowledge and emotional states (Edgar 2004:1).[1] Maria Louw (2010) shows that dreaming is perceived by her Muslim informants in Kyrgyzstan to be of great significance as sources of omens and divine revelations. As such, dreams hold peoples' fears about, and hopes for, how their lives may develop.

In recognizing dream images as omens, people enter a virtual realm: "A subjunctive state, where they can imagine and orient themselves toward various potential future scenarios and test the social and moral resonance of these scenarios; ... where they can reflect on the question of what they are able to control and change, and what has to be left to chance or fate" (Louw 2010:277). *Du'a* (prayer), dreams, and digital image-making technologies are all, I suggest, "technologies of the imagination" (Sneath et al. 2009). David Sneath and his co-authors include in "technologies" a repertoire of objects and practices that bring about imaginative effects (Sneath et al. 2009:20). Drawing on Gibson and his conceptualization of affordances, they suggest that the relationship between imagination and the technology that engenders it is neither deterministic nor teleological, but underdetermined (Sneath et al. 2009:19).[2]

In focusing on technologies of the imagination, Sneath et al. argue for renewed attention to the "external imaginary space *spanning between* persons, or *between persons and things*" (Sneath et al. 2009:14, my emphasis). The flow of images exists in the space spanning between persons, between persons and things, in techniques such as prayer, social media tactics, and magic objects, and in the space spanning between persons and their God. How can we understand the dreams of Amal, and what are the "modes" and temporalities of these dream images that are shared and discussed through smartphones and social media? Bergson calls the virtual image "pure recollection," pointing out that this is "to better distinguish it from mental images—recollection-images, dream or dreaming—with which it might be confused easily" (Bergson 1920:165, see also Deleuze 1989:89). A dream image, then, is a virtual image which is in the course of actualization in consciousness or psychological states. Building on the work of Sufi mystic and philosopher Ibn al'Arabi, William Chittick argues that in contrast to the rational faculty (*"aql*), which works by a process of stringing concepts together and drawing conclusions, and "reflection" (*fikr*), the imaginal faculty (*khayâl*) works by an inner perception that perceives ideas in sensory form. "Hence imaginal perception may be visual, but this vision does not take place with the physical eyes; it may be auditory, but things are not heard with the physical ears. Again, dreams prove that everyone has nonphysical sense experience" (Chittick 1994:70, see also Pandolfo 2018 and Stoller on *bazark* 2008).

In the reading of Laura Marks,[3] the imaginal realm (*alam al-mithâl*), "far from being an individual fantasy, accounts for the way people's collective wishes bring the unthought into the thinkable, beginning with dreams, myth and metaphor" (Marks 2016:8). Marks questions what kind of reality imagination possesses, what the difference between memory-images and fantasmatic or imaginal images is, and where imaginal images come from: "Are they created by the individual psyche, or do they come from beyond the psyche" (Marks 2016:27)? This resonates with Amira Mittermaier, who argues that certain dreams come to the dreamer as opposed to being produced by her or him (2012:248, see also Pandolfo 2018). In this sense, the dreamer is "never in charge" (2012:248, see also Pandolfo 2018:254) because dreams come from Elsewhere, troubling the notion of a unified subject and pointing toward the imaginal realm (2012:248, see also Pandolfo 2018:249, 260). According to Mittermaier's Egyptian informants, there are three kinds of dreams: *hadîth nafsi*, dreams that originate in the dreamer's self, wishes or worries; *hulm*, dreams (often nightmares) provoked by a *jinn* or evil spirit; and *ru'ya*, a divinely inspired dream-vision or waking vision that offers prophetic insight—"symbolic or literal signs for the future" (2011:110–111, 2012:249, see also Khan 2010). The women I worked with did not operate with such clear-cut distinctions. They would rather, as is the case with Louw's informants, draw on what they knew about signs and symbols, understanding the dream in the context of the big challenges in their life, or happenings in the larger circle of families and close friends, as Amal's friend who had dreamed about Isra being caught under something. The fact that it was following a *du'a*, where Amal had specifically asked for help in finding a way forward together with her husband, that she herself had experienced nightmares was a particularly bad sign. The "feel" of the dream, as well as the fact that it had returned to her several times after waking up bathed in sweat, was perceived as an omen, one that made sense only after the kidnapping.

A late night in Blaagaarden during a stay-over at Neda's place, I could not sleep as she was texting with the man she was in a (purely) online relationship with, but who she hoped would become her husband. She shared a dream with me, in which his mother had offered her a glass of water, something which she saw as a really good sign. On a similar note, Louw's informants would ask for a sign when ascertaining whether to accept a marriage proposal or not (2010), and Edgar and Henig (2010) have argued that Islam is probably the largest night dream culture in the world today (Edgar and Henig 2010:252).

According to Stefania Pandolfo, who works in the overlap between anthropology, psychoanalytic theory, and Islamic eschatology, Ibn al-Arabi distinguishes between two kinds of sleep: one that is bodily rest and another that he calls "transferal" (*intiqālī*) (2018:333). Transferal sleep is the sleep in which there are dreams. Through the experience of dreaming, transferal sleep exposes each of us to a presentiment of "the Invisible" (*al-ghayb*) (see also Bubandt et al. 2019), the divine that remains inaccessible to human perception and that can only be grasped as imagination. In transferal sleep, "the instruments of the soul are transferred from the manifest side of sense perception to the non-manifest side (*bāṭin*) in order to see what has become established in the treasury of imagination (*khizānat al- khayāl*)" (Ibn al-Arabi in Pandolfo 2018:333). Pandolfo further writes that Michel Foucault traces the tradition of the imagination as world-creating process back to Aristotle, Plotinus, Spinoza, and the mystics, an insight that is central to the Islamic tradition of dreaming and the Imagination (Pandolfo 2018:178–179, see also Sedgwick 2016). In her theoretical development of the imaginal realm, Marks links the emanation of the Neoplatonists with Deleuze and Bergson's thinking, those of Ibn al-Arabi and Mulla Sadra (1571–1641).

At the center of the ideas proposed by the Muslim philosophers (*falasifa*) mentioned in the above is God as transcendental, eternal, and unchangeable. Then there is the created world in constant flow and transformation. There is a connection between the one transcendental God and the created multiplicity *through emanation* (cf. Marks 2016; Sedgwick 2016; Simonsen 2006:179). Still, not all Islamic scholars agreed then—as today—on the question of oneness with God: For some sects and schools, it remains *shirk* (pride, self-sufficiency) in strict scriptural terms to strive for, and even claim no separation between the Creator and the created (cf. Simonsen 2006:176). These differences are much to large an issue to discuss in depth here. My informants did not discuss in these terms about God, but they did stress the importance of dreams (across Sunni and Shi'a Muslims). I therefore give attention to their dreams and discussion of them in the spirit of what Arkoun has called "the 'silent Islam'—the Islam of true believers who attach more importance to the religious relationship with the absolute of God than to the vehement demonstrations of political movements" (Arkoun 2003:19).[4]

Dreaming and imagination in the varied Muslim tradition (Chittick 1994; Corbin 1976; Ewing 1994; Henig and Edgar 2010; Khan 2010; Louw 2010; Mittermaier 2011; Pandolfo 1997, 2018) speak to—and alongside—theories on dreams and imagination in the anthropological tradition (Bateson 2000; Iain Edgar 2004; Sneath et al. 2009). Corbin introduced the concept of the imaginal realm into contemporary thought, drawing on Sohrawadi and Ibn al'Arabi and suggested "the imaginal realm" or "mundus imaginalis" as the proper translation of *alam al-mithâl* and the family of concepts related to the Arabic and Persian notion of *mithāl*: image and semblance, example, vision, witnessing (Corbin 1976; Pandolfo 2018:175).[5] Corbin saw it as problematic that the term "imaginary" was equated with the unreal, with something that is outside the framework of being and existing (Corbin 1976:3–4).[6] "The imaginal world is ontologically real: In this conception the imagination is a privileged locus of experience, transformation, and relation; not illusion and error, but the site of true knowledge. Dreaming is an experience all share that opens onto the imaginal; and … attests to the reality of the imagination" (Pandolfo 2018:175).

In the case of my informants, there were other ways of receiving a sign or guidance or dreaming, also evoking an imaginal realm as well as the "external imaginary spanning between persons and things (Sneath et al 2009:14). This could be opening a page of the Qur'an and understanding the *ayat* (verses from the Qur'an) as carrying a significance for the current situation one finds oneself in. For Shi'a Muslims, one could open a book with the poetry of poet and mystic Hafiz (1315–1390)—*Fal-e Hafiz*—with a deep wish from the soul for guidance. Informants did this in solitude as well as together. Magic objects such as amulets (*taveez*), or even a specific letter are believed to be endowed with protective powers by some. Others, however, reject these beliefs and practices as wrongful and denoted them "folk practice." One informant, Amira, told me that it was completely wrong, according to Islam, and amounted to pride (*shirk*) in a problematic way for those preparing the amulets as well as those carrying them: "As the Qur'an is perfect, one should not choose bits and pieces for amulets or "to put under the pillow." If anything, Amira would take the whole Qur'an and place under the pillow of her daughter to protect her, that would be more correct in her view. Most informants carry, or hang in their home, "the eye" (*nazars*), or "Fatimas hand" as protection from the evil eye (*al-'ayn*). Many tactics are used to avoid the *eye*, which is believed to occur when people are envious of your happiness and success. These tactics were also manifest in the digital realm. One informant, Fatima, closed down her account on Facebook after securing a really good job. She had previously been laid off, with a lot of other women that she knew, and did not want to risk anything by opening herself to envy on their part. She later re-opened her account and became more active again in social media as time had passed and she would therefore consider herself to be less vulnerable. Another woman blamed herself as her engagement was broken off, as she had been sharing and "advertising" her happiness, thereby attracting the eye. It is commonly believed that one can cast evil eyes without knowing it or having evil intentions. These practices are all in differing ways entwined in the smartphone as well as everyday more mundane activities and interactions are. As with Archambault's Mozambican informants, an everyday balancing between accessing social status and deflecting envy was pivotal and the phone integral to this, as was tactical concealment (Archambault 2017:43).

The smartphone is a relational device both connecting to and interfacing with other people, communities, and as aspects of practices and realms that have a virtual quality. Envy and the eye as phenomena do not discern between online and offline. Images flow across dreams, the digital, and the physical realms. As Pink et al. point out:

> Visualisation on the touch screen are not just *seen* but they are part of both what the hand incrementally learns and knows, and inextricable from our sensory perception of the wider environments we are in ....through the tactile screen content is necessarily experienced and engaged with corporeally. This requires it to be analysed as a sensory medium, beyond a focus on its representational or symbolic status (Pink et al. 2015).

Below I return to the digitally circulated images, infused with hopes and dreams, and how this sensory understanding opens up for a different notion of the person as embodying a composite habitus, and the women I worked with as "queer" parts of different wholes.

The composite habitus

I came to see my interlocutors' interactions in social media—attention and availability as well as the images, words, and links exchanged—as elicitations of relationships, of other persons—that make up the composite person. These "parts" are those specific relationships of which the person is constituted (parts that are also parts of others). The person understood as a microcosm (Strathern 1988, 1994; Wagner 1974, 1991), where elicitations from significant others lay claim to that person. The person is a composite—a microcosm of her social relations (Wagner 1974) that are made visible. In this analysis through attention and availability made visible in social media in the form of images and words elicited: given, received, liked, and commented on. These elicitations, or exchanges of "time given" as a gift (Derrida 1992:2–3), make up part of the young woman's composite self. Through these exchanges in social media, "invisible" social relations are made visible, and relations appear between relatives "at home" and the family members in Europe (see also Madianou and Miller 2012 on migrants' intimate ties and reciprocal relations maintained via social media).

In Blaagaarden, the radiating ties are forming a security circle with the person at the center (cf. Strathern 1994; Wagner 1974) through the affordances of the smartphone—gathering people across long distances. Put differently, the women I work with are not "hyphen-persons" made up of two discrete cultures with a hyphen connecting the two "wholes." They are "composite wholes," formed and informed by significant others, by others that make up part of them, locally and across countries, as well as by their environment, counting the physical, digital, and imaginal realm. As succinctly put by Zara in a conversation: "The children will become a remix. Take my cousin, he's a quarter Kurd, a quarter Iranian, a quarter Palestinian, a quarter Lebanese, yet he's born in Denmark and grew up here." This habitus is a composite and the culture emerging is new and part of different wholes. The women are "queer" parts of different wholes. Queer understood here as a verb, in the sense of Fatima El-Tayeb's (2011) description of how racialized Europeans (often Muslims with migrant background) challenge the construction of Europe as white and (post-) combining "queer" theory with Caribbean theories of creolization and hybridization. El-Tayeb (2017) further stresses the "ascribed permanent status as migrating" (from somewhere that is not Europe). This status is transmitted across generations and thus increasingly decoupled from the actual event of migration, shifting the meaning of 'migrant' from a term indicating movement to one indicating a static, hereditary state" (2017). This is a pivotal part of the dynamic of a double bind: Following theories on socialization, perception and adaption of most (mobile) people in the heavily mediated world of today are "composites," as we continue to be formed by our immediate environment (counting here the digital and imaginal realms) over time. The difference is that for the young women, I worked with the part of their habitus that is "European" or "Danish," is to a large extent *misrecognized*. Their self-perception thus continually out of joint with how they feel others' see them. The mirror held up to them by right-wing politicians and parts of the media is a reflection they do not recognize themselves in. They are "embodying an identity that is declared impossible, even though it is lived by millions, the experience of constantly being defined as foreign to everything one is most familiar with," in El-Tayeb's words (2017).

I argue that the smartphone is essential in allowing for *harakat* and for navigating the transcontextual situation in which the young women find themselves as differing part(s) of differently configured wholes, constantly transforming. The smartphone is a crucial relational device and opening up to virtuality for the young Muslim women from Blaagaarden, with whom I worked. The uses of social media simultaneously mirror, augment, and aid the complex condition of a habitus shaped by composite parts in which young women are informed by multiple forces and take up positions within multiple fields. The quote from Bita below alludes to the idea of a composite habitus in the Wagnerian sense, as being established in the elicitations and exchanges with significant others in the metaphor she offers of "being ten fingers":

> Most of my friends are Arab; I grew up with them; I like Arab music and Arab food. I've learned that Arabs always invite you and, if they have something, they offer you. They're generous …. Say, if I'm a person, and I'm 100 percent, or, say, I'm 10 fingers: I'm two fingers Iranian, three fingers Danish and, maybe, five fingers Arab, because I grew up here in the area. My mom regrets every day that we moved to this area and that we grew up here. If we had lived somewhere else, we would have spoken a better Danish, and we would've been better integrated and all that. We wouldn't speak this "street language." And if it wasn't because we live here, I wouldn't even bother to wear the veil.

Bita is influenced by growing up in Denmark in an Iranian household, visiting family in Teheran, watching Iranian TV, and having many Iranian "friends" and "followers" in various social media platforms. At the same time, most of her friends, whom she has known since early childhood, are Arab and Danish, and they also influence her and make up an integral part of her everyday life. When I allude to *harakat*, I do not imply that it is always successful. The notion of a composite habitus underscores the embodied "structuring structures"

(Bourdieu 1990) that you cannot sidestep or disregard, because they are only partly conscious. When the habitus is "out of joint" with its environment it "misfires," due to the "hysteresis effect" as Bourdieu would have it, ·that is, the lagging-behind of learning habitually to engage in a new habitat, or moving across different sets of expectations, values, and ideals within and from the social world(s) one is in, and continually formed by. A composite habitus assembles and develops multiple perspectives in a dialectic movement through overlapping fields or habitats. A composite habitus, however, is not necessarily flexible in the sense of being able to bend, adapt, and choose from a range of available options effortlessly. The habitus concept reminds us of how people do not simply choose consciously to disregard what they have embodied as right, wrong, and taken for granted. You cannot conveniently choose otherwise.

While a composite condition might be seen as an overall condition of modern societies, as mentioned, I argue that it is especially accentuated for young Muslim (second generation) immigrant women living in social housing areas in European cities. When thinking about a place, such as Blaagaarden, it encompasses the dimensions of the physical, digital, and imaginal realms. All of these layers, Andrew Irving points to, building on William James's insight that "the spectrum of consciousness ranges from inchoate, barely graspable and transitory forms of thinking and being that exist on the periphery of our conscious and bodily awareness to those more defined, purposeful and stable forms that are more readily articulated in language and can enable persons to establish senses of self and continuity, even amidst radically changing conditions or disruption" (Irving 2016:451). What the young Muslim women in Blaagaarden share, as mentioned above, is the feeling of being estranged from their parents' country of origin as well as their embodied habitus and worldviews from these countries of origin, similar to the experience of the informants of Sayad (1979, 2004) in the French context. The term *harakat* covers the movement—navigation—across the different sets of expectations and values, which might temporarily reconcile the struggle within, that one is experiencing in terms of how to move forward in life toward a desired future—smartphone in hand. In the moment, *harakat* also serves the purpose of entertaining one's friends, who appreciate the skill demonstrated.

What is a composite person composed of? In other words, what "parts" are a person made up of, or from which "wholes" do these parts come? On the one hand there is the relational person who makes visible the specific relations that matter, and on the other hand the person as an abstract member of a society—an individual. Both are enacted by making relations visible—relations to kin and relatives, and vis-á-vis the community as a member of it (Rasmussen 2015a, b). These two meanings are at play in understanding the constitution of the person among my informants. It ties into the discussion of individuals in a society (imagined political communities, Anderson 2006 [1983]), as members of a community and as relational persons who embody in the constitution of being, the specific sets of relationships with kin and significant others: they constitute a microcosm. The young Muslim women in Blaagaarden—growing up as *part of* Denmark, as *part of* their local (Muslim) communities, and as *part of* their families across countries—constitute themselves, or are constituted, as parts of different part-whole relations (Strathern 1988).

The young Muslim women in Blaagaarden are parts of communities and groups, loosely defined. They can be abstract members of a national society and also abstract parts of several other "communities": defined by being Muslim, being non-Danish, being from Blaagaarden, being Arab, Iranian, Pakistani, Kurdish, etc. They are parts of a society, through living in—and most of them citizens of—the Danish state. It is regularly debated whether one ever really becomes Danish (Kaur 2016, for the European case, see El-Tayeb 2011), most recently by the extreme right-wing party "Stram Kurs" (Hard Line), that will stand in the General Elections on June 5th. The party is on the ballot sheet with an explicitly racist (and un-constitutional) program of deporting Muslims residing in Denmark, and banning Islam (https://stramkurs.dk/vores-politik/udlaendinge/). The leader of the party, Rasmus Paludan, stood in the middle of Blaagaarden Square on April 14, 2019, burning the Qur'an and insulting the Prophet, provoking a riot in Noerrebro with more than seventy fires started and twenty-three arrests. Paludan started as a YouTube-phenomenon and has understood how to use the Internet, the flow of images, and fear-invoking metaphorical language to create affect.[7]

The ethno-nationalist discourse is underpinned by an essentialist notion of cultural wholes that do not see social wholes as being of a provisional kind, continually made and remade, continually in a state of becoming. When the former minister of justice, whom I quoted in Chapter B, states that "we" should be able to send "them" back home; it becomes clear that for a young Muslim in Denmark of immigrant origin the feeling that one is part of the "whole," that is Danish society, is extremely precarious. They do not have other home countries—their parents do. There is no other moment when they feel more Danish than when they visit their parents' home countries and are "called out" for being "European" or "Danish." As composites made up of the elicitations of others, and as individuals, they are situated at the nexus of various traditions, sets of expectations and values, continually in a state of becoming. Staying with the metaphor of mirror images, the young Muslim women enter into a hall of mirrors on a daily basis: who is expecting (or assuming) what? How to navigate? Through the smartphone, they gather the relations that make up who they are (becoming). They navigate being of different part-whole relations, which—as the experience in the hall of mirrors—can be quite nauseating with distorted images of oneself cast back, resulting in difficulty in orienting oneself.

By extending Bourdieu's notion of the split habitus into the notion "composite habitus," though, I underscore the creative potential of a double-bind situation— the transcontextual skilled movement, that I have denoted *harakat*. Bateson wrote that double bind theory is concerned with the "experiential component in the genesis of tangles in the rules or premises of habit," the processes of learning and adaptation that promote what he called "transcontextual syndromes"— characterized by "severe pain and maladjustment" induced by putting someone in the wrong regarding their rules for making sense of an important relationship with another, *and* he wrote further "that if this pathology is warded off or resisted, the total experience may promote creativity" (2000:276–278). This is central to my argument: The Muslim women in Blaagaarden move in a *harakat* way in which the smartphone is indispensable, to be able to withstand all of the double binds they are faced with continually—the many catch-22 situations, where there is limited room for maneuvring in a way that can "augment" their being. When there is no middle-ground between social control and state control, and the demands on being a good Muslim, pious woman, and a young woman demonstrating that she is free of constraints so as to not be perceived as subdued, then the skill for living "in" paradoxes is honed. The young women I worked with perform contextually in different groups of people, learning and adapting, applying also the smartphone in keeping apart different "selves." They bend rules occasionally so as to not break other rules in ways that are beyond repair. This is what I have denoted as *harakat*. The young women embody a composite habitus, experiencing at times pain, maladjustment *and*—most importantly—creativity is promoted as they overcome the double binds through charm, cunning, and *harakat* moves. This is a feat that is overwhelmingly impressive. In a context of marginalization and oppression, they operate *within* the law and *within* (sometimes opposing) sets of norms and values—but operating on the edges and in the interstices. Imagination, dreaming, prayer, and *sab'r* are necessary tactics that help withstand the pressures.

The flow of (mirror) images and future-making

Working across modalities and registers in body and mind and paying attention to an external imaginary space *spanning between* persons, or *between persons and things* made digital technologies and dreams appear in parallel as particular "manifestations" of the Islamic notion of an imaginal realm. The imaginal realm is also described as the world of "Images in suspense" (*mothol mo'allaqa*) (Corbin 1976:10). The analogy of images in suspense is the reflection in a mirror—describing the relation of images to the empirical world.[8] This has a resemblance to the "selfies" and other digital images in social media that my interlocutors share with others, particularly in the Snapchat platform, where an image shared will cease to exist after 10 seconds (Waltorp 2016). I find this to resonate with the notion of the virtual: "The memory seems to be to the perception what the image reflected in the mirror is to the object in front of it. The object can be touched as well as seen; acts on us as well as we on it; it is pregnant with possible actions; it is actual. The image is virtual" (1920:165).

(Non-physical) co-presence in and through digital media and image-making technologies (co)constitutes contemporary relationships across the world (Pink et al. 2016:16). Images and imaginings are often manifested in glimpses: a quote or image posted in a social media platform, or a private message presenting a "hoped for future self" rather than a "factual" present state, as in the case of Amal. Dreaming and sharing of images in social media (such as Snapchat, Instagram and Facebook) are future-making actions. The digital technologies assembled in the Internet-enabled smartphone are conducive to the flow of images in new ways—as a technology of the imagination (for good or ill) with underdetermined effects. The young women in Blaagaarden use the smartphone prolifically to consume, produce, and share images; and they use it as a relational device in specific ways.

In this book I started from the smartphone. The book, however, is not *about* the smartphone in itself, but rather about what it enables and invites, for my informants and for me, the anthropologist. Throughout the book, I have intentionally avoided the term "virtual reality" to denote the online and the digital realm, as I do not find that it does justice to what this realm constitutes and opens up to for my informants. In my fieldwork images in motion were also afforded in specific ways in-between us, allowing for knowledge to emerge in specific ways, courtesy of the smartphone and social media. Below I further discuss the (virtual and actual) images and their status, alongside Ibn al-Arabi, Mulla Sadra, Bateson, and Bergson:

Our actual existence, then, whilst it is unrolled in time, duplicates itself all along with a virtual existence, a mirror-image. Every moment of our life presents two aspects, it is actual and virtual, perception on the one side and memory on the other. Each moment of life is split up as and when it is posited. Or rather, it consists in this very splitting, for the present moment, always going forward, fleeting limit between the immediate past which is no more and the immediate future which is not yet, would be a mere abstraction were it not the moving mirror which continually reflects perception as a memory." (Bergson 1920:165) "… this duplication does not go through to the end. It is rather an oscillation between two standpoints from which one views oneself, a going and coming of the mind between perception which is only perception and perception duplicated with memory." (Bergson 1920:169)

Bergson introduced the ideas of the forking of time into actual and virtual images, and the dream-like states, while Bateson underscored that consciousness is only one way to obtain knowledge, and the limited conscious mind must be combined with the unconscious in complete synthesis. Only when thought and emotion are combined in whole is man able to obtain complete knowledge. He believed that religion and art are some of the few areas in which a man is acting as a whole individual in "complete consciousness." Occidental epistemology, according to Bateson, perpetuates a system of understanding which is purpose—or "means-to-an-end"—driven. Purpose controls attention and narrows perception, thus limiting what comes into consciousness and therefore limiting the amount of wisdom that can be generated from the perception (2000).

Seyyd Hossein Nasr summed up Mulla Sadra's notion of "*wujud*" (being) in 1972 thus: "Being is One while various determinations and ways of considering it cause man to perceive the world of multiplicity which veils Unity" (Nasr 1972:159). In the same year, 1972, Bateson published his Steps to an Ecology of Mind (2000 [1972]). From a non-religious perspective, his notion of "mind" and the systemic integrity of nature parallel the idea that being is one *and* perceived as multiplicity. As Mary Catherine Bateson, his daughter, writes in the Foreword to Steps, Bateson's theory of integrative living systems—from cells to forests to civilizations—included this idea that

mind is composed of multiple material parts, the arrangements of which allow for process and patterns. Mind is thus not separable from its material base, and traditional dualisms separating mind from body or mind from matter are erroneous. A mind can include non-living elements as well as multiple organisms … not necessarily defined by a boundary such as an envelope of skin, and consciousness, if present at all, is always only partial. (2000:xi)

Bateson's fusion of anthropology with cybernetics and feedback theory also pointed forward to current and emerging digital technology, changing everyday experiences, global economies, and cultural styles, as pointed out by Massimo Canevacci (2012). The essence of Norbert Wiener's cybernetics, in Bateson's eyes, was that "the science is the science of the whole circuit ... And you're not really concerned with an input-output, but with the events within the bigger circuit, and you're a part of the bigger circuit ... The engineer is outside the box and Wiener is inside the box ... I'm inside the box" (Bateson in Canevacci 2012:267).

The ideas of self-correcting organisms, always with the observer/knower as part of the circuit, bear resemblance to Gibson's theories (2015) of affordances and ecological psychology (the perceiver always *in* an environment), and those of Muslim philosophers of the "mystic bend" of the Islamic Golden Age, such as Corbin's work on Ibn al-Arabi's writings on the imaginal Realm (alam al-Mithal) of (Eastern) Islamic philosophy (1969, 1976) and later Mulla Sadra.[9] "Ideally, the relationships between the patterns of the biological world and our understanding of it would be one of congruence, a broader and more pervasive similarity than the ability to predict in experimental contexts that depend upon simplification and selective attention" (M.C. Bateson 2000:xiii). In Bateson's recursive epistemology, the relationship between the knower and the known is integral: knowledge looping back as knowledge of an expanded self, which has also inspired the form of this book and the notion of mirroring chapters. The mirror stage is not a stage pace Jaques lacan (1966), it is human interaction with other humans and with our environment. We mirror ourselves in others as humans, and as humans with specific technologies we do that in specific ways. "What is duplicating itself each moment into perception and memory is the totality of what we are seeing, hearing and experiencing. All that we are with all that surrounds us" (Bergson 1920:166). We are also part of a cyborg assemblage—there is a space spanning between us, an imaginary space between us, between us and things.

This book ends with an invitation to trouble the "we"—a call to be cyborgs, and seek affinity. We must move in a *harakat* way, so that we can perceive affordances differently, so that we can gain different (partial) perspectives through parallax and through staying nearby, as anthropologists. The challenge of a *harakat anthropology* that counts more realms than dualistic approaches is to dare to mirror ourselves in others, and in our surroundings—and in the cosmos. An anthropology that risks itself implodes its own mirror image and submits itself to the world and the flow of images.

I might not devolve from the same "world" as my interlocutors (or their parents'); yet, we live in the same nation, the same city, the same neighborhood: Our worlds overlap. Together we reproduce overlapping worlds: We lead parallel *and* overlapping lives (enacting hybridity). Our traditions and "cultures" might differ, but we also "invent" culture together as it emerges between us. As Wagner argues: In the act of inventing another culture, the anthropologist invents his own, and in fact he reinvents the notion of culture itself (Wagner 1981:13). It is this very premise that I allude to in the title "Mirror Images"—not a mirror image, in which we only see ourselves, when we look at the other, but in the mutual constitution and the refractions which create something new entirely, something that was virtual but is now in the process of becoming actualized. Wagner does not use "invention" in the sense of a made-up entity, but as taking "place objectively, along the lines of observing and learning, not any kind of free fantasy" (Wagner 1981:13). The quest for knowledge about others must always be accompanied by a continual questioning of "for whom" and "why" as part of an accountable knowledge making which is always at the same time future-making. In fieldwork we must "risk" ourselves, and risk being transformed. If we did not, we would be no more than an ideology sticking to our own conventions (Wagner 1981).

Pink suggests an approach that acknowledges that the digital and material are *emergent relationally* and to use digital visual research technologies and techniques to explore environments as such: "to inhabit this world in particular embodied and affective ways, that likewise move through this digital materiality … In doing so we can gain situated understandings … (of) the contingencies through which things emerge and processes occur within it, and the anticipatory modes that people use through which to contemplate their proximate and more distant futures" (Pink 2017:10–11). This resonates with the Deleuzian notion that in any assemblage we must understand how our own (the experimentalist's) body and the singularities and affects of it are meshed with those of machines, models, and material processes in order for learning to occur (Deleuze in DeLanda 2002:177, 197). As Tarek Elhaik suggests, we should take on assemblages of human and non-human form as objects of study rather than those whose voices we allegedly have to hear and care about, and frame "alongside-ness" through a different formulation of power that does not begin with the question of who is speaking on behalf of whom, or designing curative and dialogical approaches to unequal relationships found in the field (Elhaik 2013:795). The assemblage invites for another "speaking nearby." This is what I have attempted to do in asking "*Why* young Muslim women and smartphones."

I have attended to the lived realities and imaginings of the young Muslim women in Blaagaarden, how smartphones allow them to navigate double-bind, and a catch twenty-two situation in a *harakat* way *and* I have attended to what making knowledge with them has afforded in terms of new understandings of knowledge-making practices, smartphone in hand, considering further the mirror image of the Dane, the anthropologist, the Cyborg.

We need more anthropological knowledge about the mirroring taking place specifically in terms of Islam and Muslims in the Euro-American context at this specific historical time of ethno-nationalism on the rise and lurking schismogenesis (Bateson 2000). We need more anthropological knowledge about the affordances of the digital technologies we use and that use us, at this particular historical time—and how that is differently configured in specific contexts. We have a commitment to witness and communicate (Waltorp et al. 2017). In these knowledge pursuits, we need to add to our epistemological and methodological toolbox a broader understanding of "knowledge" than the conscious purpose-driven mind invites for, per the recursive epistemology of Bateson. What I hope to achieve through the presentation of ethnography and through the form of this book is an anthropological "speaking nearby" (Trinh 1989, 1991) that invites the reader to introduce her or his own associations as part of the experience of encountering the ethnographic images I have presented. This is an ethical role assigned to the receiver and consumer of the work (cf. Marks 2000). In between the ethnographic chapters about the place, the people, and the technology, recursively the attempts at displacing metaphors and questions have been pursued. This pursuit has given attention to what emerged between my interlocutors, myself, the technology, and the flow of images; The refracted questions that the ethnography invited for:

An anthropology which never leaves the boundaries of its own conventions, which disdains to invest its imagination in a world of experience, must always remain more an ideology than a science.
(Wagner 1981:14)

Notes

Introduction

1   See Ghetto strategi (2010:38); Økonomi og Indenrigsministeriet (2018). The percentage of residents of other ethnic origin than Danish in Noerrebro is 23.8, and for Copenhagen 14.6 (Blaagaardsvisionen 2016:11).

2   I am aware that the term *Middle East* did not originate from people living in that area (Marks 2015) but situates me geographically as well in the northern part of the world for whom this area becomes—relatively—the Middle East. The same goes for other geographical terms used.

3   My use of assemblage draws on the work of Gilles Deleuze (1991; see also DeLanda 2006), who in his work with Félix Guattari uses the French word *agencement*, which implies the non-reified, processual transformation between entities and the concepts they give rise to in specific connections/constellations (Deleuze and Guattari 2004).

4   Within media studies and "digital ethnography" a broad array of studies has focused on the Internet, social media, and cell phones and smartphones (boyd 2007; boyd and Crawford 2012; Horst and Miller 2012; Ito et al. 2010; Miller and Slater 2000; Miller et al. 2016; Pink et al. 2015; Pink et al. 2016) and newer studies on the relationship between intimacy and the use of mobile phones and social media among young people (cf. Archambault 2011, 2013, 2017; Costa 2018; Costa and Menin 2016). No ethnographic studies with Muslim women's use of smartphones and social media has been carried out in Denmark, though, focused on the specific assemblage, which I have sought to interrogate, tracing what smartphones make possible for young women of the second generation in a Scandinavian welfare state at this particular historical conjuncture.

5   Refraction thus—*technically*—occurs when a wave crosses a boundary from one medium to another (this is always accompanied by a wavelength and speed change).

6   Denmark is not among the 137 of the 193 members of the UN to officially recognize Palestine as a state. In Western Europe and the United States only Iceland (2011) and Sweden (2014) officially recognize Palestine.

7   Migration studies and studies of Islam in Denmark have been the topic of considerable anthropological research over the past decades, continuing a tradition by among others Klaus Ferdinand at Moesgård Museum and Department of Anthropology for research in the Middle East and Central Asia. Since then research has been focused on ethnically or nationally defined groups of

immigrants in Denmark: Turkish migrants (Pedersen and Selmer 1992), Pakistani migrants (Rytter 2013), the Iraqi community and especially women's everyday life (Pedersen 2014), and Palestinian migrants (Kublitz 2011). The concept of "integration" in discourse and practice in Denmark and the encounter between Danes and immigrants has been explored (Larsen 2011; Olwig et al. 2012; Olwig and Pærregård 2007; Rytter 2018), often focused on the institutional setting: the meeting with the asylum system (Whyte 2011); the effects of the official dispersal strategy of asylum seekers and immigrants across the country (Larsen 2011); Danish preschool and school system (Bundgaard & Gulløv 2008; Gilliam 2009; Gilliam and Kühle 2014; Olwig and Gulløv 2003); differing hospitals and healing regimes (Suhr 2013); and the social services and crime prevention and justice system (Johansen 2013). Islam scholar Garbi Schmidt has focused specifically on the area of Noerrebro and its history of immigration (Schmidt 2012, 2015). A number of ethnographic studies have focused on the media portrayal of Muslims in Denmark, and a clear picture emerges whereby Muslims have to continually prove their "Danishness," the suspicion of fundamentalism always lurking (Henkel 2014:334; Hervik 2011). See also Fibiger and Sedgwick (2016) for an overview of Danish Islam scholarship in the last decade.

8 This also depends on whether the *haraka* (singular) is written above or below the letter. In using harakat as slang, it is not discerned whether it is singular or plural, and one would never use haraka, only harakat.

Chapter A

1 This is a part of *zakat*, a tax/donation to those in need and one of the five pillars of Islam.

2 *mahram* relatives are those men a woman is never permitted to marry either because of blood ties, affinity through marriage, or other.

3 Abu-Lughod later returns to this, pointing toward a greater attention to the various forms of resistance, which she believes will "allow us to get at the ways in which intersecting and often conflicting structures of power work together these days in communities that are gradually becoming more tied to multiple and often nonlocal systems. These are central issues for theories of power which anthropologists are in a unique position to consider" (1990:42).

4 Various presentations of self might be, as Katherine Ewing reminds us, what a close observer of another in any social interaction would see—selves that "are highly context-dependent and mutually inconsistent. There is no overarching, cohesive self that is identifiable to an outside observer" (Ewing 1990:259, see also Dalsgård 2013).

5 Older forms of media, especially flow TV, also make up part of this mix as more private discussions in the home become more public and shared through social

media. Scenes that people particularly liked or disliked in popular TV series, such as "Noor" and other soap operas, were shared on Facebook or linked to on YouTube and, thereby, spurred debate on moral issues (Waltorp 2013b). The TV screen can now be taken a snap-photo of while watching a broadcast of a TV series, writing comments directly on the picture before it is sent in the Snapchat app.

Chapter a

1   Following Gregory Bateson, the communicational system "is not the physical individual but a wide network of pathways of messages. Some of these pathways happen to be located outside the physical individual, others inside; but the characteristics of the system are in no way dependent upon any boundary lines, which we may superpose upon the communicational map. It is not communicationally meaningful to ask whether the blind man's stick or the scientist's microscope are important pathways of communication and, as such, are parts of the network in which we are interested; but no boundary line—e.g., halfway up the stick—can be relevant in a description of the topology of this net" (Bateson 2000:256).

2   An afterimage is an image that continues to appear in one's vision after the exposure to the original image has ceased. An afterimage may be a normal phenomenon (physiological afterimage)—afterimages occur because photochemical activity in the retina continues even when you are no longer experiencing the original stimulus.

3   Al-Haytham's investigations into human visual perception led him to the *camera obscura* and to image inversion in the eye. He understood image formation in the eye in terms of a pinhole camera but realized that the pupil is too large to allow the eye to work precisely that way, as visual rays would intermingle and confusion would arise (Pelillo 2014).

4   Gibson rejected behaviorism early on in the 1950s, and in the late 1970s he had further developed his theory into an "ecological approach to visual perception" (Gibson 2015 (1979)), critiquing cognitivism and promoting direct perception.

5   "Big Data" research and methods building on mining the Internet allow for one kind of insights; yet, in-depth ethnographic fieldwork that follows the informants into the digital sphere as an inextricably entangled dimension of social life raises questions of another sort than "Big Data" does on its own.

Chapter B

1   Groups which all women in Danish municipalities are placed in with other women in their neighborhood giving birth around the same time. I lived across from Blaagaarden and we were therefore placed in the same group.

2   There has been a fatigue for a very long time among immigrants in Denmark toward researchers and students arriving to specific areas to do interviews and studies about them, as pointed out by a study as early as the late 1980s (Pedersen and Selmer 1992:15–18). It was important to me not to make the initial contact through the usual municipal "gatekeepers" in the area.

3   Photographs by participants (16–25 years young men and women) and a 12-minute video, filmed by three of the participants including myself, were displayed along with written texts, both on the walls and in the exhibition catalogue. The everyday stories and pictures were juxtaposed with interviews and pictures I had done in prior similar projects with young people, one in the South African township Manenberg outside Cape Town and the other in the French suburb (banlieue) Saint-Denis, north of Paris.

4   In this, I see obvious parallels to my fieldwork in a South African Cape Coloured township, where gangsterism was rife, affecting everyone in the area (Waltorp 2010; Waltorp and Jensen 2018; Waltorp and Vium 2010).

5   Through the Ghetto NO Ghetto project, I was in contact with young men who were former members of the Blaagaards Square Gang (Blaagaards Plads Banden, or BGP). After a fusion with other street gangs, BGP changed their name to Loyal to Familia (LTF). Some of these young men were ethnic Danes, even though it was commonly described as an immigrant gang. Even for those young men who kept their distance, this harsh environment, where some young men would "carry" (have a knife or gun on them for protection), could mean death.

6   In his discussion of what makes up a *Thirdspace* (1996), Edward Soja draws on Henri Lefebvre and Michel Foucault. Interested in the processes of the production of space, the formation of values, and the social production of meanings, which in turn inform spatial practices and perceptions, Soja fuses Henri Lefebvre's *spatial trialectics* (everyday practices and perceptions—*le percu*, representations or theories of space—*le concu*, and the spatial imaginary of the time—*le vecu*, 1991:23) and Michel Foucault's concept of *heterotopia* (1986). Both point to a multiplicity of spaces that are socially produced and made productive in social practices, and on the contradictory, political, conflict-filled, and heterogeneous character of the formation of space and places.

Chapter b

1   Our habitual way of accessing and communicating via keyboards and keypads has generally been ignored (Moores 2015:23, see Pink et al. 2016, though), and Moores draws our attention to this practice. Practices with keyboard, keypad, and touchscreen *do* obviously involve the body, particularly the hands and the sense of

touch; text messaging or texting requires what might be called knowledge in the thumbs, although other fingers are also involved in sliding and tapping (Moores 2015:23, see also Pink et al. 2016).

2 I especially appreciate the following quotation: "Underlying all our mystic states are corporeal techniques, biological methods of entering into communication with God," as it combines intellect, the body/corporeal, time, and the attainment of a different state through these bodily techniques over time (see Mauss 1936).

3 "Social agents are endowed with habitus, inscribed in their bodies by past experiences" (Bourdieu 2000:138), Bourdieu wrote, underscoring the habitus as a system of bodily embedded experiences that makes the individual more disposed to react in one way rather than another (Bourdieu 1990:66–96). He famously described how the habitus is a system of durable dispositions that functions as "structured structures predisposed to function as structuring structures" (Bourdieu 1990:53). And, as this embodiment of the social, the habitus feels at home in the field from which it is born—the field structures habitus as an internalized product of the immanent necessity of the field. Bourdieu's analytical concept of "field" allows an understanding of the social cosmos as composed of a range of relatively autonomous fields. These microcosms, or force fields, are to be understood as social spaces with specific logics or demands that differ from the conditions and sets of rules of other fields (Bourdieu 2000:99; Bourdieu and Waquant 2009:28, 84–85).

4 Information is conceived as available in the ambient energy flux, not as signals in a bundle of nerve fibers. It is information about both the persisting and the changing feature of the environment together (Gibson 2015:251).

Chapter C

1 Perception is learned in the world … The cultural dialectic mediates and arrests the formation of mental images through the means of collective reference points; they become epochal perceptions in conventional language space. Language, the figure-ground reversal of thought, makes it necessary that the reference points, and the perception within them be learned in the world (Wagner 1986:140–141).

2 I have consulted the English translation of the Qur'an by Abdel Haleem (2004), but follow the translations that people themselves have used.

3 Anthropological studies indicate that the appropriate direction of sexual desire seems to be universally governed in terms of incest taboos and various cultural preferences about exogamy, endogamy, and bride wealth/prize, also in a European context where these preferred "rules" might not be perceived as such (cf. Bourdieu 1977).

4   Lila Abu-Lughod's description of her time with the Awlad Ali bedouin, where she—after time—found herself veiling as a habituated, appropriate behavior socioculturally in a specific situation (Abu-Lughod 1986) suddenly resonated.

Chapter c

1   *Guardian,* July 8, 2018: https://www.theguardian.com/world/2018/jul/08/iran-woman-arrested-instagram-video-dancing?CMP=share_btn_tw
2   Which happens to also be my former agency when I was an anthropology undergraduate student *and* a model, grappling with feminist theory and performing in the fashion world simultaneously: an experience that enhanced my interest in the intersections of aesthetics, ethics, and representational politics as related to (gender) norms and ideals.
3   One context of "Pavlovian learning" may, for example, be set within a meta-context which would punish learning of this kind (Bateson 2000:250).

Chapter D

1   Parts of this case are recounted and discussed in Waltorp (2017a).
2   *Du'a* is one kind of prayer, whereas *salat* is the prayer to be performed as one of the five pillars of faith in Islam. Salat al-Istikharah is a prayer recited by Muslims in need of guidance on an issue in their life. The salat is a two *raka'ah* salat performed to completion followed by the supplications *Salat al-Istikharah.*
3   The concepts of *qadar* (fore-ordainment/fate), and *Sabr* (patience) and the particular understanding of time embedded within these concepts, are at odds with the dominant rhetoric of linear time.

Chapter d

1   At a meeting with Iain Edgar at EASA 2014, I had the privilege of discussing a few instances of informants' dreams, as well as fieldwork dreams I had had. See also Edgar (2004:93–94): He proposes a reflexive anthropology with awareness of dreaming, by informants and anthropologist(s) as a necessary part of fieldwork.
2   It is underdetermined as the virtual is to what becomes actualized. In this sense *virtuality* is different from *potentiality,* which can be realized. The mode of virtuality, in Paul Rabinow's reading of Deleuze, moves alongside potentialities and actualities so that these can be taken up and refracted in another form, another mode (Rabinow et al. 2008:49–50).

3   In her work, the imaginal realm also complements contemporary cinematic concepts from Sergei Eisenstein and Gilles Deleuze (Marks 2016).

4   Mohammed Arkoun also works on the *imaginaire* (Arkoun 2003, see also Marks 2016). Arkoun regards the *imaginaire*-concept as "unavoidable when we want to relate political, social, and cultural events to their psychological origins and impacts" (Arkoun 2003:36).

5   Corbin's life was devoted to the struggle to free the religious imagination from fundamentalisms of every kind. He sought to provide a framework for understanding the unity of the Abrahamic religions—"religions of the Book"—Judaism, Christianity, and Islam. His *Creative Imagination in the Sufism of Ibn al-Arabi* (1969) is a classic initiatory text of visionary spirituality that transcends the divisions among the three great monotheisms.

6   "Na-koja-Abad" is another term that Corbin is careful to "translate" to his Western readership: "It does not occur in any Persian dictionary, and it was coined, as far as I know, by Sohravardi himself, from the resources of the purest Persian language. Literally … it signifies the city, the country or land (abad) of No-where (Na-koja). That is why we are here in the presence of a term that, at first sight, may appear to us as the exact equivalent of the term ou-topia, which, for its part, does not occur in the classical Greek dictionaries, and was coined by Thomas Moore as an abstract noun to designate the absence of any localization, of any given situs in a space that is discoverable and verifiable by the experience of our senses. Etymologically and literally, it would perhaps be exact to translate Na-koja-Abad by outopia, utopia, and yet with regard to the concept, the intention, and the true meaning, I believe that we would be guilty of mistranslation" (Corbin 1976:3).

7   See Brian Massumi for an analysis of how the right-wing in the United States has been much more successful at this than their left-wing counterparts (Massumi 2002).

8   The philosophical Islamic ideas of the imaginal realm have interesting correspondences with Jaques Lacan's theory, yet departs with him on the crucial point of the illusion of unity, according to Marks (2016): This unity is possible to attain in states of dreaming or through meditation, whereas for Lacan it is an illusion forever felt as a lack (1966). Contrary to Lacan's approach in *The Mirror Stage* where he reformulates the conception of the ego and the imaginary within psychoanalysis, as always an illusory sense of unity, Laura Marks (2016), on the other hand, proposes that the newer work on the concept of the imaginal realm stems from a tiredness of the "unitary subject"—the illusion of unity not necessarily illusory, but actualized in experiences occurring in night dreams, vision, prayer, and ecstasy.

9   Mark Sedgwick (2016) suggests that the "intercultural transfers" point back to
     Plotinus, interpreter and developer of Plato, today less well known than Plato and
     Aristotle. His ideas and philosophy are known as Neoplatonism (to separate it from
     the earlier Platonism of Plato himself). The basic assumptions in "Emanationism"
     relate to the idea that "human souls share in the divine, and can and should
     return to the divine" (Sedgewick 2016:4). Sedgwick traces and finds intercultural
     transfer from Islam and Sufism to the west, back into Iran, Turkey, and Morocco
     (Sedgewick 2016).

Bibliography

Aaman, K. and A. Uddin (2007), *Mødom på Mode*, Copenhagen: Forlaget Gyldendal.

Abdel Haleem, M. A. S. (2004), *The Qu'ran*, Oxford: Oxford University Press.

Abu-Lughod, L. (2013), *Do Muslim Women Need Saving?*, Boston: Harvard University Press.

Abu-Lughod, L. (2002), "Do Muslim Women Really Need Saving? Anthropological Reflections on Cultural Relativism and Its Others," *American Anthropologist*, 104 (3): 783–790.

Abu-Lughod, L. (1991), "Writing against Culture," in R. G. Fox (ed), *Recapturing Anthropology: Working in the Present*, 137–162, Santa Fe: School of American Research Press.

Abu-Lughod, L. (1990), "The Romance of Resistance: Tracing Transformations of Power through Bedouin Women," *American Ethnologist*, 17 (1): 41–55.

Abu-Lughod, L. (1986), *Veiled Sentiments—Honor and Poetry in a Bedouin Society*, Berkeley: University of California Press.

Ahmad, M. and K. Waltorp (2019), "Kontroversen om Exitcirklen: Racialisering af muslimske kvinder i den danske mediedebat," *Jordens Folk*, 54 (1): 65–78.

Al-Saji, A. (2010), "The Racialization of Muslim Veils: A Philosophical Analysis," *Philosophy and Social Criticism*, 36 (8): 875–902.

Anderson, B. (2006 [1983]), *Imagined Communities: Reflections on the Origin and Spread of Nationalism*, London and New York: Verso.

Archambault, J. S. (2017), *Mobile Secrets. Youth, Intimacy and the Politics of Pretense in Mozambique*, Chicago: University of Chicago Press.

Archambault, J. S. (2013), "Cruising through Uncertainty: Cell Phones and the Politics of Display and Disguise in Inhambane, Mozambique," *Africa*, 82 (3): 392–411.

Archambault, J. S. (2011), "Breaking Up 'Because of the Phone' and the Transformative Powers of Information in Southern Mozambique," *New Media and Society*, 13 (3): 444–456.

Arkoun, M. (2003), "Rethinking Islam Today." *The ANNALS of the American Academy of Political and Social Science*, 588 (1): 18–39.

Arendt, H. (1998), *The Human Condition*, Chicago: University of Chicago Press.

Arendt, H. (1993), *Between Past and Future: Eight Exercises in Political Thought*, New York: Penguin.

Asad, T. (2009), "Free Speech, Blasphemy and Secular Criticism," in T. Asad, W. Brown, J. Butler, and S. Mahmood (eds), *Is Critique Secular? Blasphemy, Injury, and Free Speech*, 20–63, Berkeley: University of California.

Asad, T. (2002), "Muslims and European Identity: Can Europe Represent Islam?" in A. Pagden (ed), *The Idea of Europe: From Antiquity to the European Union*, 209–227, Cambridge: Cambridge University Press.

Bateson, G. (2000 [1972]), *Steps to an Ecology of Mind: Collected Essays in Anthropology, Psychiatry, Evolution and Epistemology*, Chicago: The University of Chicago Press.

Bateson, N. (2018), "The Era of Emergency Relocation—A Transcontextual Perspective." https://norabateson.wordpress.com/2018/03/22/the-era-of-emergency-relocation-a-transcontextual-perspective/ (consulted March 30, 2019).

Bauer, J. (2005), "Corrupted Alterities: Body Politics in the Time of the Iranian Diaspora," in A. Masquelier (ed), *Dirt, Undress and Difference. Critical Perspectives on the Body's Surface*, 233–249, Indianapolis: Indiana University Press.

Benjamin, W. (1986), *Illuminations. Essays and Reflections*, New York: Schocken Books.

Bergson, H. (1920), *Mind-Energy: Lectures and Essays*, London: Macmillan.

Blaagaardsvisionen (2016), https://fsb.dk/nyheder/2016/blaagardsvisionen/ (consulted October 2, 2016).

Bourdieu, P. (2000), *Pascalian Meditations*, Cambridge: Polity Press.

Bourdieu, P. (1999), *The Weight of the World*, New York: Polity Press.

Bourdieu, P. (1990), *The Logic of Practice*, Cambridge: Blackwell Publishers.

Bourdieu, P. (1977), *Outline of a Theory of Practice*, Cambridge: Cambridge University Press.

Bourdieu, P. and L. Waquant (2009), *Refleksiv Sociologi—Mål og midler*, København: Hans Reitzels Forlag.

boyd, d. (2007), "Why Youth (Heart) Social Network Sites: The Role of Networked Publics in Teenage Social Life," in D. Buckingham (ed), *MacArthur Foundation Series on Digital Learning—Youth, Identity, and Digital Media Volume*, 1–26, Cambridge: MIT Press.

boyd, d. and K. Crawford (2012), "Critical Questions for Big Data: Provocations for a Cultural, Technological, and Scholarly Phenomenon," *Information, Communication, & Society*, 15 (5): 662–679.

Boyer, D. and C. Howe (2015), "Portable Analytics and Lateral Theory," in D. Boyer, J. D. Faubion, and G. E. Marcus (eds), *Theory Can Be More Than It Used to Be. Learning Anthropology's Method in a Time of Transition*, 15–38, Ithaca: Cornell University Press.

Braagard, N. (2015), "Nørrebrobande afviser mægling." http://nyheder.Tv2.dk/article.php/id-21059916%3An%83%C2%B8rrebrobandeafviserm%C3%83%C2%A6gling.html (consulted August 5, 2016).

Brecht, B. (1964 [1936]), "Alienation Effects in Chinese Acting," in J. Willet (ed), *Brecht on Theatre: The Development of an Aesthetic*, 91–120, London: Methuen.

Bubandt, N. O., Rytter, M., and Suhr, C. (2019), A Second Look at Invisibility: Al-Ghayb, Islam, Ethnography. *Contemporary Islam*, 13 (1): 1–16.

Bundgaard, H. and E. Gulløv (2008), *Forskel og fællesskab. Minoritetsbørn i daginstitution*, København: Hans Reitzels Forlag.

Butler, J. (1990), *Gender Trouble: Feminism and the Subversion of Identity*, New York: Routledge.

Canevacci, M. (2012), "Digital Auratic Reproducibility: Ubiquitous Ethnographies and Communicational Metropolis." In Naidoo, L. (ed), *An Ethnography of Global Landscapes and Corridors*. London: IntechOpen.

Castaing-Taylor, L. (2016), "Sweetgrass. Blaaaaaaah. Bleeeeeeet," in R. Cox, A. Irving, and C. Wright (eds), *Beyond Text? Critical Practices and Sensory Anthropology*, 148–155, Manchester: Manchester University Press.

Chambers, R. (1997), *Whose Reality Counts? Putting the First Last*, London: Intermediate Technology Publications.

Chittick, W. (1994), *Imaginal Worlds: Ibn Al-'Arabi and the Problem of Religious Diversity*, Albany: State University of New York Press.

Crenshaw, K. (1991), "Mapping the Margins: Intersectionality, Identity Politics, and Violence against Women of Color," *Stanford Law Review*, 43 (6): 1241–1299.

Cooley, C. H. (1922), *Human Nature and the Social Order*, New York: Charles Scribner's Sons.

Corbin, H. (1976), *Mundus Imaginalis: Or, the Imaginary and the Imaginal*, Ipswich: Golgonooza Press.

Corbin, H. and R. Mannheim (eds) (1969), *Creative Imagination in the Sufism of Ibn al-Arabi*, Princeton: Princeton University Press.

Corzín-Jimenez, A. (2003), "On Space as a Capacity," *The Journal of the Royal Anthropological Institute*, 9 (1): 137–153.

Costa, E. (2018), "Affordances-in-practice: An Ethnographic Critique of Social Media Logic and Context Collapse," *New Media and Society*, 20 (10): 3641–3656.

Costa, E. (2016), *Social Media in Southeast Turkey: Love, kinship and Politics*. London: UCL Press.

Costa, E. and L. Menin (2016), "Introduction: Digital Intimacies: Exploring Digital Media and Intimate Lives in the Middle East and North Africa," *Middle East Journal of Culture and Communication*, 9 (2): 137–145.

Cox, R., A. Irving, and C. Wright (eds) (2016), *Beyond Text? Critical Practices and Sensory Anthropology*, Manchester: Manchester University Press.

Dahl, K. M., S. Henze-Pedersen, S. Østergaard, and J. Østergaard (eds) (2018), *Unges opfattelser af køn, krop og seksualitet*, Copenhagen: Det Nationale Forsknings- og Analysecenter for Velfærd, VIVE.

Dalsgård, A. L. (2013), "Being a Montage," in C. Suhr and R. Willerslev (eds), *Transcultural Montage*, 100–105, London: Berghahn Books.

Danmarks Statistik (2014), *Indvandrere i Danmark*. Copenhagen: PRinfoParitas.

Dattatreyan, E. G. and I. Marrero-Guillamón (2019), "Introduction: Multimodal Anthropology and the Politics of Invention," *American Anthropologist*, 121 (1): 220–228.

de Certeau, M. (1984), *The Practice of Everyday Life*, Berkeley: University of California Press.

Dehghan, S. K. (2018), *Guardian*, July 8, 2018. https://www.theguardian.com/world/2018/jul/08/iran-woman-arrested-instagram-video-dancing?CMP=share_btn_tw (consulted July 19, 2018).

Dehghan, S. (2018), "Woman Arrested in Iran over Instagram Video of Her Dancing," *The Guardian* July 9, 2018. https://www.theguardian.com/world/2018/jul/08/iran-woman-arrested-instagram-video-dancing?CMP=share_btn_tw (consulted July 19, 2018).

Dehghan, S. (2015), "Iranian Woman Wins Rights Award for Hijab Campaign," *The Guardian* February 24, 2015. https://www.theguardian.com/world/2015/feb/24/ iranian-woman-wins-rights-award-hijab-campaign (consulted July 19, 2018).

DeLanda, M. (2006), *A New Philosophy of Society: Assemblage Theory and Social Complexity*, London: Bloomsbury.

DeLanda, M. (2002), *Intensive Science and Virtual Philosophy*, London: Continuum.

Deleuze, G. (1994), *Difference and Repetition*, New York: Columbia University Press.

Deleuze, G. (1991 [1980]), *Bergsonism*, New York: Zone Books.

Deleuze, G. (1989), *Cinema 2: The Time-Image*, Minneapolis: University of Minnesota Press.

Deleuze, G. and F. Guattari (2004 [1987]), *A Thousand Plateaus: Capitalism and Schizophrenia*, London: Continuum.

Derrida, J. (1992), *Given Time: 1. Counterfeit Money*, Chicago: University of Chicago Press.

Douglas, M. (1966), *Purity & Danger: An Analysis of the Concepts of Pollution and Taboo*, New York: Routledge and Kegan Paul.

Drotner, K. (2011), *Redegørelse. Unges mediebrug. Demokrati for Fremtiden Valgretskommissionen betænkning om unges demokratiske engagement*, Copenhagen: Dansk Ungdoms Fællesråd.

Dumit, J. (2014), "Writing the Implosion: Teaching the World One Thing at a Time," *Cultural Anthropology*, 29 (2): 344–362.

Edgar, I. (2004), *Guide to Imagework: Imagination-Based Research Methods*, London: Routledge.

Edgar, I. and D. Henig (2010), "*Isthikara*: The Guidance and Practice of Islamic Dream Incubation through Ethnographic Comparison," *History and Anthropology*, 21 (3): 251–262.

El Guindi, F. (1999), *Veil. Modesty, Privacy and Resistance*, London: Bloomsbury.

Elhaik, T. (2013), "What Is Contemporary Anthropology?," *Critical Arts*, 27 (6): 784–798.

El-Tayeb, F. (2017), *European Others. EuroZine*. https://www.eurozine.com/european-others/?pdf (consulted July 19, 2018).

El-Tayeb, F. (2011), *European Others: Queering Ethnicity in Postnational Europe*, Minneapolis: University of Minnesota Press.

Estalella, A. and T. Sánchez Criado (eds) (2018), *Experimental Collaborations: Ethnography through Fieldwork Devices*, Oxford: Berghahn.

Ewing, K. P. (2006), "Revealing and Concealing: Interpersonal Dynamics and the Negotiation of Identity in the Interview," *ETHOS*, 34 (1): 89–122.

Ewing, K. P. (1994), "Dreams from a Saint: Anthropological Atheism and the Temptation to Believe," *American Anthropologist*, 96 (3): 571–583.

Ewing, K. P. (1990), "The Illusion of Wholeness: Culture, Self, and the Experience of Inconsistency," *Ethos*, 18 (3): 251–278.

Fadil, N. and M. Fernando (2015a), "Rediscovering the 'Everyday' Muslim. Notes on an Anthropological Divide," *Hau: Journal of Ethnographic Theory*, 5 (2): 59–88.

Fadil, N. and M. Fernando (2015b), "What Is Anthropology's Object of Study? A Counter-response to Schielke and Deeb," *Hau: Journal of Ethnographic Theory*, 5 (2): 97–100.

Fanon, F. (1967), *Black Skin, White Masks*, New York: Groove Press Inc.

Favero, P. S. H. and E. Theunissen (2018), "With the Smartphone as Field Assistant: Designing, Making, and Testing EthnoAlly, a Multimodal Tool for Conducting Serendipitous Ethnography in a Multisensory World," *American Anthropologist*, February 21. http://www.americananthropologist.org/2018/02/21/with-the-smartphone-as-field-assistant (consulted January 12, 2019).

Fernando, M. (2014), *The Republic Unsettled: Muslim French and the Contradictions of Secularism*, Durham: Duke University Press.

Fernando, M. (2013), "Save the Muslim Woman, Save the Republic: Ni putes Ni Soumises and the Ruse of Neoliberal Sovereignty," *Modern & Contemporary France*, 21 (2): 147–165.

Fibiger, T. and M. Sedgwick (2016), "Islamforskning på Aarhus Universitet: (snart) ti år med ICSRU," *Tidsskrift for Islamforskning*, 10 (1): 63–73.

Foucault, M. (1986), "Of Other Spaces," *Diacritics*, 16 (1): 22–27.

Foucault, M. (1975), *Discipline and Punish: The Birth of the Prison*, New York: Random House.

Gershon, I. (2011), "Un-Friend My Heart: Facebook, Promiscuity, and Heartbreak in a Neoliberal Age," *Anthropological Quarterly*, 84 (4): 865–894.

Ghetto Strategi (2010), *Ghettoen tilbage til samfundet*. www.stm.dk/publikationer/Ghetto-strategi_10/Ghettostrategi.pdf (consulted February 20, 2011).

Gibson, J. J. (2015 [1979]), *The Ecological Approach to Visual Perception*, New York: Taylor & Francis Group.

Gilliam, L. (2009), *De umulige børn og det ordentlige menneske: identitet, ballade og muslimske fællesskaber blandt etniske minoritetsbørn*, Århus: Aarhus Universitetsforlag.

Gilliam, L. and L. Kühle (2014), "Introduktion: Muslimske børn i den sekulære danske folkeskole," *Tidsskrift for Islamforskning*, 8 (2): 1–16.

Ginsburg, F. (1995), "The Parallax Effect: The Impact of Aboriginal Media on Ethnographic Film," *Visual Anthropology Review*, 11 (2): 64–76.

Gupta, A. and J. Ferguson (1997), *Culture, Power, Place: Explorations in Critical Anthropology*, Durham: Duke University Press.

Hage, G. (2014), "Eavesdropping on Bourdieu's Philosophers," in Das. V., M. Jackson, A. Kleinman, B. Singh (eds), *The Ground Between: Anthropologists Engage Philosophy*, 138–158, Durham: Duke University Press.

Hage, G. (2005), "A Not So Multi-sited Ethnography of a Not So Imagined Community," *Anthropological Theory*, 5 (4): 463–475.

Hall, S. (1980), "Encoding/decoding, in Hall," in S. D. Hobson, A. Love, and P. Willis (eds), *Culture, Media, Language*, 128–138, London: Hutchinson.

Haraway, D. (1988), "Situated Knowledges: The Science Question in Feminism and the Privilege of Partial Perspective," *Feminist Studies*, 14 (3), 575–599.

Haraway, D. (1985), "A Manifesto for Cyborgs: Science, Technology, and Socialist Feminism in the 1980s," *Socialist Review*, 15 (2): 65–107.

Henare, A., M. Holbraad, and S. Wastell (eds) (2007), *Thinking through Things: Theorising Artefacts Ethnographically*, London: Routledge.

Henkel, H. (2014), "Denmark," in Frank Peter (ed), *Islamist Movements of Europe*, 330–336, London: I.B. Tauris.

Henkel, H. (2011), "Contesting Danish Civility: The Cartoon Crisis as Transitional Drama," in K. F. Olwig and K. Pærregaard (eds), *The Question of Integration: Immigration, Exclusion and the Danish Welfare State*, 129–149, Newcastle upon Tyne: Cambridge Scholars Publishing.

Henkel, H. (2010), "Fundamentally Danish?" *Human Architecture*, 8 (2): 67–82.

Hervik P. (2011), *The Annoying Difference: The Emergence of Danish Neonationalism, Neoracism, and Populism in the Post-1989-world*, Oxford: Berghahn Books.

Hirschkind, C. (2006), *The Ethical Soundscape: Cassette Sermons and Islamic Counterpublics*, New York: Columbia University Press.

Horst, H. A. and D. Miller (eds) (2012), *Digital Anthropology*, London: Bloomsbury.

Howes, D. (2011), "Reply to Tim Ingold." *Social Anthropology*, 19: 318–322. doi: 10.1111/j.1469-8676.2011.00164.x.

Hu, T-H. (2015), *A Pre-History of the Cloud*, Cambridge: MIT Press.

Ingold, T. (2011), "Reply to David Howes." *Social Anthropology*, 19: 323–327. doi: 10.1111/j.1469-8676.2011.00165.x.

Ingold, T. (2000), *The Perception of the Environment. Essays on Livelihood, Dwelling and Skill*, London: Routledge.

Irving, A. (2017), *The Art of Life and Death: Radical Aesthetics and Ethnographic Practice*, Chicago: HAU Books.

Irving, A. (2016), "New York Stories," *Ethnos: Journal of Anthropology*, 82 (3): 437–457.

Irving, A. (2006), "The Skin of the City," *Anthropological Yearbook of European Culture*, 15: 9–36.

Ismail, A. M. (2015), "Muhajababes—Meet the New Fashionable, Attractive and Extrovert Muslim Woman. A Study of the Hijab-Practice among Individualized Young Muslim Women in Denmark," *Journal of Islamic Research*, 9 (2): 106–129.

Ito, M., S. Baumer, M. Bittanti, d. boyd, R. Cody, B. Herr-Stephenson, H. Horst, P. Lange, D. Mahendran, K. Z. Martínez, C. J. Pascoe, D. Perkel, L. Robinson, C. Sims, and L. Tripp (2010), *Hanging Out, Messing Around, and Geeking Out. Kids Living and Learning with New Media*, Cambridge: MIT Press.

Jacobsen, S. J., T. G., Jensen, K. Vitus, and K. Vebel (2012), *Analysis of Danish Media Setting and Framing of Muslims, Islam and Racism*, Copenhagen: The Danish National Centre for Social Research.

Johansen, M-L. (2013), *In the Borderland: Palestinian Parents Navigating Danish Welfare State Interventions*. PhD dissertation, School of Culture and Society, Aarhus.

Kaur, R. (2016), "Who Says You're a Dane?," *New York Times*. http://www.nytimes.com/2016/10/18/opinion/who-says-youre-a-dane.html?_r=0 (consulted December 16, 2016).

Khan, N. (2010), "Images That Come Unbidden: Some Thoughts on the Danish
    Cartoons Controversy," *Borderlands*, 9 (3). http://www.borderlands.net.au/
    vol9no3_2010/khan_images.pdf (consulted December 16, 2016).
Knappett, C. (2004), "The Affordances of Things: A Post-Gibsonian Perspective on the
    Relationality of Mind and Matter," in C. Gosden DeMarrais and C. Renfrew (eds),
    Rethinking Materiality: The Engagement of Mind with the Material World, 43–51,
    Cambridge: McDonald Institute for Archaelogical Research.
Kublitz, A. (2015), "The Cartoon Controversy: Creating Muslims in a Danish Setting,"
    in L. Meinert and B. Kapferer (eds), *In the Event: Toward an Anthropology of Generic
    Moments*, 107–125, Oxford: Berghahn Books.
Kublitz, A. (2011), *The Mutable Conflict: A Study of How the Palestinian-Israeli Conflict
    Is Actualized among Palestinians in Denmark*, PhD dissertation, Department of
    Anthropology, Copenhagen: University of Copenhagen.
Lacan, J. (1966), *Ècrits: A Selection*, New York: Norton.
Larsen, B. R. (2011), *Ind i Danmark: Skabelse af sted og tilhørsforhold blandt nyankomne
    flygtningefamilier bosat i mindre danske lokalsamfund*, PhD dissertation, Department
    of Anthropology, Copenhagen: Museum Tusculanum Press.
Lee, J. and T. Ingold (2006), "Fieldwork on Foot: Perceiving, Routing, Socializing,"
    in P. Collins and S. Coleman (eds), *Locating the Field. Space, Place and Context in
    Anthropology*, 67–86, Oxford: Berg.
Lefebvre H. (1991), *The Production of Space*, Oxford: Blackwell Publisher.
Lindström, K. and Å Ståhl (2016), "Politics of Inviting: Co-Articulations of Issues in
    Designerly Public Engagement," in R. C. Smith, K. T. Vangkilde, M. G. Kjaersgaard,
    T. Otto, J. Halse, and T. Binder (eds), *Design Anthropological Futures*, 183–198,
    London: Bloomsbury.
Lorde, A. (1983 [1981]), "An Open Letter to Mary," in C. Moraga and G. E. Anzaldúa
    (eds), *This Bridge Called My Back: Writings by Radical Women of Color*, 94–97,
    New York: Kitchen Table Women of Color Press.
Louw, M. (2010), "Dreaming Up Futures: Dream Omens and Magic in Bishkek," *History
    and Anthropology*, 21 (3): 277–292.
MacDougall, D. (2019), *The Looking Machine: Essays on Cinema, Anthropology and
    Documentary Filmmaking*, Manchester: Manchester University Press.
MacDougall D. (1998), *Transcultural Cinema*, Princeton: Princeton University Press.
Madianou, M. and D. Miller (2012), *Migration and New Media: Transnational Families
    and Polymedia*, London: Routledge.
Mahmood, S. (2012 [2004]), *Politics of Piety: The Islamic Revival and the Feminist
    Subject*, Princeton: Princeton University Press.
Mahmood, S. (2009), "Religious Reason and Secular Affect: An Incommensurable
    Divide?" in T. Asad, W. Brown, J. Butler, and S. Mahmood (eds), *Is Critique Secular?
    Blasphemy, Injury, and Free Speech*, 64–100, Berkeley: University of California.
Marcus, G. E. and M. J. Fischer (1999 [1986]), *Anthropology as Cultural Critique. An
    Experimental Moment in the Human Sciences*, Chicago: The University of Chicago
    Press.

Marks, L. U. (2016), "Real Images Flow: Mullâ Sadrâ Meets Film-Philosophy," *Film-Philosophy*, 20 (1): 24–46.

Marks, L. U. (2015), *Hanan al-Cinema: Affections for the Moving Image*, London: MIT Press.

Marks, L. U. (2010), *Enfoldment and Infinity. An Islamic Genealogy of New Media Art*, London: MIT Press.

Marks, L. U. (2000), *The Skin of the Film: Intercultural Cinema, Embodiment, and the Senses*, Durham NC: Duke University Press.

Massumi, B. (2002), *Parables of the Virtual. Movement, Affect, Sensation*, Durham and London: Duke University Press.

Masquelier, A. (ed) (2005), *Dirt, Undress and Difference. Critical Perspectives on the Body's Surface*, Indianapolis: Indiana University Press.

Mauss, M. (1936), "Les Techniques du Corps," *Journal de Psychologie*, XXXII (3–4): 1–23.

Mchangama, J. and F. Stjernfelt (2016), *Men. Ytringsfrihedens historie i Danmark*, Copenhagen: Gyldendal.

Mead, M. (2001 [1928]), *Coming of Age in Samoa: A Psychological Study of Primitive Youth for Western Civilisation*, New York: Harper Perennial.

Mead, G. H. (1962 [1934]), *Mind, Self, and Society. From the Standpoint of a Social Behaviourist*, Chicago: The University of Chicago Press.

Menin, L. (2018), "Texting Romance: Mobile Phones, Intimacy and Gendered Moralities in Central Morocco," *Contemporary Levant*, 3 (1): 66–78.

Miller, D. and D. Slater (2000), *The Internet: An Ethnographic Approach*, London: Berg.

Miller, D., E. Costa, N. Haynes, T. McDonald, R. Nicolescu, J. Sinanan, J. Spyer, S. Venkatraman, and X. Wang (2016), *How the World Changed Social Media*, London: UCL Press.

Mittermaier, A. (2012), "Dreams from Elsewhere: Muslim Subjectivities beyond the Trope of Self-cultivation," *Journal of the Royal Anthropological Institute*, 18: 247–265.

Mittermaier, A. (2011), *Dreams That Matter: Egyptian Landscapes of the Imagination*, California: University of California Press.

Moores, S. (2015), "We Find Our Way About: Everyday Media Use and 'Inhabitant Knowledge'," *Mobilities*, 10 (1): 17–35.

Moors, A. and E. Tarlo (2007), "Introduction," *Fashion Theory*, 11 (2–3): 133–141.

Narayan, K. (1993), "How Native Is a 'Native' Anthropologist," *American Anthropologist*, 95 (3): 671–686.

Nasr, S. H. (1972), *Sufi Essays*, London and Albany, New York: State University of New York Press.

Novaes, S. (1997), *The Play of Mirrors. The Representation of Self Mirrored in the Other*, Austin: University of Texas Press.

Olwig, K. F. and K. Pærregaard (eds) (2007), *Integration: antropologiske perspektiver*, Copenhagden: Museum Tusculanum Press.

Olwig, K. F. and E. Gulløv (eds) (2003), *Children's Places: Cross-cultural Perspectives*, London: Routledge.

Olwig, K. F., B. R. Larsen, and M. Rytter (eds) (2012), *Migration, Family and the Welfare State: Integrating Migrants and Refugees in Scandinavia*, London: Routledge.

Otto, T. (2016), "History In and for Design," *Journal of Design History*, 29 (1): 58–70.

Otto, T., C. Suhr, P. Crawford, K. Waltorp, A. Høgel, and C. Vium, (2018), "Camera, Intervention and Cultural Critique: An Introduction," *Journal of Visual Anthropology*, 31 (4–5): 307–317.

Ould Ahmed Salem, Z. (2001), "'Tcheb-tchib' et compagnie: lexique de la survie et figures de la réussite en Mauritanie," *Politique Africaine*, 82: v78–100.

Pandolfo, S. (2018), *Knot of the Soul: Madness, Psychoanalysis, Islam*, Chicago: University of Chicago Press.

Pandolfo, S. (1997), *Impasse of the Angels: Scenes from a Moroccan Space of Memory*, Chicago: University of Chicago Press.

Pedersen, L. and B. Selmer (1992), *Muslimsk indvandrerungdom. Kulturel identitet og migration*, Aarhus: Aarhus Universitetsforlag.

Pedersen, M. H. (2014), *Iraqi Women in Denmark: Ritual Performance and Belonging in Everyday Life*, Manchester: Manchester University Press.

Pedersen, M. H. and M. Rytter (2013), "A Decade of Suspicion: Islam and Muslims in Denmark after 9/11," *Ethnic and Racial Studies*, 37 (13): 2303–2321.

Pedersen, M. H. and M. Rytter (eds) (2011), *Islam og muslimer i Danmark. Religion, identitet og sikkerhed efter 11. september 2001*, Copenhagen: Museum Tusculanum.

Pelillo, M. (2014), "Alhazen and the Nearest Neighbor Rule," *Pattern Recognition Letters*, 38: 34–37.

Pink, S. (2017), "Ethics in a Changing World: Embracing Uncertainty, Understanding Futures, and Making Responsible Interventions," in S. Pink, V. Fors, and T. O'Dell (eds), *Working in the Between: Theoretical Scholarship and Applied Practice*, 29–52, Oxford: Berghahn.

Pink, S. (2017), "Technologies, Possibilities, Emergence and an Ethics of Responsibility: Refiguring Techniques," in E. Gómez Cruz, S. Sumartojo, and S. Pink (eds), *Refiguring Techniques in Digital Visual Research*, 1–12, London: Palgrave Macmillan.

Pink, S. (2015), *Doing Sensory Ethnography* (second ed.), London: Sage.

Pink, S. (2013), *Doing Visual Ethnography*. Revised and expanded 3rd edition, London: Sage.

Pink, S. (ed) (2012), *Advances in Visual Methodology*, London: Sage.

Pink, S. (2012), *Situating Everyday Life: Practices and Places*, London: Sage.

Pink, S. (2007), "Walking with Video," *Visual Studies*, 22 (3): 240–252.

Pink, S. (2006), *The Future of Visual Anthropology: Engaging the Senses*, London: Routledge.

Pink, S. (2004), *Home Truths: Gender, Domestic Objects and Everyday Life*, Oxford: Berg.

Pink, S. (1997), *Women and Bullfighting: Gender, Sex and the Consumption of Tradition*, Oxford: Berg.

Pink, S. and J. F. Salazar (2017), "Anthropology and Futures: Setting the Agenda," in
J. F. Salazar, S. Pink, A. Irving and J. Sjöberg (eds), *Anthropologies and Futures:
Techniques for Researching an Uncertain World*, 3–21, Oxford: Bloomsbury.

Pink, S., J. Sinanan, L. Hjorth, and H. Horst (2015), "Tactile Digital Ethnography:
Researching Mobile Media through the Hand," *Mobile Media & Communication*,
4 (2): 237–251.

Pink, S., H. Horst, J. Postill, L. Hjorth, T. Lewis, and J. Tacchi (2016), *Digital
Ethnography. Principles and Practice*, London: Sage.

Plambech, S. (2016), "Kvinder er en Kampplads," *Information*, September 10. https://www.
information.dk/moti/2016/09/kvinder-kampplads (consulted November 16, 2016).

Possing, D. H. and B. S. Johansen (2014), "Muslim Internet Sites in Denmark," in P. Frank
and O. Rafael (eds), *Islamic Movements of Europe. Public Religion and Islamophobia in
the Modern World a "European Islam,"* 294–297, New York: I.B. Tauris.

Qureshi, K. (2013), "Sabar: Body Politics among Middle-aged Pakistani Migrant
Women," *Journal of the Royal Anthropological Institute*, 19 (1): 120–137.

Rabinow, P., G. E. Marcus, J. D. Fabion, and T. Rees (2008), *Designs for an Anthropology
of the Contemporary*, Durham: Duke University Press.

Rasmussen, A. E. (2015a), *In the Absence of the Gift: New forms of Value and Personhood
in a Papua New Guinea Community*, Oxford: Berghan Books.

Rasmussen, A. E. (2015b), "Visible While Away: Migration, Personhood and the
Movement of Money amongst the Mbuke of Papua New Guinea," in Ø. Fuglerud and
L. Wainwright (eds), "Objects and Imagination: Perspectives on Materialization and
Meaning," *Material Mediations*, 3: 81–92.

Regeringen, Økonomi- og Indenrigsministeriet (2018), Ét Danmark uden
parallelsamfund. Ingen ghettoer i 2030. København.

Rouch J. and S. Feld (ed) (2003), *Ciné-Ethnography*, Minnesota: University of
Minnesota Press.

Rytter, M. (2018), "Writing against Integration: Danish Imaginaries of Culture," Race
and Belonging, Ethnos, 84: 4, 678–697.

Rytter, M. (2013), *Family Upheaval: Generation, Mobility and Relatedness among
Pakistani Migrants in Denmark*, Oxford: Berghahn Books.

Rytter, M. and M. H. Pedersen (2014), "A Decade of Suspicion: Islam and Muslims in
Denmark after 9/11," *Ethnic and Racial Studies*, 37 (13): 2303–2321.

Rytter, M. and M. H. Pedersen (eds) (2011), *Islam og muslimer I Danmark: Religion,
identitet og sikkerhed efter 11. September 2001*, Copenhagen: Museum Tusculanum.

Sabra, A. I. (1989), *The Optics of Ibn al-Haytham (Books I-III on Direct Vision)*, London:
The Warburg Institute.

Said, E. W. (1978), *Orientalism*, New York: Vintage.

Salazar, J. F., S. Pink, A. Irving, and J. Sjoberg (eds) (2017), *Anthropologies and Futures:
Techniques for Researching an Uncertain World*, Oxford: Bloomsbury.

Sayad, A. (2004), *Suffering of the Immigrant*, Cambridge: Polity Press.

Sayad, A. (1979), "Les enfants illégitimes' (1ère partie)," *Actes de la recherche en sciences
sociales*, 25: 61–81.

Schielke, S. (2015), "Living with Unresolved Differences. A Reply to Fadil and Fernando," *Hau: Journal of Ethnographic Theory*, 5 (2): 89–92.

Schielke, S. (2010), "Second Thought about the Anthropology of Islam, or How to Make Sense of Grand Schemes in Everyday Life," Working Papers 2. Centrum ModerneOrient. https://www.zmo.de/publikationen/workingpapers/schielke_2010.pdf. (consulted May 13, 2013).

Schielke, S. and L. Debevec (2012), "Introduction," in S. Schielke and L. Debevec (eds), *Ordinary Lives and Grand Schemes: An Anthropology of Everyday Religion*, 1–16, New York: Berghahn Books.

Schmidt, G. (2015), "Space, Politics and Past–present Diversities in a Copenhagen Neighbourhood," *Identities. Global Studies in Culture and Power*, 23 (1): 51–65.

Schmidt, G. (2012), "Nørrebro and 'Muslimness': A Neighbourhood Caught between National Myths-capes and Local Engagement," in J. Nielsen (ed), *Islam in Denmark: The Challenge of Diversity*, 95–114, Lanham: Lexington Books.

Scott, J. W. (2010), *The Politics of the Veil*, Princeton: Princeton University Press.

Scott, J. (1985), *Weapons of the Weak: Everyday Forms of Peasant Resistance*, Princeton: Yale University Press.

Sedgwick, M. (2016), *Western Sufism: From the Abbasids to the New Age*, New York: Oxford University Press.

Sedgwick, M. (2014), "Introduction: Families, Governments, Schools, Alternative Spaces and the Making of European Muslims," in M. Sedgewick (ed), *Making European Muslims: Religious Socialization among Young Muslims in Scandinavia and Western Europe*, 1–17, New York: Routledge.

Sharif, S. (2016), *Look. Poems*, Minneapolis: Graywolf Press.

Simonsen, J. B. (2012), "Denmark, Islam and Muslims: Socioeconomic Dynamics and the Art of Becoming," in Jørgen S. Nielsen (ed), *Islam in Denmark: The Challenge of Diversity*, 13–30, Lanham: Lexington Books.

Simonsen, J. B. (2006), *Hvad er islam*, København: Akademisk Forlag.

Simonsen, J. B. (1990), *Islam i Danmark. Muslimske institutioner i Danmark 1970–1989*, Aarhus: Aarhus Universitetsforlag.

Sneath, D., M. Holbraad, and M. Pedersen (2009), "Technologies of the Imagination: An Introduction," *Ethnos*, 74 (1): 5–30.

Soja, E. W. (1996), *Thirdspace: Journeys to Los Angeles and Other Real and Imagined Places*, Cambridge: Blackwell.

Stoller, P. (2008), *The Power of the Between: An Anthropological Odyssey*, Chicago: The University of Chicago Press.

Stoller, P. (1997), *Sensuous Scholarship*, Philadelphia: University of Pennsylvania Press.

Strathern, M. (1999), *Property, Substance and Effect: Anthropological Essays on Persons and Things*, London: Athlone.

Strathern, M. (1994), "Parts and Wholes: Refiguring Relationships," in R. Borofsky (ed), *Assessing Cultural Anthropology*, 204–217, New York: McGraw-Hill.

Strathern, M. (1988), *The Gender of the Gift: Problems with Women and Problems with Society in Melanesia*, Berkeley: University of California Press.

Suhr, C. (2013), *Descending with Angels: The Invisible in Danish Psychiatry*, PhD
dissertation, School of Culture and Society, Aarhus: Aarhus University.

Tarlo, E. (2010), *Visibly Muslim: Fashion, Politics, Faith*, Oxford: Berg.

Tarlo, E. (2007), "Hijab in London: Metamorphosis, Resonance and Effects," *Journal of Material Culture*, 12 (2): 131–156.

Tarlo, E. (2005), "Reconsidering Stereotypes: Anthropological Reflections on the Jilbab Controversy," *Anthropology Today*, 21 (6): 13–16.

Tarlo, E. and A. Moors (eds) (2013), *Islamic Fashion and Anti-Fashion: New Perspectives from Europe and North America*, London: Bloomsbury.

Thomas, M. E. (2005), "Girls, Consumption Space and the Contradictions of Hanging Out in the City," *Social Cultural Geography*, 6 (4): 587–605.

Trinh T. Minh-ha (1991), *Cinema Interval*, New York: Routledge.

Trinh T. Minh-ha (1989), *Woman, Native, Other. Writing Postcoloniality and Feminism*, Indianapolis: Indiana University Press.

Tuan Y.-F. (2004), *Place, Art, and Self*, Santa Fe: University of Virginia Press.

Vigh, H. (2009), "Motion Squared: A Second Look at the Concept of Social Navigation," *Anthropological Theory*, 9 (4): 419–438.

Vigh, H. (2006), *Navigating Terrains of War: Youth and Soldiering in Guinea-Bissau*, Oxford: Berghahn.

Vium, C. (2017), "Fixating a Fluid Field: Photography as Anthropology in Migration Research," A. Elliot, R. Norum, and N. Salazar (eds), *Methodologies of Mobility: Ethnography and Experiment*, 172–194, London: Berghahn.

Vium, C. (2016), "Enacting Immanent Potentialities: Tcheb-Tchib Strategies at the Centre of the Urban Fringe in Nouakchott, Mauritania," *Singapore Journal of Tropical Geography*, 37 (3): 343–363.

Vium, C. (2014), "Icons of Becoming: Documenting Undocumented Migration from West Africa to Europe," *Cahiers d'Etudes Africaines*, LIV (213–214): 217–240.

Wagner, R. (2012 [1987]), "Figure-ground Reversal among the Barok," *HAU: Journal of Ethnographic Theory*, 2 (1): 535–542.

Wagner, R. (1991), "The Fractal Person," in M. Godelier and M. Strathern (eds), *Big Men and Great Men: Personifications of Power in Melanesia*, 159–173, Cambridge: Cambridge University Press.

Wagner, R. (1986), *Symbols That Stand for Themselves*, Chicago: University of Chicago Press.

Wagner, R. (1981 [1976]), *The Invention of Culture*, Chicago: University of Chicago Press.

Wagner, R. (1974), "Are There Social Groups in the New Guinea Highlands?" in Murray et al. *Frontiers of Anthropology: An Introduction to Anthropological Thinking*, 95–122, New York: Van Nostrand.

Waltorp, K. (2018a), "Fieldwork as Interface: Digital Technologies, Moral Worlds and Zones of Encounter," in A. Estalella and Tomás Sánchez-Criado (eds), *Experimental Collaborations: Ethnography through Fieldwork Devices*, 114–131, London: Berghahn Books.

Waltorp, K. (2018b), "Intimacy, Concealment and Unconscious Optics: Filmmaking with Young Muslim Women in Copenhagen," *Journal of Visual Anthropology*, 31 (4): 394–407.

Waltorp, K. (2017a), "Digital Technologies, Dreams, and Disconcertment in Anthropological Worldmaking," in J. Salazar, S. Pink, A. Irving, and J. Sjöberg (eds), *Anthropologies and Futures: Researching Emerging and Uncertain Worlds*, 101–116, London: Bloomsbury Publishing.

Waltorp, K. (2017b), *Joyous Are the Eyes That See You* (film), Aarhus: WaltorpVium & Aarhus University.

Waltorp, K. (2016), "A Snapchat Essay on Mutuality, Utopia and Non-innocent Conversations," *Journal of the Anthropological Society of Oxford*, 8 (1): 251–273.

Waltorp, K. (2015), "Keeping Cool, Staying Virtuous—Social Media and the Composite Habitus of Young Muslim Women in Copenhagen," *MedieKultur, Journal of Media & Communication*, 58: 49–67.

Waltorp, K. (2013a), "Sæbeopera som forestillingsgenererende teknologi," *Tidskriftet Antropologi*, 67: 139–155.

Waltorp, K. (2013b), "Public/private Negotiations in the Media Uses of Young Muslim Women in Copenhagen: Gendered Social Control and the Technology-enabled Moral Laboratories of a Multicultural City," *International Communication Gazette*, 75 (5–6): 555–572.

Waltorp, K. (2010), "Uddannelse & Opposition," *Tidsskriftet Antropologi*, 62: 127–151.

Waltorp, K. (2011), Ghetto NO Ghetto: udstillingskatalog, Avant Afro Micro Press, 43.

Waltorp, K. (Accepted/In press), "Multimodal Sorting: The Flow of Images across Social Media and Anthropological Analysis," in B. Winthereik and A. Ballestero (eds), *The Ethnographic Effect: A Companion to Analysis*, Duke University Press.

Waltorp, K. and S. E. Jensen (2018), "Awkward Entanglements: Kinship, Morality and Survival in Cape Town's Prison-township Circuit," *Ethnos. Journal of Anthropology*, 84 (1): 41–55.

Waltorp, K. and C. Vium (2010), *MANENBERG: Growing Up in the Shadows of Apartheid*, (film), distributed by DR International sales/Royal Anthropological Institute.

Waltorp, K., C. Vium, and C. Suhr (2017), "Witnessing and Creating the World Audio-Visually: Aesthetics, Politics, Anthropology," *Visuel Arkivering*, 10: 46–51.

Weiner, J. (1997), "Televisualist Anthropology. Representation, Aesthetics, Politics," *Current Anthropology*, 38 (2): 197–235.

Whyte, Z. (2011), "Asyl, insh'allah: Tro og mistro i det danske asylsystem," in M. H. Pedersen and M. Rytter (eds), "Islam og muslimer i Danmark. Religion, identitet og sikkerhed efter 11. september 2001," København: Muesum Tusculanum.

Wright, C. (2013), *"The Echo of Things": The Lives of Photographs in the Solomon Islands*, Durham: Duke University Press.

Yaeger, L. (2019), "Ilhan Omar Is Poised to Be the First Muslim Woman to Wear a Hijab in Congress Tomorrow," *Vogue* (US edition), January 3. https://www.vogue.com/article/ilhan-omar-democratic-representative-minnesota-hijab-congress-headgear-ban (consulted February 2).

Zigon, J. (2009), "Within a Range of Possibilities: Morality and Ethics in Social Life," *Ethnos*, 74 (2): 251–276.

Index

Printed in the United States
by Baker & Taylor Publisher Services